Leading and Managing Continuing Professional Development

Second Edition

Leading and Managing Continuing Professional Development

Second Edition

Sara Bubb and Peter Earley

Paul Chapman Publishing

Paul Chapman Publishing
A SAGE Publications Company
1 Oliver's Yard
55 City Road
London EC1Y 1SP

SAGE Publications Inc
2455 Teller Road
Thousand Oaks, California 91320

SAGE Publications India Pvt Ltd
B 1/I1 Mohan Cooperative Industrial Area
Mathura Road, Post Bag 7
New Delhi 110 044

SAGE Publications Asia – Pacific Pte Ltd
33 Pekin Street #02-01
Far East Square
Singapore 048763

Library of Congress Control Number: 2007924114

British Library Cataloguing in Publication Data
A catalogue record for this book is available from the British Library

ISBN-978-1-4129-4827-2
ISBN 978-1-4129-4828-9 (pbk)

Typeset by Pantek Arts Ltd, Maidstone, Kent
Printed in Great Britain by the Cromwell Press, Trowbridge, Wiltshire
Printed on paper from sustainable resources

*We would like to dedicate this book
to the late Ray Bolam whose work in this
field has been inspirational.*

CONTENTS

List of Figures

List of Tables

Acknowledgements

We would like to thank all those who helped and contributed in some way to the writing of this book, particularly Graham Handscomb for writing Chapter 7. We would also like to thank all the teachers who come on our CPD and higher degree courses. They stimulate thought and help keep our feet on the ground!

Most of all, we must thank our families – especially Paul, Julian, Miranda and Oliver – for their encouragement and tolerance.

Publisher's note

Preface

This book has been written for those who lead and manage continuing professional development (CPD). Continuing professional development co-ordinators hold a key role and one that needs to be developed further in many schools and colleges. We hope that this book helps people think more deeply about the professional development and training of staff – all staff – in schools and other organizations. We hope, too, that it will lead to even better practice.

The last decade or so has seen a growing recognition, in schools and colleges, that people matter and that attention must be given to their needs, especially those concerning their professional and personal development and growth. This is perhaps best epitomized by the government's emphasis on lifelong learning and the introduction in 2001 of a strategy for continuing professional development. In 2004, the (then) Teacher Training Agency (TTA) was asked to expand its remit and to bring its expertise to bear in three new areas: (a) to improve the training and development of the wider workforce in schools; (b) to provide more co-ordinated and coherent support for the continuing professional development of teachers and support staff; and, (c) to link all its work to the emerging children's agenda. With the increase in mentoring and coaching, devolved funding to schools and professional standards that recognize the contribution of teachers to the learning of their colleagues, the school's role in leading and supporting staff learning is more crucial than ever before with remodelling as a vital tool to help schools adopt creative, innovative solutions to enhance their capacity to develop as learning-centred communities. Alongside this recognition of the importance of people there has been a growing awareness that schools do not always manage their staff – their human resources – as well as perhaps they might. The quality and quantity of professional development that individuals experience is hugely variable, largely depending on what school they are in.

We hope that this book will help improve human resource development and its management and leadership so that more people get a better deal and that CPD is given the attention it merits.

In writing this book we have tried to do two things. First, we have summarized the most recent relevant research – some of which we have been personally involved in – to highlight the issues and current state of affairs. This gives a firm foundation for CPD co-ordinators leading and managing professional development. Secondly, we have given examples and case studies of good practice drawn from a wide range of schools.

The book is made up of two parts. After an introductory chapter which examines the notion of continuing professional development, locating it within the wider context of human resource development, Part I is entitled 'Professional development for school improvement'. We argue that individual professional development is crucially important and that the professional growth and learning of staff is crucial to school improvement. How adults and schools learn is the focus of Chapter 2, which also examines the notion of the learning-centred community and effective professional development. It is important to remember that development cannot be forced and that teachers and other staff who are excited and motivated by the experience of their own learning are likely to communicate that excitement to the pupils.

What we know about effective leadership and management of CPD is the theme of Chapter 3 where the training and development cycle is introduced. This cycle – of needs identification, meeting the training and development needs of staff, and monitoring and evaluating the impact of CPD (what Ofsted has termed 'the logical chain') – forms the substance of the next three chapters, whilst the final chapter of Part I, written by Graham Handscomb, examines the importance of collaborative enquiry, the sharing of practice and the growth of the self-researching or the 'research-engaged' school. In all of these chapters, indeed throughout the book, we draw upon latest research and examples of good practice, where possible giving case studies and pen portraits.

Part II of the book – 'Leading and managing the CPD of specific groups' – examines the implications of the training and development cycle for those who work in schools. We look at specific groups or categories in schools – support staff, newly qualified teachers (NQTs), teachers in the first five years, supply teachers, middle managers, school leaders and governors. The issues around their roles and development needs are considered and we suggest ways in which they might be met.

Although our focus is predominantly on schools we argue throughout the book that for CPD to be effective it has to be well led and managed at three levels, that of the school, the local authority and at a national level. The key goal of all educational organizations is pupil learning, whereas the on-going learning of teachers, support staff and other employees is not always prioritized or adequately resourced. Creating a culture of learning is crucial and this is shaped essentially by the attitude and approach of school leaders and governors towards CPD. There is a need to ensure that individual or personal development is not marginalized as it is crucial to teacher effectiveness and thus to the success of the school. Schools need to achieve a healthy complementarity or interrelationship between system and individual needs – something that has been absent over the past two decades. The balance needs to be right.

We hope those in schools who are responsible for leading and managing CPD will find the book helpful. For if one of the keys to effective CPD is to ensure it is effectively led and managed, then the role of CPD co-ordinators needs to be given the kudos and time it requires to be done well. The book has been written with this in mind.

Sara Bubb and Peter Earley
Institute of Education, University of London
June 2007

About the Authors

Sara Bubb is an experienced London teacher who helps staff in schools develop. She does this in many ways: through leading professional development, assessing, developing schemes, researching and writing.

With a national and international reputation in the induction of new teachers and professional development, Sara speaks at conferences and runs courses throughout the country and abroad (e.g. Norway, Taiwan) on topics such as helping staff develop, observation skills, induction, developing pedagogical skills, leading CPD, subject leadership, monitoring teaching and implementing performance management. She has featured on and been a consultant for eight Teachers TV programmes. She trains a broad range of people, including inspectors, assessors, advisers, consultants, Fasttrack, TeachFirst and advanced skills teachers.

Sara assesses advanced skills, excellent, overseas trained and graduate teachers and higher level teaching assistants and was an external assessor for Threshold. She has inspected over 25 primary schools.

As a senior lecturer at the Institue of Education (0.2) she works on PGCE and Masters programmes and set up the employment based routes (OTT and GTP) to QTS. She is lead director of the CfBT Educational Trust-funded Sef2Si – 'From Self Evaluation to School Improvement: the role of effective professional development' project. She co-directed the DfES-funded national research *Project on the Effectiveness of the Induction Year*, was deputy director of the TTA systematic review of induction research and helped the Northern Ireland GTC revise their teacher competences.

On a 0.2 secondment to the (then) DfES London Challenge team, Sara is the consultant for Chartered London Teacher status – a scheme involving over 38,600 teachers. She is the London Gifted and Talented Early Years network leader, working with staff in reception and nursery classes to enhance their provision for all children, especially the most able.

She has written books and numerous articles on induction, professional development, workload, and performance management. She is the new teacher expert at the *Times Educational Supplement*, and writes articles, a weekly advice column and answers questions on its website.

Professor Peter Earley is Head of Education Leadership and Management Programmes at the London Centre for Leadership in Learning at the Institute of Education, University of London. A central research interest is leadership and he has recently completed a series of studies of school leaders. Other research interests include school governing bodies, school inspection, self-evaluation and professional development. He is currently co-ordinating projects entitled 'From Self Evaluation to School Improvement: the role of effective professional development' and 'Future Leaders: an evaluation of a pilot project'.

In addition he co-edits the practitioner journal *Professional Development Today*. He was the course leader for the Institute's Educational Leadership and Management MA and currently is co-ordinating the EdD specialist module on 'Leadership and Learning in Educational Organisations'. He was until recently a school governor and a member of the executive of the National Association of School Governors.

He has published widely and his previous books for PCP/Sage include, *Understanding School Leadership* (2004) (with Dick Weindling), *Managing Teacher Workload: Work-life balance and wellbeing* (2004) (with Sara Bubb), and *Improving Schools and Inspection: The Self-inspecting School* (2000) (with Neil Ferguson). He has also written, *Improving Schools and Governing Bodies* (1999) (with Michael Creese), Routledge and *Leadership and Management in Education: Cultures, Change and Context* (2005) (with Marianne Coleman), Oxford University Press.

Graham Handscomb is Principal Adviser in Essex Schools, Children and Families Directorate and has held a number of Local Authority senior management roles. He previously taught for eighteen years and was a secondary deputy headteacher. He leads Essex's policy and practice on initial teacher training and the continuing professional development of teachers. He is an associate tutor with the University of Cambridge, and Senior Member of Hughes Hall College, Cambridge. He founded the Essex Forum for Learning and Research Enquiry (FLARE) which pioneered work on the concept of the Research-Engaged School.

Graham is editor of *Professional Development Today*, and a member of the editorial board of *Teaching Thinking* magazine; he has written extensively on professional development. He is a member of numerous national bodies including the DfES Steering Group on a three-year research project looking at the impact of school leadership on learning; the national Thinking Skills Strategy Group, and Professional Development Board. Graham also does work with the General Teaching Council and the Training and Development Agency.

Abbreviations

AST Advanced skills teacher
BECTA British Educational Communications and Technology Agency
BTEC Business and Technology Education Council
CEA Cambridge Education Associates
CEDP Career Entry and Development Profile
CLT Chartered London Teacher
CIPD Chartered Institute of Personnel and Development
CPD Continuing professional development
CSBM Certificate of School Business Management
DfEE Department for Education and Employment
DfES Department for Education and Skills
DRB Designated Recommending Body
DSBM Diploma of School Business Management
EAL English as an additional language
EDP Education development plan
EFQM European Foundation for Quality Management
EPD Early professional development
ESS Education Standard Spending
FLARE Forum for Learning and Research Enquiry
GTC General Teaching Council
GTP Graduate Teacher Programme
HEADLAMP Headteacher Leadership and Management Programme
HEI Higher education institution
HIP Headteacher Induction Programme
HLTA Higher level teaching assistant
HMCI Her Majesty's Chief Inspector
HMI Her Majesty's Inspectorate
HoD Head of department
HRD Human resource development
HRM Human resource management
ICT Information and communications technology
IEP Individual education plan
IiP Investors in People
ILP Individual learning plan
INSET In-service education and training
IPDP Individual professional development plans
IPPR Institute of Public Policy Research
ITET Initial teacher education and training
ITT Initial Teacher Training
IWB Interactive whiteboard
LA Local authority
LEA Local education authority
LftM Leading from the Middle
LiG Leadership Incentive Grant
LMS Local management of schools
LPSH Leadership Programme for Serving Headteachers
LSA Learning support assistant
LSC Learning and Skills Council
MFL Modern foreign languages
MPS Main pay scale

NAGM National Association of Governors and Managers
NAHT National Association of Head Teachers
NARIC National Academic Recognition Information Centre
NC National Curriculum
NCSL National College for School Leadership
NCT Non-contact time
NERF National Education Research Forum
NFER National Foundation for Educational Research
NLC Networked Learning Communities
NOS National Occupational Standards
NPQH National Professional Qualification for Headship
NVQ National vocational qualification
NQT Newly qualified teacher
Ofsted Office for Standards in Education
OSHLI Out of School Hours Learning Initiative
OTT Overseas-trained teacher
PDC Professional development centre
PDP Professional development profile
PGCE Postgraduate certificate in education
PM Performance management
PSLN Primary School Learning Network
QTS Qualified teacher status
RB Recommending body
RE Religious education
SCITT School-centred initial teacher training
SDP School development plan
SEF Self-evaluation form
SEN Special educational needs
SENCO Special educational needs co-ordinator
SHA Secondary Heads Association
SMT Senior management team
SNA Special needs assistant
STA Specialist teacher assistant
SWOT Strengths, weaknesses, opportunities and threats
TA Teaching assistant
TDA Training and Development Agency for Schools
TDLB Training development lead body
TES Times Educational Supplement
TIPD Teachers' international professional development
TPLF Teachers' Professional Learning Framework
TTA Teacher Training Agency
VRQ Vocationally relevant qualification

1

Introduction: CPD Matters

♦ People matter

♦ What is continuing professional development?

♦ Is the focus on CPD new?

♦ Taking CPD seriously

♦ An entitlement to CPD

The improvement of training and development of heads, teachers and support staff is high on both national and local educational agendas, particularly as delegated budgets and devolved funding have enabled all schools to become self-managing and increasingly autonomous. Teachers, researchers, policy analysts and politicians argue that professionalism must increase if education is to improve. Throughout the western world, the professionalism of teachers has been placed under considerable pressure by the move towards centralized curricula and assessment, and the use of performance data and outcome measures as a means to account for and improve what goes on in classrooms.

This chapter provides the context and rationale for the book arguing strongly that for schools and colleges to improve urgent attention must be given to their main resource – their people. It attempts to define continuing professional development (CPD) and to show that the focus on it is not new. This introductory chapter also provides a strong case or rationale for taking the management and leadership of CPD seriously, whilst also offering a framework for understanding CPD. Finally, it concludes that an entitlement to CPD or lifelong learning is the proper way forward and that all employees have a right to work in a learning-centred community.

PEOPLE MATTER

Educational reform, especially over the last 20 years, has made imperative the need for urgent and high-quality staff development and training. Teachers have delivered unparalleled curricular change including the introduction of a 'National Curriculum' in 1988; Key Stage 2 literacy and numeracy strategies ten years later and, more recently, the Key Stage 3 and Secondary strategy, thus placing well-documented strain on the profession, and promoting national concerns about teacher recruitment, retention and morale. The pivotal role of teachers in the delivery of the government's reform agenda was acknowledged when it was clearly stated that 'all our ambitions for education depend on teachers doing well in the classroom' (DfEE, 2001a: 3).

There is a growing recognition that the management and development of people – human resource management (HRM) and human resource development (HRD) – is more effective in enhancing the performance of organizations, including schools and colleges, than any other factor. For example, the Chartered Institute of Personnel and Development (CIPD) argue for the careful management of people as the prime resource of the organization, claiming that managers get better results (in terms of productivity, customer satisfaction, profitability and employee retention) by managing and developing people better. Within the sphere of education, Riches and Morgan were probably the first to recognize that the truly key and scarce organizational resource was not finance or money but excellent people when they stated:

> Of all the resources at the disposal of a person or an organisation it is only people who can grow and develop and be motivated to achieve certain desired ends. The attaining of targets for the organization is in *their* hands and it is the way *people* are managed so that maximum performance is matched as closely as possible with satisfaction for the individuals doing the performing, which is at the heart of HRM and optimum management. (1989: 1 original emphases)

People and their training and development – their continuing professional development – must be seen as an investment and it is therefore essential that each school establishes not only a CPD or HRD policy but also the means of its implementation through effective management and leadership. As funds and responsibilities are progressively transferred to schools they can be deployed in more varied and creative ways, leading to more responsive and effective systems of CPD. Schools and their governing bodies take the main responsibility for developing the quality, motivation and performance of their people – for managing and developing the human resources. The approach to CPD and its management presented in this book is to regard the training and development of staff as both a collective and individual responsibility – institutional and individual needs have to be regarded in a complementary and holistic way. Schools operating in this manner are likely to have a better motivated and higher-performing workforce.

Schools that do not look after their staff's professional development usually lose the best people. The arguments for professional development are clear. We believe that it:

- helps everyone be more effective in their jobs, so pupils learn and behave better and achieve higher standards;
- improves retention and recruitment – word gets around about the places where you are looked after, and where you are not;
- contributes to a positive ethos where people feel valued and motivated;
- makes for a learning-centred community – the pupils are learning and so are the staff;
- is a professional responsibility and entitlement;
- saves money – the costs of recruiting and inducting a new teacher are high.

If the expertise and experience of staff are increasingly seen as a school's most precious resource then the management and leadership of CPD must be seen as an integral part of managing the total resources available to the school. Some have linked CPD to objectives as identified in both school development and personal development plans. In this way it is likely that an appropriate balance will be retained between school (and group) needs and the personal and professional needs of the individual. Staff will always feel the need to be valued, and this should not be forgotten when considering the balance between identifying and meeting individual and institutional needs. The effective management of CPD should ensure that support is available and conditions created which enable staff to work together and to develop and improve their workplace performance. By head-teachers, CPD co-ordinators and other staff helping to create a climate or culture which is conducive to learning – of both staff and pupils – schools are well on the road to becoming learning-centred communities where investment in people is given the priority it deserves. Student or pupil learning is a key goal of all schools, whereas often the on-going learning of staff is not always prioritized or adequately resourced.

WHAT IS CONTINUING PROFESSIONAL DEVELOPMENT?

One of the hallmarks of being identified as a professional is to continue to learn throughout a career. The professions, broadly defined, now cover over 20 per cent of the workforce – more if managers are included – and most are employed in large companies or the public sector. They range from the well established and powerful to those who are still trying to establish their professional status. The strongest are those of over 80 professions regulated by law, public authority and royal charter, where membership or registration is necessary to practise. Continuing professional development has become the phrase widely used for on-going education and training for the professions, whilst 'workforce development' is the more general term. If teaching is seen as a profession – and a case for this has long been argued – an important characteristic or hallmark of a member of a profession is the commitment shown towards self-improvement or development. This is not, however, for its own sake but to ensure that the beneficiaries or clients – in our case pupils and parents – are provided with the best possible service. The prime responsibility for securing individual professional development of staff is not, however, the exclusive concern of the employer – staff themselves must expect to play a key role – and professional development opportunities must be available for individuals to help them become better practitioners.

But what do we mean by the term CPD and is it different from *personal development* or *staff development* or *in-service education and training* (INSET)? Broadly speaking, continuing professional development encompasses all formal and informal learning that enables individuals to improve their own practice. Professional development is an aspect of personal development and, wherever possible, the two should interact and complement each other. The former is mainly about occupational role development, whereas personal development is about the development of the person, often the 'whole' person, and it almost always involves changes in self-awareness. As Waters explains: 'It is the development that can occur when teachers are construed first and foremost as people, and is predicated on the premise that people are always much more than the roles they play' (1998: 30).

A definition of CPD might refer to: 'any professional development activities engaged in by teachers which enhance their knowledge and skills and enable them to consider their attitudes and approaches to the education of children, with a view to improve the quality of the teaching and learning process' (Bolam, 1993: 3). In this sense it is perhaps little different to how some have defined in-service training or staff development. The seminal *James Report* (DES, 1972) defined INSET as: 'the whole range of activities by which teachers can extend their personal education, develop their professional competence and improve their understanding of education principles and techniques'.

An analysis of the literature does, however, reveal a number of nuances and slight differences for the different concepts used. A simple but most useful conceptual breakdown is offered by Bolam in his publication for the General Teaching Council where he makes use of a threefold distinction among:

- *professional training*, for example, short courses, workshops and conferences emphasizing practical information and skills;
- *professional education*, for example, long courses and secondments emphasizing theory and research-based knowledge;
- *professional support*, for example, activities that aim to develop on the job experience and performance. (Bolam, 1993)

Continuing professional development is an on-going process building upon initial teacher training (ITT) and induction, including development and training opportunities throughout a career and concluding with preparation for retirement. At different times and at different stages one or other may be given priority, but the totality can be referred to as continuing professional development. Development – as noted earlier – is about improvement, both individual and school improvement.

Continuing professional development embraces those education, training and support activities engaged in by teachers following their initial certification which aim to add to their professional knowledge; improve their professional skills; help clarify their professional values; and enable pupils to be educated more effectively (Bolam, 1993).

In their survey of continuing education for the professions, Madden and Mitchell (1993) state that CPD can fulfil three functions:

- updating and extending the professional's knowledge and skills on new developments and new areas of practice – to ensure continuing competence in the current job;

- training for new responsibilities and for a changing role (for example, management, budgeting, teaching) – developing new areas of competence in preparation for a more senior post;

- developing personal and professional effectiveness and increasing job satisfaction – increasing competence in a wider context with benefits to both professional and personal roles.

Our definition of CPD is also wide-ranging and goes well beyond the mere acquisition of knowledge or skills. For us staff development is:

> an on-going process encompassing all formal and informal learning experiences that enable all staff in schools, individually and with others, to think about what they are doing, enhance their knowledge and skills and improve ways of working so that pupil learning and wellbeing are enhanced as a result. It should achieve a balance between individual, group, school and national needs; encourage a commitment to professional and personal growth; and increase resilience, self-confidence, job satisfaction and enthusiasm for working with children and colleagues. (Based on Bubb and Earley, 2005)

Or, put more simply, it is about creating opportunities for adult learning, ultimately for the purpose of enhancing the quality of education in the classroom. To summarize, CPD is an on-going process of education, training, learning and support activities which is:

- taking place in either external or work-based settings;

- engaged in by qualified, educational professionals;

- aimed mainly at promoting learning and development of their professional knowledge, skills and values;

- to help decide and implement valued changes in their teaching and learning behaviour so that they can educate their students more effectively thus achieving an agreed balance between individual, school and national needs (based on Bolam, 2003).

It is clear that long gone are the days when initial training and induction were seen as a total or final preparation for a career in teaching; nowadays they have to be seen as merely providing a platform on which further or continuing professional development will be built. Nevertheless, the initial period in teaching is crucial as the experience of the first year is most formative. There is therefore a need to set high expectations and standards when there is the greatest receptiveness and willingness to learn and develop. It is during the induction period, for example, that the support of others is crucial if new entrants to the profession are to develop the competences, the confidence and the attitudes that will serve as the basis for on-going professional development.

Perhaps the single most important feature of CPD is to encourage and promote a commitment on the part of the individual to professional growth. Leading and managing people development – making CPD work – therefore means providing structures and procedures to coordinate developmental opportunities so as to promote such growth and to help staff develop and improve their workplace performance.

IS THE FOCUS ON CPD NEW?

Ideas about the central importance of CPD to education are not new, although they are of fairly recent origin:

> The first national enquiry into in-service education training was not mounted until 1970, which seems to suggest that it had broadly been assumed that initial education and training would suffice for a professional lifetime. It is an assumption rooted in a view, perhaps held subconsciously rather than formalized as 'policy', that the task of the teacher remained constant. (H. Tomlinson, 1993)

The *James Report*, published as long ago as 1972, was aware of the need to change such outmoded views and recognize the social and cultural changes that were affecting the education system. As a result, the further professional development of staff became a national issue. The report, which is perhaps best known for its suggestion that teachers should be entitled to the equivalent of one term's release for training and development every seven years, stressed the importance of in-service education and training, and stated that each school should regard the continued training of its teachers as an essential part of its task for which all members of staff share responsibility. Every school was seen as needing a 'professional tutor' to coordinate training and development, and to compile and maintain 'a training programme for the staff of the school, which would take account of the curricular needs of the school and of the professional needs of the teachers' (DES, 1972). As Williams (1993) notes in his overview of changing policies and practices, the strength of these proposals was their focus on teachers and schools, seeing responsibility for CPD to be that of individual staff and the schools in which they worked.

The *James Report* also made reference to the now widely used and accepted continuum of professional development – the so-called 'three Is' of initial teacher training, induction and INSET. Continuing professional development should ensure that individuals progress from 'novice' or 'advanced beginner' status to that of an 'expert'. However, expert status is not a once and for all achievement. It is on-going – new demands, a changing curriculum and various other changes mean that learning and development are never ending.

At the time of the *James Report*, training and development were seen very much as the individual's concern and they were not perceived as important by all staff or their employers, the local (education) authorities (LAs). The report was followed by a number of policy and discussion documents, culminating in what has been termed 'the INSET revolution' so that now CPD has 'gradually become a priority within the education system paralleling the rise of "human resource development" in other large organisations in the public and private sectors' (Oldroyd and Hall, 1991). The point has been made, however, that the predominant view of INSET over the recent past is that it is centrally funded and used largely to 'retool' and 'retrain' teachers so they can 'deliver' the government's reforms, particularly those associated with the 1988 Education Reform Act and the national strategies for primary and secondary schools. John Tomlinson, for example, identifies the early 1980s as a turning point: 'between a time when INSET was almost entirely left to be pursued by the individual teacher and the present view that it must also, indeed predominantly, serve the needs of the schools and the system as well as the personal or professional development of the individual' (1993). We shall return in a later chapter to this shifting emphasis of CPD provision and consider how the needs of the 'system', the 'institution' and the 'individual' might be catered for.

TAKING CPD SERIOUSLY

The 2006 GTC(E) survey of teachers found clear differences in experiences of CPD that related to professional role:

> There was a gradient in response with headteachers being the most satisfied that their needs were met; having engaged in the most different types of CPD activity; and being the most con-fident that CPD was valued in their school and taken into account in decision-making, while class teachers were less satisfied that their needs had been met, had experienced less variety in CPD activity; and were less confident that CPD was valued and taken into account in their schools. (Hutchings et al., 2006: vii)

Continuing professional development has to be seen as a collective responsibility – the responsibility of both individual staff and the schools and colleges in which they work. Individuals and their places of employment should take joint responsibility for profes-sional development and training, which should be for the benefit of both. Growing atten-tion has been given to organizational 'cultures' and the emphasis that may or may not be given to the training and development or the 'learning' of its members. The experience and expertise of staff – both teaching and support – are generally recognized to be the school's most important and most expensive resource (Earley, 1995). The term 'learning organiza-tion' or 'learning community' is becoming more commonly known and attempts are being made – through such initiatives as Investors in People and the school inspection frame-work (Ofsted, 2003a; 2005) – to ensure that more schools are aware of what this means for themselves. Leading and managing people and their development have to be seen as a central part of the responsibility of managing the school's total resources.

A learning community – or what we prefer to call a 'learning-centred community' (see next chapter) – is sensitive to its environment and constantly evolving, making use of the skills and talents of all of its people to greatest benefit. It develops a learning cul-ture where learning and development are valued and seen as an integral part of effective performance, and where people are regarded as assets rather than costs to be reduced. The term is particularly appropriate to education. In a school, for instance, the question has to be asked how can the idea of learning be central to it if its own staff are not engaged in that process themselves? There are two groups of learners within schools – young people and adults – and we neglect either at our peril. If teachers and other staff are not seen as continuous learners by the school itself, how can adults engage young-sters in any meaningful pursuit of learning?

As any teacher who has worked in more than one school will attest, the training and development culture may be quite different from one establishment to another. In some schools staff's on-going professional development is seen as integral, given great signif-icance and very closely linked to the school improvement plan (SIP). In such places there is an expectation that individuals and their managers will take a collective respon-sibility for both individual and institutional development. In this sense 'good schools' are said to make 'good teachers' as much as the other way around. A school wishing to become a learning-centred community would therefore take its CPD responsibilities most seriously and strive to secure effective learning for both its pupils and staff. It would subscribe heavily to a development culture and give training and development – and its effective leadership and management – a high priority.

Investors in People – a national standard for training and development – is at the fore-front in helping schools and colleges to embrace a development culture and become 'learn-ing-centred' or 'thinking' schools. The learning-centred community is capable of developing itself and its workforce, and a culture of training and development – of CPD – will imbue the organization and be embedded in both its structures and processes. The fact that a significant number of schools and colleges have been awarded Investors in People status is a formal recognition of this. Chapter 3 considers Investors in People in more detail.

AN ENTITLEMENT TO CPD

The notion of an entitlement to CPD is something that has been promoted in England and Wales by the General Teaching Councils. It sees an entitlement to professional development as 'career long and sustained so that on entry to the profession a teacher has a clear expectation of continuing, relevant and planned professional development'. England's General Teaching Council (GTC) has drawn up an entitlement to professional learning within its *Teachers' Professional Learning Framework (TPLF)* that was published in March 2003 (GTC[E], 2003). The GTC(E) believes that there should be a personal entitlement to professional development throughout a teacher's career and one that is not linked solely to school targets.

Teachers need the opportunity to:

- Have structured time to engage in sustained reflection and structured learning;
- Create learning opportunities from everyday practice such as planning and assessing for learning;
- Develop their ability to identify their own learning and development needs and those of others;
- Develop an individual learning plan;
- Have school-based learning as well as course participation, recognized for accreditation;
- Develop self-evaluation, observation and peer review skills;
- Develop mentoring and coaching skills and their ability to offer professional dialogue and feedback;
- Plan their longer-term career aspirations. (GTC[E], 2003: 6)

So, there is a great lever for professional development in the *Teachers' Professional Learning Framework* but, as noted earlier, anyone who has worked in more than one school will know that the training and development culture may vary from one place to another. Carol Adams, the (then) chief executive of the GTC (England), was clear about the need for a high quality CPD entitlement, seeing the necessity to transform the meaning of CPD so that:

> teachers and providers come to see it as lifelong access to high quality experiences that enhance teaching for teachers and learning for learners; opportunities for teachers' needs to be met as and when they arise. This model stands in stark contrast with one of being 'sent' on a course. Activities like observing teaching and learning in a range of colleagues' classes is valued by teachers and those who lead them and is an important component in the GTC's vision. (Cordingley, 2001: 80)

In Wales the GTC considers that teachers and employers have different but complementary responsibilities in relation to CPD (see Jones, 2003):

- *employers* – to provide professional development opportunities for teachers to support a broad range of priorities which occur during the normal work cycle and an entitlement to professional development which focuses on the individual professional and personal needs and objectives of the teacher is emphasized;

- *teachers* – to develop themselves as 'reflective professionals' by reflecting on their work and by identifying new ways of working. These activities should be undertaken as part of a teacher's work.

The GTC(W) argues that teachers need CPD opportunities based on three priority areas (see Figure 1.1):

- *Individually focused* – these activities should focus on a teacher's own needs and be identified by the individual teacher as supporting their professional development and/or career objectives. Appropriate CPD activities might include attending courses, mentoring, developing a new teaching activity, exchanging ideas and good practice with colleagues, and exchange visits.

- *School focused* – these activities should primarily be targeted at the requirements of the school that currently employs the teacher. The CPD requirements would be identified from the school development plan and relevant activities should largely be undertaken during the statutory non-pupil contact days, with any additional identified school-focused activities financed from school budgets.

- *National/Local authority (including diocesan authorities)* focused – these CPD activities would meet the demands of national and local initiatives. They could involve activities organized on a cross-school basis such as cluster meetings or around a national priority.

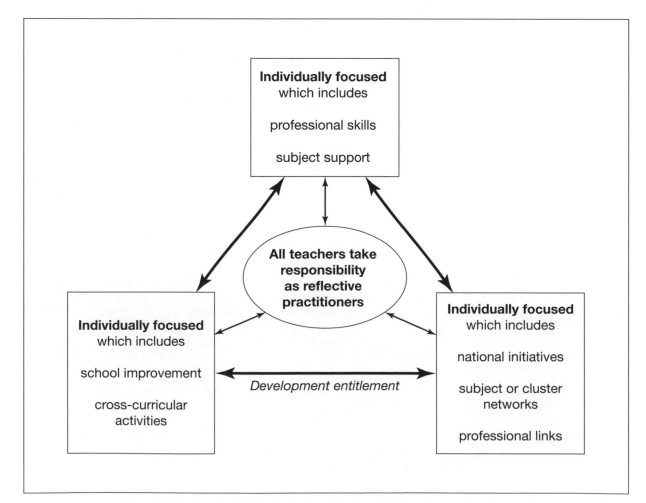

FIGURE 1.1 CONTINUING PROFESSIONAL DEVELOPMENT FRAMEWORK (JONES, 2003: 37)

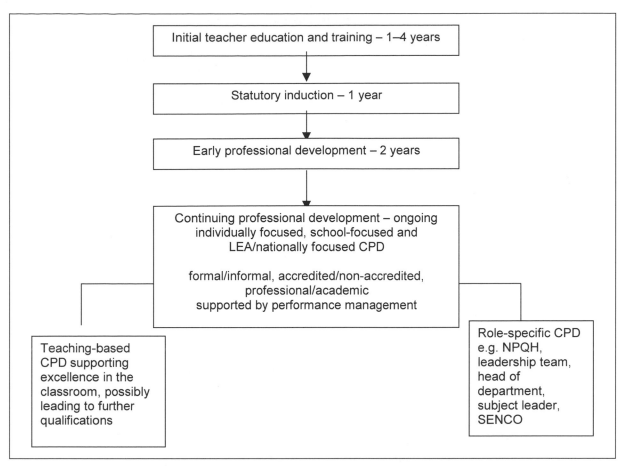

FIGURE 1.2 A CAREER-LONG PROFESSIONAL DEVELOPMENT ENTITLEMENT (JONES, 2003: 38)

As Jones notes, 'teachers require a career-long entitlement to professional development opportunities, with clear opportunities for teachers at different stages of their careers' (2003: 38). The advice from the GTC (W) proposes a continuum of opportunity from initial teacher education and training (ITET) throughout a teacher's career (see Figure 1.2).

An entitlement to CPD – and not only for teachers – is a notion whose time has clearly come! The rest of this book is devoted to an analysis and portrayal of the key areas and issues around the successful leadership and management of continuing professional development, a better understanding of which it is hoped will help realize that entitlement.

RESPONSIBILITIES

Professional development is a responsibility throughout teachers' careers, as can be seen in the *Teacher Standards Framework* (TDA, 2007). One of the standards that people have to demonstrate in order to get qualified teacher status (QTS) is that they:

> Q7 (a) Reflect on and improve their practice, and take responsibility for identifying and meeting their developing professional needs.

In order to pass induction, teachers have to:

> C7 Evaluate their performance and be committed to improving their practice through appropriate professional development.
> C9 Act upon advice and feedback and be open to coaching and mentoring.

The post-threshold standards require people to:

> P10 Contribute to the professional development of colleagues through coaching and mentoring, demonstrating effective practice, and providing advice and feedback.

Higher Level Teaching Assistants (HLTAs) are required to demonstrate that,

> 7. Improve their own knowledge and practice including responding to advice and feedback. (TDA, 2007b: 2)

With the change of emphasis on the importance of training and development and greater control from the centre, there has been a corresponding move towards a higher degree of prescription and statutory requirements regarding CPD. The late 1980s, for example, saw the introduction of the Teachers Pay and Conditions of Service Act (1987), which for the first time specified teachers' professional duties. These included, amongst many other things, 'participating in arrangements for his [sic] further training and professional development as a teacher'. It did not, however, make it a statutory requirement for teachers 'to show any official evidence of developing, updating or even maintaining their professional knowledge and competence' (H. Tomlinson, 1993). The legislation also introduced the notion of 'directed' time (1,265 hours) and 'non-contact' days. The latter – consisting of five days when teachers met without pupils being on site – were for the purpose of preparation, planning, assessment (PPA), review and in-service training. Research into the use of these five days – of which at least three are recommended to be used for CPD – suggests that they have not always been used productively by schools (Harland et al., 1999). There is still much variation in how effectively these training days are being used for development purposes and the introduction, through workforce remodelling, has meant PPA should be done at other times.

In some other professions there is specified mandatory CPD for all its members. The Royal Institute of British Architects, for example, has an obligatory requirement that members undertake certain amounts of CPD each year. A survey of 20 professional bodies found that 13 specified a certain number of hours – a median of 30 hours a year (Madden and Mitchell, 1993). Professional bodies can be located on a continuum from full mandatory CPD requirements to individuals taking responsibility voluntarily for their own on-going development. Teachers are perhaps found somewhere in the middle of the continuum. Within the teaching profession there has been no shortage of calls for CPD to be taken more seriously, whether as a reward (the benefits model), or as compliance (the sanctions model), and for certain 'entitlements' to be enshrined in legislation. However, the problem with any voluntary scheme is that those with most to gain from CPD are often the least likely to do so, whilst mandatory policies may lead to a lack of individuality, although the latter do ensure all members have the opportunity to develop.

CONCLUSION

Continuing professional development is about on-going or lifelong learning which will help us respond to ever-changing situations and exercise judgement in informed and creative ways but, as Pachler and Field remind us, it should also be seen as a means for us 'to rejuvenate practice, to expand our professional repertoire, increase our self-esteem, self-confidence and enthusiasm for teaching or, for example, our level of criticality and, thereby, achieve enhanced job satisfaction' (2004: 2). This book is about all of these and more!

PART I:

PROFESSIONAL DEVELOPMENT FOR SCHOOL IMPROVEMENT

2

Learning People – Learning Schools

♦ How adults learn

♦ Learning-centred communities

♦ What is effective CPD?

♦ The Standards Framework

♦ Professional development portfolios

Professional development is crucial for organizational growth and school improvement. The professional growth of teachers and other staff is a key component of developing children's learning. Roland Barthes, a former US principal and well-known writer on school improvement, remarked: 'Probably nothing within a school has more impact on students in terms of skills development, self-confidence, or classroom behaviour than the personal and professional development of their teachers' (1990: 49). This is quite an assertion, but the fundamental point he was making has been supported by research and inspection evidence. But how does adult development and learning occur and is there anything different about how adults learn compared to children? What do we know about how adults best learn? Also what sort of organizational settings and cultures are most conducive to adult or teacher development and growth? What do we know about learning organizations or communities of learners? How do staff and schools learn? These questions form the main themes of this chapter.

HOW ADULTS LEARN

Thinking about how adults learn is crucial for anyone involved in CPD. The way that we understand learning will affect the provision of activities we make for people to learn, and the accuracy of our understanding will affect the effectiveness of the learning that takes place. Those who work in schools and other educational organizations come from a variety of backgrounds and experiences. This needs to be recognized and built upon. Adults have a wide variety of previous experiences, knowledge, skills, interests and competences. Some prefer informal learning situations, others more formal ones. The American writer Knowles (1984) used the term 'andragogy' (as opposed to pedagogy) and noted the following characteristics of adult learners:

- They are largely self-directed and require a climate of trust, openness, respect and collaboration to learn effectively.

- The previous experience of the learner has to be implicit in the learning process (it is too significant to ignore).

- The adult learner needs to accept the need to learn.

- They are biased towards problem-solving as a learning activity.

- Practical relevance is a significant factor in gaining commitment.

- They only internalize learning if motivated by intrinsic factors.

It is interesting to reflect on how many of these characteristics are found in most educational organizations.

Eileen Carnell, as part of research conducted over six years, found that teachers said that effective learning experiences:

- are linked inextricably with day to day work contexts, for example, in the classroom or working with groups of colleagues in their school;

- are challenging, developmental and take place over an extended period of time;

- arise when people feel in control, have ownership, develop shared aims and reciprocity – supporting and being supported by respected colleagues;

- are participatory; the more people are engaged in activities and the more interaction with colleagues, the more effective the activities are seen;

- are practical and relevant with opportunities for reflection, learning and change;

- happen in a trusting, non-hierarchical environment;

- include pupil and peer learning dialogue;

- occur when staff work together in social exchange, reflecting, planning and developing actions for change;

- focus explicitly on their own learning. (2001: 44)

The most appropriate model for thinking about professional development is one based on experiential learning. This stresses the importance of workplace learning and learning by doing, sharing, reviewing and applying. Dennison and Kirk (1990) talk about a learning cycle of 'do, review, learn and apply' that is illustrated in Figure 2.1. So, someone who wants to get better at taking assembly, for instance, might usefully go through the cycle in this way:

Do   Observe someone that I admire take assembly.
Review   Think about it and discuss it with them afterwards.
Learn   Learn some key techniques for taking assembly.
Apply   Try them out when I take assembly.
Do   Get someone to observe me taking assembly and give me feedback.

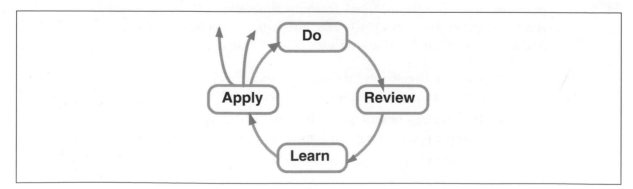

FIGURE 2.1 A LEARNING CYCLE (DENNISON AND KIRK, 1990)

■ LEARNING STYLES

Howard Gardner's theory of multiple intelligences and our awareness of visual, auditory or kinaesthetic learning styles are useful in teaching children. Similarly, different adults learn in different ways and have preferred learning styles. Probably the best known analysis of this is that of Honey and Mumford (2006a). They identify four types of learners: theorists, pragmatists, activists and reflectors.

- *The theorist* likes to learn using abstract conceptualization and reflective observation (lectures, papers, analogies) and asks such questions as: 'How does this relate to that?' Training approach: case studies, theory readings, thinking alone.

- *The pragmatist* likes to learn using abstract conceptualization and active experimentation (laboratories, fieldwork, observations). Pragmatists ask: 'How can I apply this in practice?' Training approach: peer feedback and activities that apply skills.

- *The activist* likes to learn using concrete experience and active experimentation (simulations, case studies, homework). Activists tell themselves: 'I'm game for anything.' Training approach: practising the skill, problem-solving, small group discussions, peer feedback.

- *The reflector* likes to learn using reflective observation and concrete experience (logs, journals, brainstorming). Reflectors like time to think about the subject. Training approach: lectures with plenty of reflection time.

Honey and Mumford (2006b) have a questionnaire designed to help people pinpoint their learning preferences so that they are in a better position to select learning experiences that suit them. Few people fall neatly into one category, but have a leaning towards one or two. However, it is useful to know where their preferences lie and for people organizing professional development to take this into account. For some people the form of the training activity may be a significant factor: if this is not compatible with the way they learn then they may be hostile to the content or message of the training. So, the next time you see people being stroppy, self-centred and argumentative during an INSET day ask them whether their learning style is incompatible with the training!

However, Frank Coffield, a colleague of ours at London University's Institute of Education, has reviewed different learning style theories, and is sceptical about the whole business:

> Some of the learning styles instruments – many of them well-known commercial products – make extravagant claims of success which are not upheld when subjected to scrutiny. People may take the results too seriously and come to think in stereotypes and live up to their label. (Bubb, 2005a: 15)

He believes that different approaches are needed for different things: it depends what you need to learn.

The difference between the learning of most adults and the learning of staff in schools is significant because it relates so closely to their core activity at work – helping others to learn. It is analogous to the health of doctors. If individuals understand how they learn and can appreciate that others have different learning styles, then they will be more able to support the learning of both young people and colleagues.

People learn in different ways and have preferred learning styles but learning takes place in a variety of ways and in different settings. It can be formal or informal, within the workplace or off site. Types of informal learning for example could be:

- planned – but other things may be learned too;
- reactive and unplanned – the day to day learning from doing;
- implicit – learning that the individual is unaware of, but which has taken place and which others may notice (Williams, 2002).

One can also think of learning in vertical and horizontal dimensions:

- vertical – knowing more, new learning and experiences;
- horizontal – the same knowledge applied in different contexts, deeper understanding.

So people do not always have to learn new things to be developing professionally.

There is no easy answer to the question 'what needs to be done to help adults become better learners?' but the following are worth asking:

- How open are individuals to new experiences?
- Are they seen as opportunities for learning?
- Do individuals learn from mistakes that may have been made?
- Is becoming a better learner largely a state of mind?
- Does the school help or hinder learning?

For change to occur in practices then priority must be given to the personal resources and capacity for learning of individuals. Responding to new demands requires a range of skills and qualities (for example, problem-solving, stress management, interpersonal skills) and effective CPD is about empowering staff so they can prepare for change. It is as much concerned with the affective as the cognitive; process skills as with outcomes; and personal growth as much as technical competence (West-Burnham and O'Sullivan, 1998). The VITAE project (Day et al., 2006) recommended that any CPD should target both instrumental needs and those designed to support individuals' commitment and resilience. It needs to support rather than erode staff's sense of positive identity and contribute to their wellbeing, job satisfaction, sense of achievement and capacities to maintain upward trajectories of commitment.

■ LEARNING STAFF

The role of CPD in the development of learning-centred communities has focused discussion on the ways in which staff learn most successfully. Eileen Carnell has drawn up features of teachers who make good progress in their learning (see Table 2.1).

People need time after any development activity to consolidate thoughts into new and novel contexts. Small-scale action research or teacher practitioner projects undertaken after the development activity are likely to have a powerful impact on staff, as is shown in Chapter 7. An Ofsted report on CPD (Ofsted, 2002a) also draws attention to the importance of preparation time before professional development, and consolidation time afterwards.

The Hay Group's 'iceberg' model (see Figure 2.2) is useful in illustrating the importance of looking at the whole person. Personalized learning shouldn't just be for pupils but for staff too, so we need to look below the surface at people's motives, personality, self-esteem and roles outside school. Professional development that takes these into account will be very powerful.

A key task of managers of CPD is to encourage and develop 'learning adults' and to facilitate planned learning and development opportunities. This can be done in a variety of ways but especially by offering a structured programme of on-the-job, close-to-the-job and off-the-job opportunities, and a culture of development within which staff feel valued in the job they do. All of the above are likely to be found within learning-centred communities.

TABLE 2.1 CHARACTERISTICS OF LEARNING TEACHERS

Learning teachers	Explanation
... have a lifelong commitment to learning and change	This commitment is evidenced in teachers' willingness to take risks and promote new ideas. There is concern to seek out ways to improve professional growth, including evidence of a system for continuous inquiry and complex decision-making. They keep up with professional knowledge and new conceptions; they grow personally as well as professionally.
... collaborate with young people and colleagues	Learning teachers create collaborative working relationships with pupils and colleagues. They are able to maintain collegial support groups and manage the classroom in collaboration with pupils. They are able to demonstrate reciprocity, self-disclosure and mutual respect.
... have a commitment to increasing the effectiveness of teaching and learning	This commitment is exhibited in their strong motivation to be involved in things they care about, their ways of creating more adaptive ways of teaching and learning in their ability to reflect and understand assumptions, beliefs and values. This commitment includes understanding and respecting the diversity of their pupils.
... have an holistic, multi-perspective view of teaching, young people and relationships	Taking a holistic view of teaching and learning requires seeing pupils as whole human beings. Understanding interactions and the impact of interactions upon one's self and others is important as is self-knowledge and the ability to think critically. Teachers who take an holistic view exhibit empathy, flexibility and high levels of humane and democratic values, appreciate multiple possibilities, multiple perspectives and interdependency of relationships. They encourage complex learning.

Source: Carnell, 2001: 49

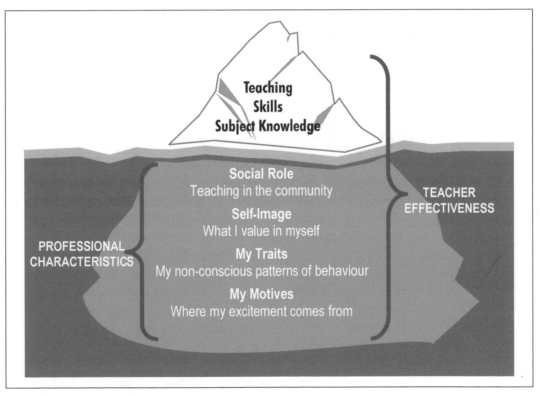

FIGURE 2.2 THE ICEBERG MODEL (AFTER HAY MCBER, 2000)

LEARNING-CENTRED COMMUNITIES

Training and development cultures differ; they may be quite different from one establishment to another. In some schools or departments within schools the on-going professional development of all staff is seen as integral, given great significance and is very closely linked to the school development plan. In other places nothing could be further from the truth. In the most effective schools, the adults are learning and collaborating, as are the pupils – they are learning-centred communities. Such schools have a positive impact on pupils' learning and benefits are usually found in staff's work lives, classroom practice and in improvement in general across the school. The GTC believes that: 'Teachers who collaborate, learn together, share ideas and model best practice are more likely to remain in teaching. They feel valued and supported in their development and in their work' (GTC, 2003: 3).

A learning-centred community is constantly evolving, making use of the skills and talents of its entire people to greatest benefit. The importance of professional development cannot be overstated and a learning-centred community would subscribe heavily to a development culture and give training and development – and its effective leadership and management – a high priority. Leaders of such communities engender an ethos that all pupils, teachers and support staff in a school are seen as learners in their own right. They also seek everyone's views and involve all in decision-making processes, supporting, developing and empowering them to feel a sense of ownership in the future direction of their organization. Staff discuss their work openly and seek to improve and develop their pedagogy through collaborative enquiry and the sharing of good practice. Can we ensure that what may be an effective learning environment in the classroom is mirrored in the staffroom or school as a whole?

An early example of research into the nature of learning-centred communities – although they were not labelled as such – was that of the American educational researcher Susan Rosenholtz (1989). In her classic study she identified two types of school, what she referred to as 'moving' schools and 'stuck' schools. The former were 'learning enriched' and the latter 'learning impoverished' (see Table 2.2).

TABLE 2.2 TYPES OF 'LEARNING' SCHOOLS

'Learning impoverished'	'Learning enriched'
• Teacher isolation	• Collaboration and sharing
• Teachers compete with each other	• Continuous teacher talk about practice
• Lack of positive feedback	• A common focus
• Pulling in different directions	• A sense of efficacy
• Avoidance of risk-taking	• A belief in lifelong learning
• A sense of powerlessness	• Looking out as well as in
• Made to do CPD	• Focus on improving things for pupils
• Professional development treated negatively	• Feedback is welcomed
	• Safe to take risks and try out new things
	• Teachers share values

Source: adapted from Rosenholtz, 1989

Rosenholtz's simple twofold classification of schools has since been developed further by those researchers interested in school effectiveness and school improvement. Using the four headings of effective and ineffective, and improving and declining, a number of categories have been defined such as 'coasting' or 'cruising', 'struggling' or 'sinking' and 'strolling' schools (see Stoll and Fink, 1996).

The importance of this classification of schools is perhaps clearer when we consider the question posed by another American educationist, Judith Warren Little. She remarked: 'Imagine that you could become a better teacher just by virtue of being on the staff of a particular school – just that fact alone' (Little, 1990). This is a key question, but how is a school transformed from one type ('learning impoverished') to another ('learning enriched'), particularly when the members of 'stuck' schools may be quite happy and not wish to move? How can a learning-centred community be established?

Nobody would argue with the idea of schools developing as learning communities but getting there is hard because it requires changing the culture. And here is where Stoll and colleagues' (2006) pack of documents about professional learning communities

(PLCs) is a godsend to busy professional development co-ordinators. The pack contains a sheet explaining what PLCs are, a user guide, and a route map to assist in planning your journey through the 13 booklets. After some activities that help deepen understanding about PLCs, these materials give step by step suggestions of how to audit an organization, plan its development, ideas for action, and lastly how to monitor and evaluate its impact.

Across the pack there are a range of different activities such as reading short articles, auditing current practice and sorting quotations into different characteristics of PLCs. Identifying your present school culture is a sensible place to start and these materials suggest fun ways to do so, such as looking at what messages the entrance area conveys, asking pupils to take photos, and getting staff to think of metaphors for what their learning community is like.

The isolation that most teachers experience needs to be replaced with a climate that encourages observation, sharing teaching strategies, trying out new ways of teaching, getting feedback, and redesigning curriculum and methods of instruction (Bezzina, 2002). People in such groups become a 'community of practice' (Wenger, 1998).

Research tells us there are eight key characteristics of effective professional learning communities:

1. shared values and vision;
2. collective responsibility for pupils' learning;
3. collaboration focused on learning;
4. individual and collective professional learning;
5. reflective professional enquiry;
6. openness, networks and partnerships;
7. inclusive membership;
8. mutual trust, respect and support (Bolam et al., 2005).

PLCs are created, managed and sustained through four processes: optimizing resources and structures; promoting individual and collective learning; explicitly promoting, monitoring and sustaining the learning community; and leading and managing CPD well. The following play an important role:

- school-based formal professional development opportunities – a solid basis of expert knowledge and skills and practical tools for implementing CPD (for example, professional development profiles, coaching and mentoring);

- work-based and incidental learning opportunities, based on theories of adult learning (for example, experimenting with and reflecting on pedagogical practices, experiential learning, problem-based learning and meta-learning);

- teamwork at both group and whole-school level (for example, problem-solving and creative activities within departments, key stage and pastoral groups, strategic leadership groups, teams developing whole-school policies or leading school improvement activities);

- self-evaluation and inquiry, action research, and using evidence to inform practice (for example, Ofsted reports, pupil and teacher surveys, assessment of pupils' progress, eliciting feedback from parents);

- partnerships with people from LAs, higher education, local businesses, and so on, involving a rethinking of the way each institution operates as well as how staff might work as part of this partnership;

- external professional development opportunities, including courses, higher degrees, membership of local working parties;

- networking through teachers and other members of school communities linking up with each other to share ideas, disseminate good practice, discuss and resolve problems, challenge each other's thinking and create new knowledge;

- critical friendships involving external agents who play a role in promoting inquiry-mindedness in school communities by helping those in schools to interpret and use data, bringing an outsider's eye to school activities and supportively challenging assumptions;

- leadership, management and co-ordination of professional activities (Stoll et al., 2003: 5–6. See also Stoll et al., 2006).

Effective leaders help shape the culture of a school by their behaviour. They lead the learning. This might be by constantly questioning the status quo to find better ways of achieving goals, creating environments where positive results and credits are celebrated; evaluating and affirming people; or by thinking positively and realizing that every problem presents a learning opportunity. Groups of staff who correspond outside of school, either electronically or in face-to-face groups or meetings or networks, show great potential as sites for focused, on-going and self-directed inquiry.

NETWORKED LEARNING COMMUNITIES

In England, the National College for School Leadership (NCSL) has encouraged networked learning communities to promote change through learning at multiple levels of the education system. The networks are made up of at least six schools and a higher education institution, and the underpinning notion is that the learning is from each other, with each other and on behalf of each other. An example of a networked learning community is offered by Kellow (2003) who describes the origins of the Primary Schools Learning Network (PSLN) in Milton Keynes.

Networks provide:

- opportunities for staff to both gain and generate knowledge;

- a variety of collaborative structures;

- flexibility and informality;

- discussion of problems that have no agreed-upon solutions;

- ideas that challenge staff rather than merely prescribing generic solutions;

- an organizational structure that can be independent of, yet attached to, schools or universities;

- a chance to work across schools and district/local authority lines;

- a vision of reform that excites and encourages risk-taking in a supportive environment;

- a community that respects teachers' knowledge as well as knowledge from research and reform (Lieberman, 1999).

The NCSL website (www.ncsl.org.uk) has many useful resources related to networked learning communities. There are six interconnected levels of learning, which are the foundations for each network:

- *pupil learning* – pupils tell us about themselves as learners;
- *adult learning* – through joint work, adults teach each other the art and craft of teaching;
- *leadership for learning and leadership development* – leaders coach and facilitate others to lead;
- *school-wide learning* – adults become better every year at supporting pupil learning, just because they work in this school and network;
- *school-to-school learning* – our schools learn more because they are learning together;
- *network-to-network learning* – we feel part of a learning profession.

WHAT IS EFFECTIVE CPD?

Any discussion of what constitutes effective professional development needs to begin by asking effective for whom – the individual, the school and its pupils, or the education system as a whole? And for what? The beneficiaries of CPD may not always over-lap, although in many cases they will; what is helpful for an individual is also likely to be of benefit both for pupils and the school. On the other hand, training to meet the latest government initiative may be effective for implementing a particular strategy but not necessarily for the overall long-term development of staff. Effective CPD is likely to consist of that which first and foremost enhances pupil outcomes, but which also helps to bring about changes in practice and improves teaching, management and leadership skills and qualities. It should be 'fit for purpose' and add something to the school's overall capacity to develop; the school should be able to build upon the collective learning of its people. Exposure to and participation in a wide range of professional development opportunities are likely to bring about change to individuals' beliefs, values, attitudes and behaviours, and these may well lead to changes in classroom and school practices. Any change should, however, lead to improvement; we are not talking about change for change's sake!

Ultimately, effective CPD should lead to improvements in the five outcomes of the *Every Child Matters* agenda through supporting all children to:

1 Be healthy.
2 Stay safe.
3 Enjoy and achieve.
4 Make a positive contribution.
5 Achieve economic wellbeing.

Much has been written about what constitutes effective CPD (e.g. a series of EPPI reviews conducted by Cordingley et al., 2004, 2005, 2006) but it should be remembered that the characteristics influencing effectiveness are multiple and highly complex. We should therefore begin with an important caveat: the technical and methodological problems of measuring the direct effects or impact of CPD especially on classroom performance – of both staff and pupils – are considerable. This is, amongst other reasons, because the term embraces a wide variety of modes and methods, and includes professional training, education and support. The number of variables to be taken into account is considerable. In Chapter 6, for example, we show how the 'impact' of a course or a piece of training may be mediated through a number of factors.

Continuing professional development can only have an indirect impact on pupil learning and outcomes. Very few research studies have considered the relationship between the characteristics of professional development and any change in classroom teaching practice or the gains in pupil achievement or learning outcomes more broadly. Despite this, there is a growing body of research evidence and informed professional judgement that gives a broad indication of the essential characteristics of effective CPD.

An early National Foundation for Educational Research (NFER) study found effective CPD could take a variety of forms but had a number of key characteristics. These included the clear identification of aims and objectives, along with an analysis of training needs to ensure training and development activities matched existing levels of expertise. Training needs were identified at school level following appraisal (performance management) and/or the drawing up of the school development plan. Opportunities for reflection were also important, as were action research, on-going evaluation and follow-up work. Effective training was seen to form part of a coherent programme and was not a 'one-off' activity. The optimum use of existing resources and facilities was most likely when CPD activities were well planned, helping to promote targeted and tailor-made training, avoiding overload and minimizing disruption (Brown and Earley, 1990).

In 2002, Her Majesty's Inspectors found that:

> Teachers, line managers and CPD co-ordinators rarely assembled an array of CPD activities to form a coherent individual training plan, designed to bring about specific improvement in a teacher's knowledge and skills. More often teachers worked on a range of loosely related activities that did not always provide good value or achieve the intended outcome. (Ofsted, 2002a: 3)

The report concluded that schools 'failed to allow enough time to support effective professional development and to ensure that acquired knowledge and skills were consolidated, implemented and shared with other teachers' (Ofsted, 2002a: 3).

More recently, Ofsted describes the management of professional development as a logical chain of procedures, which entails 'identifying school and staff needs, planning to meet those needs, providing varied and relevant activities, involving support staff alongside teachers, monitoring progress and evaluating the impact of the professional development'. They note that schools which had designed their CPD effectively and integrated it with their improvement plans found that teaching and learning improved and standards rose (Ofsted, 2006: 2).

Fragmented 'one-shot' workshops and conferences at which staff listen passively to 'experts' rarely make a difference. As Boyle and colleagues point out, these traditional approaches to professional development appear insufficient to foster learning which fundamentally alters what teachers teach or how they teach. The following types of professional development activities are more likely to offer sustained learning opportunities:

- study groups in which staff are engaged on regular, structured and collaborative interactions around topics identified by the group;
- observation – observing others and being observed;
- coaching or mentoring arrangements, where staff work one-on-one with an equally or more experienced teacher;
- networks, which link people either in person or electronically, to explore and discuss topics of interest, pursue common goals, share information and address common concerns;
- immersion in inquiry, in which people engage in the kinds of learning that they are expected to practise with their students (Boyle et al., 2003: 3).

Involvement in development activities by staff is, to a large extent, voluntary but there are a number of factors that will encourage participation. Boring, repetitive and dependent work discourages professional development and growth, whereas challenging, variable and independent work encourages it – certainly there are parallels with the classroom here. Equally personal factors and life changes can cause individuals to reconsider career priorities and goals. Professional development can help enhance performance through improved self-esteem – this, along with personal wellbeing and a sense of professional control, are all essential components of job satisfaction.

The CfBT/Lincolnshire model uses nine characteristics of a school to judge the quality of its CPD: ethos, school support, the role of the CPD leader, systems, needs identification, approaches, evaluation, dissemination and professional recognition (see Table 2.3). Thomas Guskey (2002) helped to develop the Standards for Staff Development published by the National Staff Development Council. These consist of context, process and content standards.

TABLE 2.3 CHARACTERISTICS OF A SCHOOL WITH OUTSTANDING CPD

Feature	Qualities
Ethos	Strong sense of 'learning community' Whole school community heavily involved in CPD Staff enthusiastic and positive about CPD Entitlements/guarantees ensure equality of opportunity Staff take responsibility for their own CPD
School support	Strong support for CPD from the school leaders and governors School devotes sizeable resources to CPD and monitors and evaluates their use
Role of CPD leader	Clearly defined and attracts status and respect
Systems	Systems are effective and not excessively bureaucratic CPD policy and systems are fully understood by all and seen as an integral part of school improvement and morale
Needs identification	Reliable systems to identify needs and aspirations effectively using existing data such as self-evaluation and PM information Views of the workforce are actively sought and considered
Approaches	Recognizes benefits of different kinds of training and support Wide repertoire of approaches suitably differentiated to reflect needs Workforce aware of what is most effective for them CPD available addresses school, national and personal needs School effectively develops its own staff to contribute as well as receive CPD Good use is made of in-house expertise as well as external provision
Evaluation	Considerable attention is devoted to measuring the impact of CPD Range of criteria used such as objective and less-easily measured aspects such as self-esteem, confidence and risk-taking
Dissemination	Good grasp of what proves successful and effective with regard to CPD Dissemination carefully planned for and given adequate time and other resources Role of sustaining and embedding is seen as very important
Professional recognition	Strong encouragement for the workforce to earn professional recognition including accreditation

Source: CfBT/Lincs, 2006: 42

CONTEXT STANDARDS

Staff development that improves the learning of all students:

- Organizes adults into learning communities whose goals are aligned with those of the school and district.

- Requires skilful school and district leaders who guide continuous instructional improvement.

- Requires resources to support adult learning and collaboration.

PROCESS STANDARDS

Staff development that improves the learning of all students:

- Uses disaggregated student data to determine adult learning priorities, monitor progress, and help sustain continuous improvement.
- Uses multiple sources of information to guide improvement and demonstrate its impact.
- Prepares educators to apply research to decision-making.
- Uses learning strategies appropriate to the intended goal.
- Applies knowledge about human learning and change.
- Provides educators with the knowledge and skills to collaborate.

CONTENT STANDARDS

Staff development that improves the learning of all students:

- Prepares educators to understand and appreciate all students, create safe, orderly and supportive learning environments, and hold high expectations for their academic achievement.
- Deepens educators' content knowledge, provides them with research-based instructional strategies to assist students in meeting rigorous academic standards, and prepares them to use various types of classroom assessments appropriately.
- Provides educators with knowledge and skills to involve families and other stakeholders appropriately (NSDC, 2001).

THE STANDARDS FRAMEWORK

In 2007, the Training and Development Agency for Schools (TDA) brought coherence to the framework of professional and occupational standards for classroom teachers in England and introduced new standards for qualified teacher status (Q), induction (the core, C), post-threshold (P), excellent teacher (E) and advanced skills teacher (A). All the standards are underpinned by the five key outcomes for children and young people identified in *Every Child Matters* and the six areas of the *Common core of skills and knowledge for the children's workforce* (see Figure 8.1). They are arranged in three interrelated sections:

a) Professional attributes
b) Professional knowledge and understanding
c) Professional skills.

They are organized like a tree with the QTS and core standards being the trunk off which the other standards grow (see Table 2.4). Each set of standards builds on the previous set, so that a teacher being considered for the threshold would need to satisfy the threshold standards (P) and continue to meet the core standards (C); a teacher aspiring to become an Excellent Teacher would need to satisfy the standards that are specific to that status (E) and continue to meet the preceding relevant standards (C and P); and a teacher aspiring to become an AST would need to satisfy the standards that are specific to that status (A) as well as meeting the preceding relevant standards (C, P and E), although they can apply for an AST post before going through the threshold.

TABLE 2.4 AN EXTRACT FROM THE TEACHERS' STANDARDS FRAMEWORK

1. Professional attributes				
Those recommended for the award of QTS (Q) should:	All teachers (C) should:	Post-threshold teachers (P) should:	Excellent teachers (E) should:	Advanced skills teachers (A) should:
Q3 (a) Be aware of the professional duties of teachers and the statutory framework within which they work. (b) Be aware of the policies and practices of the workplace and share in collective responsibility for their implementation.	**C3** Maintain an up-to-date knowledge and understanding of the professional duties of teachers and the statutory framework within which they work, and contribute to the development, implementation and evaluation of the policies and practice of their workplace, including those designed to promote equality of opportunity. **P1** Contribute significantly, where appropriate, to implementing workplace policies and practice and to promoting collective responsibility for their implementation.		**E1** Be prepared to take a leading role in developing workplace policies and practice and in promoting collective responsibility for their implementation.	**A1** Be prepared to take on a strategic leadership role in developing workplace policies and practice and in promoting collective responsibility for their implementation in their own and other workplaces.

Source: TDA, 2007a

The framework of standards is progressive, reflecting the development of teachers' professional attributes, knowledge and understanding and skills. Post-threshold teachers are expected to act as role models for teaching and learning, make a distinctive contribution to raising standards across the school and provide regular coaching and mentoring to less experienced teachers. Excellent Teachers provide an exemplary model to others through their professional expertise, have a leading role in raising standards by supporting improvements in teaching practice and support and help their colleagues to improve their effectiveness and to address their development needs through highly effective coaching and mentoring. Advanced Skills Teachers provide models of excellent and innovative teaching and use their skills to enhance teaching and learning by undertaking and leading school improvement activities and continuing professional development (CPD) for other teachers. They support staff in other schools one day a week and draw on the experience they gain elsewhere to improve practice in their own and other schools.

The framework may also help to develop a clearer and more relevant job description or career path. Teachers' careers can and do follow a huge variety of different routes. Some teachers never want to take on management responsibilities but make extremely valuable contributions to their pupils and their schools by the quality of their teaching in the classroom. Some move through different leadership roles and eventually become headteachers. In between there are many different combinations and sequences of roles – including moves into and out of other areas of education, or other areas of employment more generally. Effective CPD needs to meet all these needs.

PROFESSIONAL DEVELOPMENT PORTFOLIOS

Staff need a receptacle for all professional development and performance management related paperwork. A professional development portfolio is useful in chronicling where one has been and planning where one wants to go. It is not a requirement but many people are now keeping such a folder. Many new teachers start them in training. There are many models around but all embody the wider idea of the responsible and reflective professional who keeps an on-going record of professional development. It is a receptacle for all objectives, action plans, reflections and assessments that can stay with the teacher for their whole career and be used for induction, performance management, threshold and job applications.

People who keep professional development portfolios say how useful they are. Here are some soundbites from teachers:

> The portfolio does make you think differently about yourself. You recognise the things that you do and it makes you feel good about the things that you do. It's very easy to become frustrated by what you are not achieving rather than by what you are achieving. And, it's so easy to forget. The portfolio is one of those ways to look at what you have achieved. I think parents should see the teacher's portfolio. It would blow their mind.
>
> I love doing my portfolio! I find it really satisfying, especially to look back at. (Berrill and Whalen, 2003: 5)

Some portfolios are kept electronically. Keeping Track (www.teachernet.gov.uk/development) has been the professional and career development section of the Teachernet website since 2004. The great thing about Keeping Track is that it is free but it has disadvantages: it is only designed to be used by individual staff so it would involve a lot of cutting and pasting to enable a CPD manager to collate people's professional development. However, Keeping Track provides individuals with the opportunity to build and maintain an electronic professional portfolio (an e-portfolio) by:

- showing individuals how to keep track of their own professional development;

- enabling individuals to record milestones and achievements as a basis for reflecting on progress and further development needs;

- making it easier for individuals to maintain and update CPD records, and their CV.

Once individuals have logged in, using a password, all of the information they record on the site is confidential and saved in their 'filing cabinet'. However, they can print off a copy; copy the document from the on-line filing cabinet and attach it to an e-mail; or ask a colleague to read individual entries on screen. Alternatively, staff may just use some features such as the CPD log or CV. These come in either a template or a free form.

There is much on this website for CPD co-ordinators to dip into and use selectively to augment their work. The templates section has questionnaires, self-audits, and a learning journal, that CPD co-ordinators might wish to use or modify. Some of these could be used as part of the basic CPD structures within a school and others as optional extras. Different people record experiences in different ways – some love learning journals and others think they're a waste of time.

The case studies are structured to show different career routes and how these were chosen. They describe the experiences of a range of teachers in all phases, from NQTs, career changers, middle and senior managers, right up to Her Majesty's Chief Inspector. This might inspire staff in schools to discuss their career routes and why they made certain choices. 'Starting Points' identifies the characteristics of effective teachers in the context of the Threshold Standards, and invites individuals to use questionnaires to compare their progress and performance against these.

Companies such as Blue and Ascon have produced software systems that unify both the individual and school level professional development with performance management, and so could be very useful for CPD managers. Both cater for all staff, not just the teachers, and have testimonials from schools that have used them. The downside is the cost but if the system works well this would easily be recompensed for by the time saved. Schools would need to ensure that:

- the system worked alongside existing software;
- it was easy to use by people with a range of ICT skills;
- time was given to training people in the system;
- the running costs (for getting updates and troubleshooting) were reasonable.

CONCLUSION

How can we disseminate good practice within school? Recognizing its existence and its importance is a good start. We also need to remind ourselves of the finding from school effectiveness research that individual teachers in their classrooms matter three or four times more than headteachers or other school 'effects'. So focusing on best practice at classroom level is essential. David Reynolds (2003) states that we need to rid ourselves of the notion that the way to improve the system is through school-to-school transfer of good practice – the belief which underlies training and specialist schools, for example. It is, he argues, much more sensible for schools not to be dependent on others helping them out but from learning from their own best practice. He claims that 'every school, no matter how well it is doing overall, has practitioners relatively better than others, many schools will have excellent teachers defined in national terms, and a significant proportion of schools will have world-class people' (ibid.: 23).

Helping people learn from others in their schools is so much easier (and cheaper) than learning from someone 20 miles away. 'When you are "buddied" with a colleague who is doing better than you with the same children in the same school, that is when the alibis stop' (ibid: 23).

We need to get people from the same department or school working closely together, talking and sharing experiences. But we also need to be aware of the limitations of such an approach if it is taken up to the exclusion of all else. Good schools welcome the contribution of outsiders – critical friends from the local university and the local authority, for example – and there is a real danger of schools 'recycling their own inadequacies' without it. Pachler and Field state that:

> CPD is dependent upon debate, discussion, sharing and joint learning and therefore we must be prepared to use our work context and the people therein as a resource for our learning, but also be prepared to assist in the 'generation' of sharable examples to enable the transferral and adaptation of good ideas to others. (2004: 6)

Nevertheless, Reynolds' plea for a new emphasis on internal good practice is a valid one. It is also a central feature of a learning-centred community. More recently, Michael Fielding and colleagues (2005) in a study of factors influencing the transfer of 'good practice' prefer to use the term 'joint practice development' as a more accurate and appropriate description of how staff learn.

The role of CPD managers and school leaders in all this is crucial as they encourage staff to think about their own learning. Professional development managers and school leaders themselves need to be up to date and demonstrate a commitment to CPD, to be 'lead learners' promoting a learning climate or culture and monitoring and evaluating the progress of staff professional development and training. It is difficult not to be a learning adult in a learning-centred school! But such schools have to be managed and it is to the management and leadership of CPD that we turn to in the next chapter.

3

Leading and Managing CPD

- ◆ The professional development co-ordinator role
- ◆ The training and development cycle
- ◆ Investors in People
- ◆ CPD policy
- ◆ Budgets
- ◆ Training and development for CPD co-ordinators

Professional development does not just happen – it has to be managed and led, and done so effectively ensuring it has a positive impact and represents good value for money. Research (Hustler et al., 2003) on teachers' attitudes to CPD found that the status, knowledge and approach of the CPD co-ordinator (and the leadership team or senior management team more generally) could radically affect, positively or negatively, staff attitudes towards and understandings of professional development. The Office for Standards in Education found that:

> Teachers, line managers and CPD co-ordinators rarely assembled an array of CPD activities to form a coherent individual training plan, designed to bring about specific improvement in a teacher's knowledge and skills. More often teachers worked on a range of loosely related activities that did not always provide good value or achieve the intended outcome. (Ofsted, 2002a: 3)

The CPD co-ordinator role is both crucial and often underdeveloped – many could benefit from professional development in order to do their job better. If one of the keys to effective CPD is to ensure it is well led and managed, then the role of CPD co-ordinator needs to be given the kudos and time it requires to be done well. We need to move from an administrative role to that of facilitator and staff supporter.

The Training and Development Agency for schools (TDA) wants to build stronger infrastructures in schools. The GTC(E) have formed an online network of CPD co-ordinators called 'Connect'. This has rightly raised their status because they have the power to make a significant difference to their colleagues and thereby raise pupil achievement, but they also risk wasting a great deal of time and money. How many people have had training in how to lead and manage professional development? It has to be done effectively so that CPD gives good value for money and has a positive impact.

Schools often link CPD to objectives or targets as identified in both school improvement and personal development plans, and these in turn are related to a system of performance management or staff appraisal. In this way it is likely that an appropriate balance will be retained between school (and group) needs and the personal and professional needs of the individual – between what has been referred to, more generally, as 'hard' and 'soft' aspects of human resource management. Staff will always feel the need to be valued and this should not be forgotten when considering the balance between identifying and meeting individual and school needs.

The effective management of CPD should ensure that support is available and conditions created which enable staff to work together and to develop and improve their workplace performance. Through headteachers, CPD co-ordinators and other staff helping to create a climate or culture which is conducive to learning – of both staff and pupils – schools and colleges are well on the road to becoming learning-centred communities where investment in people is given the priority it deserves. Student learning is a key goal of all educational organizations, whereas the on-going learning of teachers, support staff and other paid employees is not always prioritized or adequately resourced.

Creating a culture of learning is crucial and this is going to be shaped by the attitude and approach of educational leaders towards CPD. What messages are headteachers and other educational leaders giving about the importance of professional development? Are they themselves participating in training, particularly in school-based events, are they 'leading the learning'? If it is true that 'children learn more from adults' deeds than their words' and that 'in order to develop a love of learning in students, teachers must first be learners themselves' (Jallongo, 1991: 48), then this is equally true of teachers and others working in the organization.

This chapter considers how schools and educational systems are approaching the leadership and management of CPD. It draws upon existing research and inspection findings to illuminate some of the key issues that need to be given consideration by educational leaders. It commences with an examination of the role of the professional development co-ordinator.

THE PROFESSIONAL DEVELOPMENT CO-ORDINATOR ROLE

It could be argued that leading and managing professional development to help bring about a learning-centred community, for all that work or study within it, is everybody's responsibility. However, formally the responsibility is most likely to belong to the professional development or CPD co-ordinator or leader. The person undertaking this responsibility is usually a senior member of staff, often a deputy or assistant head, or in primary schools (especially small ones) the headteacher. The responsibility for managing CPD may be part of the post holder's wider 'human resources' or personnel function, but it will always be one of several management responsibilities held.

No longer is CPD co-ordination about collating all the thousands of fliers and booking courses: the role is expanding to cover many of the core functions within a school (see an example of a CPD co-ordinator job description in Figure 3.1). Capacity building and change management processes to enable schools to become learning-centred communities are central to the role, as are auditing and organizing opportunities to meet the learning needs of staff as they are identified through performance management (and other processes) and linked to individual and school improvement plans.

At the moment job titles have a combination of these words:

- CPD/professional development/staff development/INSET/human resources
- Co-ordinator/leader/manager/officer/administrator.

More often the role is subsumed under the title 'head', 'deputy' or 'assistant head'. This is indicative of the confusion around the role – and how much is expected from it. For instance, contributors (LA and school CPD co-ordinators) to *London's Learning* (DfES, 2005a) consider that a school has a good basis to be a learning-centred community when the CPD leader:

- is a member of the school's leadership team;
- empowers individual staff to be responsible for their own professional development;

- empowers team leaders to be responsible for their team's learning programmes;
- has an overview of the learning of all staff in the school and its impact on standards and school improvement;
- ensures that CPD and performance management are integral to the improvement cycle of the school;
- ensures the characteristics of high quality professional learning are applied to development opportunities available to all staff;
- promotes the link between effective professional learning and the standards of teaching and learning;
- integrates local, regional and national opportunities into staff learning plans and relates these to school priorities;
- uses CPD resources strategically to bring about school improvement;
- ensures all staff contribute to effective school evaluation and improvement processes (DfES, 2005a).

As national standards are being developed across the teaching profession from teaching assistants, to NQTs to headteachers, should there be a set for CPD co-ordinators? It is difficult because while we agree with Goodall et al.'s (2005) recommendation that the CPD leader role should be undertaken by a senior member of staff, we believe that such a statement is misleading because one person cannot do the job alone. It would be more accurate to say that *overall responsibility* should lie with a senior member of staff because the job needs more than one person – unless they don't do anything else! Clear job descriptions are needed to define exactly who does what and where priorities lie. Many of the tasks – the budget, booking cover and courses – are administrative and don't need a teacher to undertake them. Below is a list of tasks that needs to be broken down and parts allocated to appropriate people:

- to identify school training and development needs in the context of the school development plan;
- to assure the identification of individual development needs in accordance with the staff development policy and procedures;
- to compile the school's training and development plan;
- to determine resource needs and allocate resources in accordance with the staff development policy;
- to design training programmes in accordance with effective learning principles and to assist others in this task;
- to co-ordinate the provision of training in accordance with the school's training plan;
- to monitor resource expenditure on staff development and to ensure expenditure stays within budget;
- to support and advise other managers in their staff development role;
- to promote the monitoring and assessment of staff learning and performance, ensuring that such activities are used to steer development and enhance performance;
- to collect information on performance and to assist other managers in this task, so as to contribute to evaluation;
- to evaluate and improve the school's training and development programmes and processes (based on Baxter and Chambers, 1998).

1 The school will have a named CPD co-ordinator who shall be deemed to be fulfilling a leadership and management responsibility in relation to this post. The CPD co-ordinator will receive training as appropriate in order to fulfil this role effectively and attend useful providers sessions;

2 The CPD co-ordinator shall be responsible for identifying the school's CPD needs and those of the staff working within it. CPD will be an integral part of the school's development plan and be based on a range of information:

- the needs of the school as identified through its self-evaluation;

- issues identified through other monitoring, e.g. Ofsted, quality standards such as Investors in People;

- national and local priorities, e.g. national strategies, the LA's EDP, local community priorities;

- Performance Management;

- feedback from staff and others including governors, pupils and parents;

3 The CPD co-ordinator will be responsible annually for discussing with the headteacher and governing body the main CPD priorities and the likely budgetary implications of addressing these needs. They will advise on issues such as the benefits of service agreements with appropriate providers;

4 CPD issues will be addressed at governing body meetings and be included as part of the headteacher report. The CPD co-ordinator shall attend governing body meetings and those of the curriculum committee as appropriate including the presentation annually of a report on the provision and impact of CPD;

5 Requests for accessing CPD should be addressed to the CPD co-ordinator who will decide on the most effective means, e.g. deciding whether to offer to a single member of the school community or whether there would be benefits in more having direct access;

6 The CPD co-ordinator should provide and update details of the range of CPD opportunities available and be responsible for communicating relevant opportunities to appropriate staff, e.g. relevant courses, partnership groups, distance learning materials. The information will be kept updated and made accessible and available to staff;

7 The CPD co-ordinator shall be responsible for ensuring that appropriate opportunities are provided for all groups in the school community;

8 The CPD co-ordinator will maintain a list of accredited providers and will use only those who have accredited status;

9 There will be annual discussion between staff and the CPD co-ordinator to discuss within the context of school priorities:

- needs and aspirations;

- methods of accessing CPD provision including appropriate bursaries;

- accreditation opportunities;

- ways of disseminating the training.

Where appropriate, this will be combined with the Performance Management process.

10 The CPD co-ordinator will be responsible for ensuring the efficient organizing of opportunities, e.g. booking, replacement cover arrangements, circulating relevant materials;

11 The CPD co-ordinator will be responsible for providing appropriate support to CPD, e.g. training videos, organizing membership and subscriptions of appropriate bodies such as subject associations, school improvement organizations;

12 Where the school is either offered an opportunity or where a member of the school community recommends participating in a school improvement project or initiative, the CPD co-ordinator will be responsible for investigating the benefits and for reporting to the headteacher and governing body.

FIGURE 3.1 A CPD CO-ORDINATOR JOB DESCRIPTION (FROM CfBT/LINCS, 2006: 120)

We suggest that new terms would raise the profile of and give clarity to the role, perhaps in a similar way to the changes that occurred when the term 'SENco' started to be used. The STADco would be the Staff Training and Development Co-ordinator; the STADle, the leader; STADman, the manager; and STADadmin, the administrator. The word 'staff' is used rather than 'professional' to emphasize that we're looking at the whole school workforce not just the teachers (the professionals). The phrase 'training and development' can be used both as a catch-all and to distinguish between formal training and more holistic development.

Does the CPD co-ordinator need to be a teacher? We have come across someone in the role whose background is in administration and who is also the headteacher's PA.

CASE STUDY 3.1: HEATH PARK TECHNOLOGY COLLEGE, WELLS

Rita Chase, the full-time Training School and CPD Manager at Heath Park Technology College in Corby, is an example of the potential of workforce remodelling. Young and with a background in project management rather than teaching, she is an unusual appointment but she successfully manages the training school budget and organizes the professional development of all staff, from the bespoke to whole school training. Offering amongst other things voice coaching and sessions on body language run by a teacher from the drama department, she works closely with trainee and newly qualified teachers. She is very good at keeping track of who's done what and offers a menu of professional development activities that takes account of money, time and resources. Tim Hobbs, part of the leadership team, can't speak highly enough of her: 'Because Rita is doing this I can spend time on things that really require a teacher'. He is Rita's link to the staff. For instance, she wants to introduce 360 degree feedback so Tim gives advice on how to circumvent the cynics.

Baxter and Chambers (1998) have drawn upon the national standards developed by the training and development lead body (TDLB) to examine systematically the role of the CPD co-ordinator in schools. Such guidelines would allow CPD leaders to 'set their own targets and goals, and would allow for recognition of the importance of embedding evaluative practices' (Goodall et al., 2005: 10).

Although there is no judgement specifically on developing the workforce in inspection reports, inspectors will assess the extent to which the performance management, deployment and development of staff are effective in bringing about improvement in the areas identified through the school's self-evaluation form (SEF). Schools are asked to grade themselves on their SEF on a four point scale (Grade 1: Outstanding; Grade 2: Good; Grade 3: Satisfactory; Grade 4: Inadequate) on each of these aspects:

- Learners' achievement and standards in their work
- Learners' personal development and wellbeing
- Quality of teaching and learning
- Quality of the curriculum and other activities
- Quality of care, guidance and support for learners
- Effectiveness and efficiency of leadership and management
- Overall effectiveness
- Capacity to make further improvement
- Improvement since the last inspection
- Quality and standards in the Foundation Stage (Ofsted, 2007).

Inspectors will consider the investment the school makes in its staff to raise pupil standards and the extent to which coherent professional development strategies are linked with improvement planning and performance management. Understanding the training and development cycle is key to the CPD co-ordinator role.

THE TRAINING AND DEVELOPMENT CYCLE

Managing CPD in any organization, be it a small or medium-sized primary school or a large multi-purpose college, requires an understanding and knowledge of many things. These include the processes by which adults best learn and the devising of plans and policies to underpin effective practice. It is also crucially important to understand the training and development cycle illustrated in Figure 3.2. This model consists of six stages, all of which are broadly subsumed within the CPD co-ordinator's job description. Each of the stages will be examined in the next three chapters. The stages are:

- identifying and analysing training needs – Chapter 4;
- planning and designing programmes, their implementation or delivery – Chapter 5;
- monitoring and evaluation: the impact of CPD – Chapter 6.

Ofsted (2006) talks of a similar approach to understanding the cycle of training and development when it talks about 'a logical chain' of CPD processes which entails:

> identifying school and staff needs, planning to meet those needs, providing varied and relevant activities, involving support staff alongside teachers, monitoring progress and evaluating the impact of the professional development. (2006: 2)

Overall HMI, who conducted the study, found that CPD was 'most effective in the schools where the senior managers fully understood the connections between each link in the chain' (ibid: 2).

The chain or the cycle is complex, but we hope that the next three chapters will help.

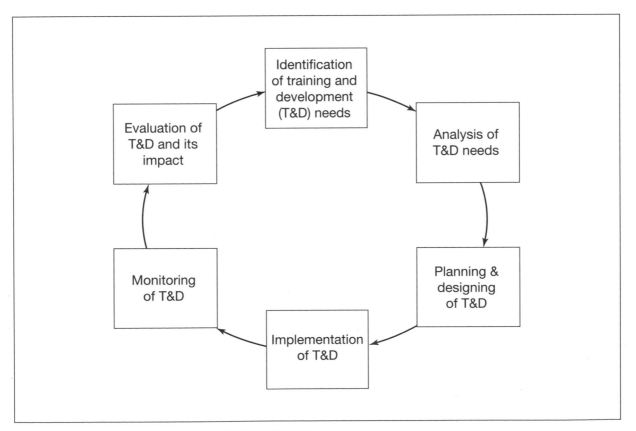

FIGURE 3.2 TRAINING AND DEVELOPMENT CYCLE

INVESTORS IN PEOPLE

How can you tell that your investment in people is making a difference? Having processes in place may be important, but will not necessarily lead to the results you desire. Many schools and colleges have instituted a major review of continuing professional development under the impetus of applying for Investors in People recognition. This is a national quality standard (Figure 3.3) that sets a level of good practice for improving an organization's performance through its people. This national standard for training and development is at the forefront in helping schools and colleges to embrace a development culture and become learning-centred communities capable of developing themselves and their workforce. Most importantly, there is plenty of evidence to show that it has helped to ensure that a culture of training and development is embedded within the organization's CPD structures and processes.

Developing strategies to improve the performance of the organization
1   A strategy for improving the performance of the organization is clearly defined and understood.
2   Learning and development are planned to achieve the organization's objectives.
3   Strategies for managing people are designed to promote quality of opportunity in the development of the organization's people.
4   The capabilities managers need to lead, manage and develop people effectively are clearly defined and understood.

Taking action to improve the performance of the organization
5   Managers are effective in leading, managing and developing people.
6   People's contribution to the organization is recognized and valued.
7   People are encouraged to take ownership and responsibility by being involved in decision-making.
8   People learn and develop effectively.

Evaluating the impact on the performance of the organization
9   Investment in people improves the performance of the organization.
10   Improvements are continually made to the way people are managed and developed.

FIGURE 3.3 THE INVESTORS IN PEOPLE NATIONAL STANDARD (IiP, 2006)

Investors in People has presented schools and colleges with a number of challenges especially evaluating the impact of its investment in people on its performance (see Chapter 6). Research into Investors in People in the education sector has also demonstrated three other factors of significance, namely:

- the need to address the training and development requirements of support staff as well as teachers;

- for all those staff with management responsibilities to see this as including the need to take responsibility for the development of other people (their staff development role);

- that there is not necessarily a conflict between the needs of schools and colleges and that of individuals working within them (Earley, 1996).

CPD POLICY

Leaders and co-ordinators of CPD need systems to help them do their job and raise the status of professional development in the school. One of the ways that Ash Manor School in Surrey does this is to have a professional development committee. As well as the co-ordinator, it consists of the head; the deputy head; a support staff representative; a department head; a main scale teacher; and one other member of staff. The committee decides the school's annual professional development targets, which fit in with the

SDP. It is helpful to be able to discuss CPD issues with others – things like how to spend money efficiently, choosing from the bewildering array of consultants and courses, how not to add to staff workload and how to meet the needs of a very disparate group of people. Continuing professional development policies are useful in making clear expectations and entitlements. Here are some headings that might prove useful in structuring one:

- Rationale and purpose of CPD; people covered by the policy.
- The range of CPD opportunities in the school, close to the school and outside the school.
- Roles of people involved in CPD.
- Procedures – applications, funding, monitoring, impact, etc.
- Related school documents e.g. performance management, induction, etc.

Have a look in *The CPD Co-ordinator's Toolkit* by Sue Kelly (Paul Chapman Publishing, 2006) for some examples.

? POINTS FOR REFLECTION

Application and evaluation forms can carry subliminal messages. Can you see what messages are being conveyed in the form in Figure 3.4?

BUDGETS

Professional development co-ordinators – like everyone else – have to work within budgetary constraints, and sometimes one may find oneself awash with money and at other times there are massive cuts or other priorities. There has been a move away from ring-fenced training grants and centrally run programmes so that all the funding for CPD is devolved to schools. How much of the general school budget will be dedicated to training and development, and which staff members will benefit from it, are decisions for schools to make (see Kelly, 2006: 64 for a handy spreadsheet). Funding has to cover a host of people's professional developments and there are difficult decisions to be made. The potential for individuals to feel hard done by is great. Consider this teacher's point of view made on the *Times Educational Supplement (TES)* Website Professional Development Forum:

> Is attending a headteachers' conference really more important than four training days for staff? Which adds more to raising standards? Which would have more impact: a very stressed teacher who is enduring appalling behavioural problems attending training aimed at supporting teachers in that situation or a headteacher attending the same course and cascading useful information in a five minute soundbite at a staff meeting?

Managing CPD is a complex affair in which many priorities compete for attention. Procedures followed can often come to reflect custom and habit rather than a considered response to changing circumstances. It is important, to step back and ask such questions as:

- Why are we doing this?
- What do we need to achieve?
- Is this method the most economical, efficient and effective?
- What is in the best interests of our pupils?
- What is the evidence about levels of need?

CPD EVALUATION   Please return to ....

Ref. no:

Name:	Development activity:
Type of CPD (circle):	Observation/Visit/Course/Conference/Study time/Meeting time/Other (please specify)

Venue:	Organization: Address:	Date:	Time:

Cost:	Cover required:	Travel/subsistence cost:	Total:

Links to targets

PM: Standards: SIP: Other:

What do you want to achieve?

Predicted impact and dissemination – discuss with a colleague

Predicted impact: Predicted dissemination:	WHEN?	TO WHOM?

Team Leader's comments: I agree to the application and confirm funding arrangements are correct.		
Signed Team Leader:	Funding source	Date:
Signed Applicant:		Date:

YOUR REQUEST HAS BEEN/NOT BEEN APPROVED

The CPD activity has been booked by .... on .... (date)

The cover arrangements are as follows: ....

Signature: .... (CPD co-ordinator)

CPD EVALUATION

Ref. no:

SECTION 1 – EVALUATION – complete within five working days of the activity

Did the CPD activity take place as planned? Yes/No. If No, please state why

A. How would you rate the CPD activity on a 1–4 scale? Interest ☐ Relevance ☐ Value for money ☐
1 = Excellent   4 = Poor

Comments

What did you gain?
Unexpected gains?
Networks made: (name, contact details)

Impact and dissemination – What are you going to do as a result of this CPD activity? What help do you need? What are you going to disseminate, when and to whom?

Impact planned:	WHEN?	TO WHOM?
Dissemination:		

SECTION 2 – TEAM LEADER EVALUATION to be completed after six weeks

Has the dissemination happened? YES/NO To whom? Date:

Comments:

What impact has it had on the individual and/or the subject/team/school?

What has been the impact on teaching and learning?

Next steps:

Signed: Date:

FIGURE 3.4 CPD APPLICATION AND EVALUATION FORMS

Leading and Managing Continuing Professional Development by Bubb and Earley, PCP 2007

- Are there better ways of achieving the desired results?
- Could another organization do this for us more effectively and economically?
- Are our procedures competitive compared with possible alternatives?

It is helpful to consider the principles of best value known familiarly as the four Cs:

Challenge – is the professional development pitched at the right level for all participants?
Compare – how does your school's CPD compare with other schools and between parts of the school? Are you getting good value for money from your spending of the CPD budget?
Consult – listen to the views of staff especially over the use of CPD funding; ask around for the best forms of CPD, the best providers, consultants, etc.
Compete – as a means of securing efficient and effective CPD.

CfBT in Lincolnshire have drawn up a value for money analysis to consider the benefits and drawbacks of different types of workforce development (Figure 3.5), and offer suggestions for maximising efficiency.

CPD PROCESS	COST	BENEFITS	DRAWBACKS	MAXIMIZING EFFICIENCY
Attendance at a lecture, course or conference	High	Input from specialists or experts; Sharing ideas; Possible supporting resources.	Disruptive of time; Cover usually needed; Not all external provision is of good quality; Often lacks personalization to needs of school and individual; Inefficient dissemination to colleagues.	Needs to ensure clarity of purpose of provision in advance; School needs quality assurance evidence; Possibly more than one to attend from the school; School needs effective system of dissemination; School needs efficient implementation systems.
Working within a learning team (in a dept, KS or on a cross-school theme)	Low	Encourages teamwork and sharing of good practice; Sense of working towards a common goal is stimulating.	Can be viewed merely as an extension to the 'day job' and not as CPD.	Clear focus needs to be established in order to avoid over-generalization; Ground rules needed to ensure that all colleagues are able to have ownership and make a valid contribution.
Observing colleagues teaching	Medium	Close analysis of practice; Analysis of effectiveness leads to improvement in practice.	Needs cover if done effectively; Depends on coaching and mentoring skills; Can mismatch colleagues.	Needs clear focus; good match of colleagues; School system of coaching and mentoring; Time to engage with fully; And time to follow up and implement.

FIGURE 3.5 VALUE FOR MONEY: MEASURING THE BENEFITS OF DIFFERENT TYPES OF WORKFORCE DEVELOPMENT (BASED ON CfBT/LINCS, 2006)

TRAINING AND DEVELOPMENT FOR CPD CO-ORDINATORS

Our research has found that there continues to be little CPD provided specifically for co-ordinators. Some local authorities and private providers offer one-day courses supplemented by newsletters, update meetings and conferences. One of us (SB) has been involved in the development of an innovative course. The NUT piloted a four-day course on *Leading and Managing CPD* that took the form of two, two-day residentials in November and April with two 10-day online chatrooms in January and March. Between the taught sessions, participants had to:

1 Identify the professional development needs of one or more people in their school. What do they want? What do they need? How do you know?

2 Negotiate some professional development for the target people to do based on your analysis of their needs.

3 Evaluate the impact of the target people's CPD, at different levels.

Sustaining the course over three terms and having tasks to do enabled participants to embed practices in their own school settings. The overnight stay gave them time to reflect and carry on discussing and networking, while feeling pampered by the hotel atmosphere. One said, 'our "learning conversations" have been good'. The course had a powerful impact. People said,

> It's given us the big picture and made us aware of all the CPD options. I now feel up to date. I used to think about CPD in a simplistic way – now I see that that can do more damage than good.

There were people from across the country and from primary, secondary and special schools. This opened up opportunities for primary colleagues to hear about secondary materials, and vice versa. The combination of all these aspects gave the participants not only more confidence but also more status:

> Attending this four-day course has given me the kudos to bring about change – people listen to me about budget allocations. (Bubb, 2005b: 36)

Jenny Reeves (2005) says that teachers need a 'third space', a temporal or physical place where they can work out how to implement the new things that they have learned. It seems that the online chatroom provided this third space because benefits included:

> Being able to use it to bounce ideas around, to encourage creative thought and move towards new methodologies and practices.
> Being provoked and thus encouraged to read newspaper articles and [watch] Teachers TV programmes that people referred to.

In addition to training we have seen the development of support materials for those who lead and manage CPD. For example, two 'toolkits' from consortia of LAs, one from the East Midlands (SDSA, 2005), and the other from London (DfES, 2005a), have been produced. The outcomes of the DfES-funded project 'Evaluating the impact of CPD' (Goodall et al., 2005) have also included a 25-page 'route map' to help CPD co-ordinators go about their task of leading and managing training and development, whilst findings from another DfES-funded research project – Effective Professional Learning Communities (Bolam et al., 2005) – have been used to develop materials for schools to use (Stoll et al., 2006).

CONCLUSION

Perhaps the single most important feature of leading and managing CPD is to encourage and promote a commitment on the part of the individual and the school to professional and personal growth. Leading and managing people's development – making CPD work – therefore means providing structures and procedures to co-ordinate developmental opportunities so as to promote such growth and help staff develop and improve their workplace performance. An understanding of how adults learn and the training and development cycle – 'the logical chain' – can help here, but it also means creating a culture where learning is seen as central to everything that is done, where there is a community of learners or a learning-centred community.

On-going professional development should be fully integrated into the life of the school, not seen as something brought in from the outside by 'experts', and there should be clear and consistent means of identifying the needs for CPD and assessing its effectiveness. Continuing professional development co-ordinators need to balance the development needs of the individual and the institution, and promote a positive and participative attitude to CPD from all educational managers. It is also important, as discussed in the previous chapter, that there is an understanding of how adults learn and what constitutes effective learning.

People in charge of CPD in their schools have a great responsibility. They have the power to make a significant difference to their colleagues' working lives and thereby raise pupil achievement – but they also risk wasting time and money. The CPD co-ordinator role needs to be addressed creatively and given kudos and time, for leading and managing professional development is a complex affair in which many priorities compete for attention. The role is crucial but often underdeveloped. Co-ordinators have responsibility for managing the training and development cycle of identifying and analysing needs, designing and implementing support programmes and evaluating their impact. It is the first part of the cycle – needs identification – that is the subject of the next chapter.

> ## ❓ POINTS FOR REFLECTION
>
> Often the most effective professional development is acquired within the school itself. Consider keeping a 'professional development log' for a week. Take it to all meetings, planning sessions, and even have it with you in the staffroom. Make a note of all reflections that you have and new understandings you gain. This is a useful way to become aware of the professional expertise and insights that are available in the course of your everyday life in and around school.

4

Identifying Training and Development Needs

◆ Individual or school needs

◆ Personal development

◆ Taking account of workload and wellbeing

◆ Finding out what CPD staff want and need

◆ Catering for a range of people

◆ Performance management

◆ Choosing objectives

The first two stages of the staff development cycle are concerned with the identification of staff needs and their analysis. The measurable discrepancy between the present state of affairs and the desired state of affairs is the first and pivotal issue of CPD or staff development management. No CPD should be undertaken without taking into account what teachers and other staff already know and can do. It is therefore important to identify individuals' needs (rather than wants) along with those of the school and the education system. Needs identification is about discovering individuals' needs for training and in which particular areas it might be most effective.

INDIVIDUAL OR SCHOOL NEEDS

Continuing professional development co-ordinators and other educational leaders have to ensure that training and development programmes meet the needs of both individual staff and their schools, minimizing any tensions that may exist between system needs and priorities (the school development or improvement plan) and those of individuals (the individual development plan). Continuing professional development has to meet several, sometimes competing, needs:

- the school's agenda in the form of its development or improvement plan;
- school teams (e.g. department or year group);
- government initiatives;
- local authority initiatives;
- individuals' needs – which can be broken down into the professional, personal and propersonal.

To make best use of time and money, there needs to be 'joined up' thinking across all these areas. This is not easy: Her Majesty's Inspectorate (HMI) (Ofsted, 2002b) found, for instance, that the link between performance management and the school's other planning cycles and procedures was weak in around three-fifths of the schools they visited.

One of the key issues that CPD co-ordinators have to consider is managing the tension between the demands of the school (as reflected in school improvement plans), the latest government or local initiatives and the needs of individuals. In the past, professional development has been more focused on addressing school needs than individuals' needs. Schools are better at identifying their own needs than those of their staff. As HMI note:

> Although senior managers identified their school's needs systematically and accurately, the identification of individual teachers' needs was not always so rigorous. As a result, planning for the professional development of individuals was often weak. (Ofsted, 2006: 2)

However, CPD can only be effective if it is rooted in a commitment to evaluate and move forward individuals' basic teaching competence. Without this, school development is unlikely to occur and certainly not at the speed required to ensure continuing improvement. Individual and school needs have to be brought together. This has to be managed within a finite budget.

The different approaches to the management of people (or HRM) that schools take will make a difference here. Is the human resource approach one of 'hard' economic utilitarianism or more of a 'soft' developmental humanism where staff are valued, morale is high and they are likely to be well motivated? Interestingly, the Ofsted handbook (of 2003) told inspectors that 'professional development should reflect the professional and career needs of the individual, as well as the needs of the school' (2003a: 48). It is important to remember that professional development can serve both individual and system needs – it is not always a case of serving one or the other. Fortunately, to make matters easier, the two often go together – individuals' needs very often overlap with those of the school. Also, it is important to remember that development cannot be forced – it is the person who develops (active) and not the person who is developed (passive). People who are excited and motivated by the experience of their own learning are likely to communicate that excitement to pupils.

One of the issues to consider is the degree to which training provision, particularly off-site courses, can effectively meet individual professional development needs. Balancing the needs of individuals with those of the school, especially with limited CPD budgets, has already been alluded to. School development and other plans will clearly show priorities but Connor argues that 'without a clear analysis of individual need, strategies for corporate development can fall on barren ground' (1997: 49). He gives the example of a department in a secondary school:

> Let us assume the English department has identified the need to strengthen its teaching of media. The second in department is sent on a course run by an external provider. An adviser is brought to a team meeting and does a splendid job of outlining a creative, activity based approach to the teaching of the subject centred on the concept of pupils doing things: making newspapers, editing TV news bulletins, writing comment columns and the like. So far, so good. But what of the two newly qualified members of the department who struggle to achieve purposeful order with group work? What of the teacher of 30 years' experience who does not perceive the need at his time of life to master the skills of desktop publishing and what has that got to do with English teaching anyway, thank you very much? (ibid.: 49)

Each individual is different and a 'one size fits all' approach to meeting development needs is unlikely to be successful. A more 'personalized' approach is needed for CPD to be effective but this is not without its own challenges.

PERSONAL DEVELOPMENT

But what about *personal* development? Managers and leaders of CPD need to ensure that personal development is not marginalized as it is crucial to teacher effectiveness and school success. Research makes a compelling case for personal development as a key component of teacher development. In the introductory chapter professional development was defined as the knowledge and skills relating to 'occupational role development' and personal development as the development of 'the person, often the "whole person"' (Waters, 1998: 30), and that personal development was 'often necessary to complement and "complete" professional development' (ibid.: 35).

Also personal development can have wider benefits. As Davey suggests: 'An individual's personal development may not be used immediately within an institution but often constitutes a resource which can be drawn upon in the future to the benefit of the wider education service' (2000: 34).

The more common approach to personal development adopted by schools is best described by Waters' term 'propersonal development'. This is development that is not genuinely 'personal' in its focus but is personal development for professional development purposes (Waters, 1998: 35). Teachers and educational leaders are increasingly being asked to acquire and develop their emotional intelligence as well as their knowledge and skills. Research, especially into highly effective leaders, is pointing to the importance of this and it reinforces Waters' exhortation for teacher development which links improved personal management with increased professional efficacy. The importance of 'resilience' has also been noted as crucial to teacher effectiveness (Day et al., 2006). Do most schools' CPD policies and practices recognize fully that professional and personal spheres are mutually supportive and beneficial?

As we have seen, the stance of individual schools to developing and supporting their people resource is crucially important but it needs to include elements of personal development. This has been recognized by another government initiative, the *Staff Health and Wellbeing* project, which states its preferred school HRM policy as one that clarifies the personal developmental needs of teachers in the same way as in other professions:

> The business world is recognizing that there is a link between health and wellbeing of employees and the productivity of an organization. There is a compelling business case to be made for investing in the wellbeing of employees. Similarly it could be argued that the health of a school community and its capacity to be effective is, in part, a product of the health of the staff who work there. (DfES, 2002a: 7)

However, meeting the needs of individuals makes the CPD co-ordinator's role yet harder. There are many different people taking many different roles in schools. Each person will have different needs, different learning styles and will be at a different stage of development. Table 4.1 illustrates five stages that new teachers typically go through. Clearly there is no point in planning professional development requiring someone to think deeply about assessment for instance, when they are in the 'Survival' stage battling for control. Equally, teachers at the 'Moving On' stage will want more than quick tips.

Hustler et al. have drawn pen portraits of types of teacher saying, 'It is clear that the "person" a teacher is, makes a difference, revealed from the somewhat differing learning styles, personality characteristics, and social situations reflected' (2003: 220).

TAKING ACCOUNT OF WORKLOAD AND WELLBEING

We have explored the issues of workload and wellbeing in detail elsewhere (Bubb and Earley, 2004) but both are important to consider in relation to professional development. We all remember how a course became a beacon to look forward to and how we returned from it with a spring in our step. To a degree, CPD co-ordinators need to look at the potential of CPD to motivate, refresh and reward. There may be teachers for whom some inspiring CPD will really help keep them in the job and being effective.

TABLE 4.1 FIVE STAGES THAT TEACHERS GO THROUGH

Stage	Characteristics
Early idealism	Feeling that everything is possible and having a strong picture of how you want to teach ('I'll never shout'). This is a fantasy stage where you imagine pupils hanging on your every word.
Survival	Reality strikes. You live from day to day, needing quick fixes and tips. You find it hard to solve problems because there are so many of them. Behaviour management is of particular concern – you have nightmares about losing control. You are too stressed and busy to reflect. Colds and sore throats seem permanent.
Recognizing difficulties	You can see problems more clearly. You can identify difficulties and think of solutions because there is some space in your life. You move forward.
Hitting the plateau	Key problems, such as behaviour management and organization, have been solved so you feel things are going well. You feel you are mastering teaching. You begin to enjoy it and do not find it too hard, but you do not want to tackle anything different or take on any radical new initiatives. If forced you will pay lip service to new developments. Some teachers spend the rest of their career at this stage.
Moving on	You are ready for further challenges. You want to try out different styles of teaching, new age groups, take more responsibilities.

Source: Bubb, 2003a: 63

For instance, some schools, mainly in the independent sector, give a term's sabbatical for teachers with more than 20 years' service. Teachers have to plan what they are going to do with the time, but they are encouraged to follow personal interests not things to do with their job. So they spend a term not working but travelling or reading all the works of William Shakespeare or walking the length of the Thames in chunks of a day or two. The school expects nothing from this other than a refreshed teacher – a reward for those rare people who stay in the same school for 20 years.

Many teachers work over 60 hours per week in term time and simply do not feel that they have the time for professional development, that it will be another thing to do – a burden. Training during the day causes extra work in preparing lessons for others to teach, having to deal with problems afterwards and not getting the curriculum taught and course work done to a good standard. We have seen the growth of 'non-disruptive' forms of CPD partly as a response to this (see Chapter 5). Continuing professional development in twilight sessions is hard because people are tired. The venue for professional development is important to consider. Courses are held in a range of rooms and buildings, not all of which are conducive to professional development. They can be judged in terms of the quality of the food rather than the learning, which is not to dismiss the importance of feel-good factors. Training in hotels tends to offer a pampering touch, which might be worth the extra expense but may not. Some courses are held in places that are hard to get to, especially on public transport. All these things need to be considered so that the professional development meets individual needs and circumstances.

Some schools offer teachers flexibility in how they spend their CPD time. Many CPD opportunities are arranged for after school either within the school or nearby at the professional development centre. Teachers agree to attend at least 15 hours of CPD outside of the school day, and they log this. In recompense the school allows those teachers to do what they like on three of the five statutory training days. Staff like this flexibility in meeting their specific needs when they want. It is seen as preferable to a 'one size fits all' approach to school INSET days. Other schools pay staff for professional development activities that take place at weekends or holidays. This is explained in *School Teachers' Pay and Conditions* (DfES, 2006).

FINDING OUT WHAT CPD STAFF WANT AND NEED

So how are the training and development needs of individuals gleaned? How does one know what one doesn't know? Connor describes what is a common school pattern around placing CPD within the context of team and school development or improvement plans:

> Much of this is based around the most important management set piece in the school, a series of formal review meetings between team leaders, the headteacher and a linked deputy. At these meetings development priorities are discussed and agreed within the structure of the whole school needs and action is formulated. This then provides the context for team leaders and the school to plan their professional development activities for the year. (1997: 48)

The most used methods for assessing the training and development needs of individuals are interviews and questionnaires. A good example in relation to ICT need identification is given by Adams (2005). Performance management reviews can be extremely useful to elicit participants' views of their needs, but are not always helpful because it is often difficult for staff to think about those areas of their own practice where they feel least knowledgeable, skilled and competent. Teachers and other staff are likely to be better at identifying 'wants' rather than 'needs'!

Effective needs assessment is an important factor in contributing to the success of training programmes. This cannot always be derived from interviews and questionnaires – some people do not know what they need. Monitoring of teaching, such as observation, is useful in such cases. The time and effort put into identifying needs accurately is well worthwhile but according to HMI:

> Arrangements for identifying staff's individual needs were too subjective in about a third of the survey schools. These schools relied too heavily on staff's own perception of their needs and on the effectiveness of individual subject leaders to identify needs accurately. (Ofsted, 2006: 4)

The role of individuals in the identification of their needs has often been a minor one. Indeed, there is evidence that where they do choose the professional development they undertake, it can be in a random and ad hoc way:

> It involved them glancing through a list or booklet of advertised professional development courses prepared by their employing schools or professional association. They selected a course to attend based on criteria such as their interest in the topic, when and where it was to be held, and/or its cost, and whether or not the school or employer will meet these costs. The linking of the course to their actual professional development needs appeared to be of minor significance. (Harris, 2000: 26)

Professional development portfolios are useful in chronicling where one has been and planning where one wants to go (see Chapter 2) and helping individuals to be greater advocates for their own learning needs. Some people draw up individual professional development plans.

CATERING FOR A RANGE OF PEOPLE

Any school or college will have a range of people working within it who will have varying preferred learning styles (see Chapter 2). An audit of learning styles may help to explain people's perceptions and expectations of the training they receive, and to support schools in recognizing and facilitating different ways to support individuals' learning. If one looks just at teachers, there will be people with a range of experience and needs, and who vary in how effective their teaching is. Our colleague Kathryn Riley (2003) distinguishes two broad groups of teachers, which she calls the 'glow-worms' and 'skylarks'.

Many of the 'glow-worms' find it difficult to think beyond the confines of their classroom. Locked into a dependency culture by prescriptive reforms, they are cautious and lack spontaneity, caught up in a 'painting by numbers approach to teaching'. They find it difficult to see how they can take responsibility for their own professionalism. Nevertheless, the 'glow' of teaching is still there, however dimly lit and however intermittent. They occasionally get excited about new things such as interactive whiteboards that they see having a direct impact on pupils. To 'glow' again, this group will need to be fanned and nurtured.

The 'skylarks' recognize some of the difficulties created by the centralized reform process. However, they seem less constrained and less likely to see themselves as prisoners of the government's agenda than the glow-worms. Skylarks talk about the need to put the 'sparkle' back into teaching. They are keen on sharing good practice with colleagues in other schools, having sabbaticals and secondments; participating in international and professional exchange programmes. They want 'professional learning' that is distinctively different from the 'professional development through courses' model typically available to teachers. The skylarks want time and space to develop.

The challenge for CPD co-ordinators is to ensure that all groups and types of people get the professional development that will move them on. In any size of school this is difficult, but in a large one there will be more people to liaise with. Do you ask people what they want or wait for them to ask? You will find yourself torn between government and local initiatives, where the school wants to go and team and individual needs.

One way to look at what staff need, and whom to invest in, is to use the performance and attitude to improvement grid (Figure 4.1). Use the horizontal and vertical axis to look at how well someone is doing their job and how keen they are to improve. You may see four broad categories of staff:

(A) Someone who is doing their job well but doesn't want to improve needs motivation.

(B) Someone who is doing their job well and wants to improve probably doesn't need training so much as resources, such as time, to enable them to develop.

(C) Someone who is not doing their job well and doesn't want to improve probably needs a new job, either in the same school or somewhere else.

(D) Someone who is not doing their job well and wants to improve is an ideal person to invest in training that is likely to help them do their job better.

Spending most time and money on people in Group D, who are not doing their job very effectively but who want to improve, is likely to have the most impact on whole-school improvement. This is one of the reasons why new teachers are worth investing in.

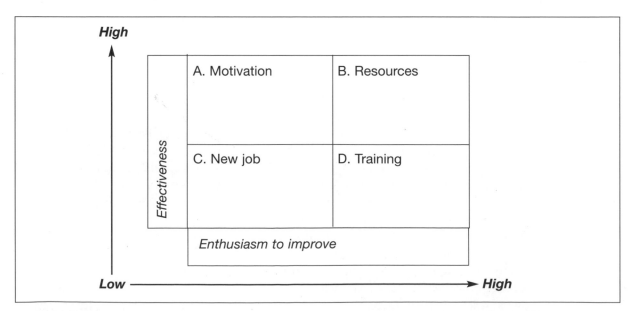

FIGURE 4.1: THE PERFORMANCE AND ATTITUDE TO IMPROVEMENT GRID (BASED ON GLASER'S PERFORMANCE ANALYSIS GRID, 2002: 4)

PERFORMANCE MANAGEMENT

Schools and colleges which integrate performance management, school self-evaluation and CPD into a coherent cycle of planning improve the quality of teaching and raise standards (Ofsted, 2006: 4). Participation in CPD is an essential part of any performance management (PM) cycle with teachers seeing 'performance management as their right and continuing professional development as their duty' (Miliband, 2003: 6). Effective performance management arrangements provide schools with a route to better reconciliation between the individual's and the school's priorities for development. They allow individual, departmental or section and whole-school developmental priorities to be identified and enable individuals to see how their own development fits into and contributes to the wider agenda.

The notion of managing performance is controversial, however. In unsound hands, performance management can be used to control, to ensure uniformity and to de-professionalize; in sound hands it can be used to support, coach and validate good practice, whilst respecting and promoting proper autonomy, creativity and variety. Used with flair the process can be used to support the school's vision and help develop pupils and staff alike; it is an effective instrument but it is only as effective as the person who uses it. Individuals whose team leader does not get round to holding individual meetings or does not carry them out well will suffer. One secondary deputy, in charge of performance management and CPD, gets frustrated: 'You have to chase, chase, chase and don't take no for an answer. It's worse than getting the kids to get their course work in'. He now sets a training day aside for the interviews to make sure that they happen.

Performance management is an ideal forum for discussing individuals' needs but schools vary in how well it works. Clearly it should be a forum to discuss professional development, but some schools and teachers do not take it very seriously, as illustrated in this posting from a teacher on the *TES* website: 'Ninety per cent of the time it is toothless ticky-box bollocks. I was appraised a year ago and got a good report, which highlighted some training needs about which I have asked about at three monthly intervals since but without result. What nonsense it all is!' (Bubb, 2003c).

Her Majesty's Inspectorate's report into PM found that there was scope for improvement in objectives related to teachers' professional development in at least half of the schools they visited (Ofsted, 2002b). There was a tendency for objectives to be activities or tasks, such as 'produce a report', 'attend a training course'. They often did not detail the strategies or the support needed, including resources and training, to help progress. Training plans are one of the weakest features of performance management practice.

Performance management is the statutory procedure (DfES, 2006a) for making sure that all teachers (except NQTs on induction) discuss their teaching, career plans and how to be more effective. Done well, it should make people feel valued, give them a clear picture about their work and help them develop but it takes time, skills and commitment: on the part of the reviewer and reviewee. Coaching can also help (see Chapter 5).

Worth Primary School in Cheshire (see Case study 4.1) has made great efforts to give professional development the high priority it deserves and to link it closely with performance management and other planning processes. It has also endeavoured to ensure that value for money linked to effective CPD and pupil outcomes is paramount.

HOW PM WORKS

Someone who knows a person's work will be nominated to be the 'reviewer'. They will have one formal meeting each year, which has two parts: reviewing the past year then planning the next. These may be useful prompts:

(A) REVIEW THE PAST YEAR

What's gone well? Look at the main elements of the job description, previous objectives and professional development to consider not only what the person has done but their impact. Use evidence from as broad a base as possible, such as:

CASE STUDY 4.1: WORTH PRIMARY SCHOOL

The senior leadership team, governors and all staff of Worth Primary School are highly committed to, and greatly value, training, development and coaching and fund it appropriately. The school believes that receiving and providing high-quality, effective training, development and coaching enables the organization and individuals continuously to improve and develop. Well-trained, well-motivated and effective staff, governors and trainees are a valuable resource that can be used to provide a first-class education for all pupils. We aim to recruit good quality people with the right 'skill set and mind set' coach them well, then create space for them to shine!

The school unashamedly puts performance management (and performance coaching) at the heart of professional development, it sees performance management as a structured, professional dialogue that reviews and enhances organizational effectiveness, staff motivation and professional development. Team leaders at Worth see PM as a key tool in moving an organization from being a series of processes, structures and separate groups of individuals to an effective, flexible and focused learning organization. There is a direct linkage between pupil progress targets, professional development targets, action plans and the school development plan; one informs the other in a cycle of growth and development.

The Performance Management process has evolved into Performance Coaching. The process still follows nationally recognized guidelines and statutes but the feel of the process is professional, agreed and applies coaching skills. The appraisal interview in particular is very much a coaching dialogue as our staff are very positive. The leadership team reserve the legal right to disagree with team members and press a point but this has never happened to date.

Training is consciously reduced in quantity but enhanced in terms of quality, impact and monitoring. For professional development to be regarded as effective it must impact on the individual member of staff, change a behaviour or process and be seen to impact on pupils and colleagues. Virtually all professional development is organized within set training days or a few twilight sessions; ad hoc training and meetings are unpopular and are strongly discouraged. This ruthless focus on that which is needed saves precious time, goodwill and funds that are so often wasted in so many organizations. Every event and development has an 'opportunity cost'; these must be reviewed and all resources placed where and when they are most effective.

Source: Taylor, 2004

- feedback from pupils, parents and colleagues;
- analysis of test results;
- self-evaluation;
- observations;
- planning and evaluations;
- work samples showing progress and the impact of assessment for learning.

Use benchmarking data to compare the impact with others in a similar context nationally and locally. For instance, in London the *Family of Schools* data (DfES, 2006b) can be used to compare impact on pupils with other schools with a similar pupil profile.

(B) PLANNING THE NEXT YEAR

- What would the person like to improve?
- Why? What's the current picture? (What's the evidence?)
- How does this fit in with the school improvement plan?
- How does this fit in with career plans and any standards that are being worked towards?
- How will you know that things have improved, in about a year?

- What does the person need to do to meet this objective?
- What support from the school, including professional development, will help?
- How should progress and impact be monitored?

An outcome of this meeting is the draft performance review statement, which should be given for agreement within five days. The completed review statement is passed to the headteacher within ten days. During the year, the reviewer should keep an eye on your progress towards the objectives and take any supportive action needed. At the end of the year, there is a formal review of progress and then some more objectives are set for the next year (based on Bubb, 2007).

CHOOSING OBJECTIVES

Under the 2007 PM arrangements in England people can have as many or as few objectives as they like and they don't have to relate to any particular area. One objective is enough but people may want to use a model of choosing one to do with teaching, another relating to other roles in the school and perhaps another about them as a person. This last point is important. Performance management, and the professional development that goes with it, need to support and increase wellbeing, physical and emotional resilience, job satisfaction, sense of achievement and commitment. This is particularly relevant when teaching in challenging conditions.

How many times have we been told that objectives should be SMART: Specific, Measurable, Achievable, Relevant and Time-bound? This is of course also true of learning objectives in lesson plans or targets on Individual Education Plans (IEPs) but it's easier said than done. A frequent problem with objectives is that they are not made specific enough, which can lead to failure. Research on NQTs (Bubb, 2003b) found that many objectives were too large so that they had to be repeated. 'Improve control' may be too general and benefit from being more specific about what needs most urgent attention, such as 'To improve control, particularly during transitions, after breaktimes, in independent activities and at tidying-up time'.

It makes sense for individuals' objectives to link in with other developments in the school, where possible. But be sure that the intended impact is focused on the impact of development. For instance, in a school where the priority was 'Improve the quality of teaching in mathematics' an individual's objective was: 'Participate in training in the teaching of mathematics through school-based courses, self study and observation of others'. This objective is confused with the activity: will participation mean that learning takes place and will there be an impact in the classroom? Not necessarily!

It's useful to think of how much better things will be in a year's time: aim high but be realistic. These points then become the success criteria around which an action plan is drawn up of what needs to be done when. When the professional development co-ordinator has the big picture of everyone's needs, INSET days or training can be organized around common areas. Table 4.2 illustrates the process of setting an objective, success criteria and how progress is to be monitored.

The benefit of objective-setting as a way to manage steady improvement by children and adults is well recognized. Objectives provide a framework for staff doing a complex job at a very fast pace. They encourage people to prioritize tasks and make best use of time and other resources, and feel a sense of achievement when objectives are met. However, if the processes of reflection, setting an objective, drawing up an action plan and evaluating the impact of the learning do not take place, professional development may be reduced to the level of ad hoc activities. The very act of writing things down causes people to consider whether they are the real priorities and gives them something to focus on.

TABLE 4.2 THE PROCESS OF SETTING AN OBJECTIVE AND SUCCESS CRITERIA

Questions	Examples of answers
What would you like to be better at?	Challenging more able pupils.
Why? What's the current picture? (What's the evidence?)	Test results, work samples and my gut feeling show that average pupils and those with special needs are making better progress in comparison with other classes at this school and others. My more able pupils' results were disappointing: they could have done better. Their parents are not as pleased as others. Some of the very able pupils mess around and avoid working.
How does this fit in with the school development plan?	Perfectly! The school is trying to raise the achievement of all pupils.
How does this fit in with your career plan and any standards you're working towards?	It will help me be a better teacher, and help me meet the upper pay scale standards.
How will you know that things have improved?	Higher attainers will be engaged in lessons, will produce good work and will make more than two NC sublevels progress in a year. Maybe, they will pull up the achievement of the rest of the class.
What do you need to do to meet this objective?	Identify pupils with potential for high achievement – I may have missed some. Plan more challenging work. Where possible, set pupils purposeful problems to solve. Raise expectations of what they can achieve. Develop my questioning skills so that I can really get them thinking. Consider organizing mentoring by older successful pupils. Look for opportunities for pupils to extend themselves outside school. Get involved in any competitions or projects.
What support from the school, including professional development, will help you?	Time to discuss strategies and resources with G&T co-ordinator, including how to use Bloom's taxonomy of questioning. Find ideas from websites such as www.londongt.org. Observe two teachers (one in this school, one in a higher achieving school) with a reputation for challenging more able pupils, and discuss strategies.
How should your progress and its impact be monitored?	Keep track that activities happen by the dates agreed. In 3rd week of March, the reviewer should observe a lesson and look at the work of three pupils to see impact.

Source: Bubb, 2007: 5

■ DIAGNOSING A PROBLEM AREA

Some teachers and other staff have suffered from not having areas for development accurately diagnosed. It is very hard to decide what to work on when things are not going right because each problem has a huge knock-on effect. Always remember that objectives should be able to be met, while containing a degree of challenge, but setting ones which will be useful and that contain the right amount of challenge is not easy. Particularly when someone has a problem, it needs to be reflected upon and diagnosed accurately in order to draw up the most useful objectives and plan of action. Brainstorm its features and results. For instance, Rachel's control problems include the following:

- Her voice is thin and becomes screechy when raised.
- Sometimes she comes down hard on the pupils and at other times she lets them get away with things.
- She takes a long time to get attention.
- She runs out of time so plenaries are missed, the class is late to assembly, and so on.
- Pupils call out.
- Pupils are too noisy.
- A small group of pupils is behaving badly.
- Even the usually well-behaved pupils are being naughty.

Look at your list. Does it seem a fair picture? It is easy to be too hard or too generous. Then list some positive features, relating to the problem area. For instance, Rachel:

- really likes and cares for the pupils;
- speaks to them with respect;
- plans interesting work for them;
- is very effective when working with individuals or small groups;
- has better control in the early part of the day, and works hard.

Think about why things go well. Reflection on successes is very powerful. The process of analysing strengths is very helpful and this positive thinking can now be used to reflect on problems. Try to tease out the reasons for the problem. Think of actions to remedy situations – they can be surprisingly easy. It is often the small things that make a difference.

Rachel completed a very detailed action plan (see Figure 4.2) because she had such problems. Such detail is not always necessary, although it illustrates how breaking a problem into manageable chunks helps.

Name: Rachel　　　　Date: 1 Nov　　　　　　　Date objective to be met: 16 Dec

Objective:　　　To improve control, particularly after playtimes, in independent literacy activities, at tidying-up time, and home-time

Success criteria	Actions	When	Progress
Gets attention more quickly	Brainstorm attention-getting devices with other teachers Use triangle, etc. to get attention	4.11	7.11 Triangle made children more noisy – try cymbal
Rarely shouts	Voice management course Project the voice Don't talk over children	19.11	23.11 Using more range in voice – working!
Plans for behaviour management	Glean ideas from other teachers through discussion and observation Watch videos on behaviour management strategies Write notes for behaviour management on plans	4.11	12.11 Improvement through lots of tips, staying calm and being more positive. Not perfect and exhausting but better.
Successful procedures for sorting out disputes after playtimes	Glean ideas from other teachers Ask playground supervisors to note serious incidents Children to post messages in incident box	11.11	18.11 Incident box really working for those who can write and I can now tell when there's a serious problem.
Successful procedures for tidying	Discuss what other teachers do Start tidying earlier and time it with reward for beating record. Sanctions for the lazy	18.11	25.11 Sandtimer for tidying working well though still a few children not helping. Might try minutes off playtime.
Successful procedures for home-time	Discuss ideas with other teachers Monitors to organize things to take home Start home-time procedures earlier and time them (with rewards?)	25.11	2.12 Changed routine so tidy earlier. Some Y6 children helping give out things to take home.
Children succeed in independent literacy activities	Ideas from literacy co-ordinator Change seating for groups Differentiate work Discuss with additional adults	2.12	9.12 All class doing same independent activity working better. Mrs H helping.

FIGURE 4.2 AN ACTION PLAN TO MEET AN OBJECTIVE (BUBB ET AL., 2002: 111)

CONCLUSION

Identifying and analysing needs can be time-consuming but, like any in-depth look at pupils' learning needs, the effort is worthwhile. The next challenge is to find the best way to meet needs – the topic of the next chapter.

? **POINTS FOR REFLECTION**

Reflect on your current classroom experience. Are there aspects to do with work schemes or the work and progress of the children that you teach that are an issue for you? Consider what new information about this issue might be useful in order to tackle it, and how you would go about seeking this information?

? **POINTS FOR REFLECTION**

Think of an example in your wider school community where there needs to be better liaison between professionals from different backgrounds (e.g. education, health, social services). What could be done to increase understanding of each other's work? What kind of professional development activity would be useful to jointly undertake?

Meeting CPD Needs

- ◆ The range of professional development activities
- ◆ Good value CPD
- ◆ Learning with and from each other
- ◆ Coaching and mentoring
- ◆ Observation
- ◆ Teachers TV
- ◆ Courses
- ◆ Masters courses and further study
- ◆ Learning conversations – online
- ◆ Running training yourself

The Training and Development Agency has argued that school staff are too rarely engaged in a systematic analysis of their needs, and that both they and their schools too rarely assess the type of CPD that is likely to be most effective in meeting identified needs (Tabberer, 2005). Indeed, meeting professional development needs is a key task. Collating everyone's CPD needs is important so that you can identify areas of commonality and get the whole picture. The data gathered about training needs, at both individual and school level, will need to be analysed and, most likely, a report written and presented to the headteacher and governing body. Table 5.1 is an extract from a secondary school co-ordinator's logging system. This relates to courses attended, the twilight INSET training that the school runs and the informal ways that relate specifically to identified performance management needs.

The GTC Teacher Learning Academy (TLA) offers professional recognition for teachers' learning through development work in school. TLA Professional Recognition is achieved by addressing each of six core dimensions:

1 Engagement with a knowledge base.
2 Assessing peer and coaching support.
3 Planning a change activity.
4 Carrying out the activity.
5 Evaluating.
6 Disseminating.

The learning process undertaken is grounded in what is known to be effective CPD. Teachers can work on projects individually or collaboratively, in their own schools or across institutions. Mentoring, coaching and peer support are considered essential to professional learning and these are built into the process and criteria. Verification of the quality for acceptance within the TLA should be carried out by peers who are fellow professionals, and who have been trained on a national GTC(E) programme. The TLA is independent of any university, but the scheme has been developed so that university accreditation is an option for teachers who make successful submissions at Stages 2 or 3. For more information go to www.gtce.org.uk.

Meeting individuals' needs whilst also addressing whole school and collective needs is a challenge. HMI in their report on the 'logical chain' note that school 'plans gave suitable emphasis to staff's individual needs and career aspirations, though managers did not simply agree to their staff's requests for training unless there was a clear benefit for the school' (Ofsted, 2006: 10). But a more personalized approach is crucial if we are to ensure our limited CPD funds are deployed most effectively. We need to ensure that we take account of individuals' previous knowledge and experience and that we respond, if possible, to individuals' preferences and learning styles. Bolam and Weindling (2006), in a review for the GTC(E) of 20 research studies into CPD, state that their findings provide strong evidence 'that the more influence teachers have over their own CPD the more likely they are to consider it effective. More generally, the (findings) lend support to the importance of teachers' professionalism and agency as key components of effective CPD' (2006: 3).

TABLE 5.1 PROFESSIONAL DEVELOPMENT NEEDS IDENTIFIED THROUGH PERFORMANCE MANAGEMENT

Teacher	Professional development need	External CPD	Internal CPD	Informal
A	Leadership development for middle managers NQT mentoring	LftM Induction tutor course	Observation skills	Books on induction, etc.
B	Public examination officer Connect 3 Network Manager		Course	Discussion with previous exam officer
C	AS Drama Unit 3 PGCE mentoring	PGCE mentor training		HoD; other schools
D	See Career Entry Profile		NQT Induction	
E	Connexions training	Visit other schools		
F	AS/A2 PE Sports Leadership Award Sports Co-ordinator Learning styles	Exam board course LEA meetings	Learning styles	Reading
G	CAD/CAM GCSE Electronic Products, Systems & Control	Course	HoD	
H	SEN Code of Practice Co-ordination of work of outside agencies	SEN meetings; network with SENCOs	Ed Psych session	
I	KS3 National Strategy Performance Management for non-teaching staff	LA courses		Coaching from deputy
J	GNVQ Computer-generated report writing Liaison with outside agencies Use of PowerPoint Citizenship	Course	Report session	Self-study on PP
K	Getting QTS	OTT course		Develop portfolio
L	Intranet	Visit schools with intranets	Science Dept	
M	AS/A2 German Interactive whiteboard	IoE course		Self-study
N	KS3 NLS Target-setting	LA courses	Eng Dept	

Once the schools had identified their needs, the next link in the chain, as HMI note, was to plan a range of relevant professional development activities to tackle them. They note:

> Good CPD plans covered all levels of staff: teachers, middle and senior managers, and support staff. It was clearly based on the school's improvement objectives; it identified actions, the people responsible, and how the objectives would be achieved through the most suitable type of CPD; it allocated adequate financial and other resources; it identified clear outcomes for the activities; and it built in time for reflection, discussion and evaluation. (Ofsted, 2006: 9)

So what then are the various CPD options available to meet both school and individual needs and how can school staff, such as Advanced Skills Teachers or Excellent Teachers, be deployed to best effect?

THE RANGE OF PROFESSIONAL DEVELOPMENT ACTIVITIES

The range of professional development activities is huge and offers on-the-job, off-the-job and close-to-the-job opportunities. Developing a culture of development and enquiry has been the key to many schools' success, and this is explored further in Chapters 2 and 7. People often think only of courses but here are some ideas for self-study, observations, extending your professional practice and working with pupils.

SELF-STUDY

1 Reflecting on progress so far.

2 Reading the educational press.

3 Learning more about strategies for teaching pupils with special needs.

4 Learning more about strategies for teaching pupils with English as an additional language (EAL).

5 Learning more about strategies for teaching very able pupils.

6 Visiting local education centres, museums and venues for outings.

7 Looking at the educational possibilities of the local environment.

8 Working with the SENCO on writing individual education plans.

9 Improving subject knowledge through reading, observation, discussion, and so on.

10 Analysing planning systems in order to improve your own.

11 Analysing marking and record-keeping systems to improve your own.

OBSERVING OTHER PRACTITIONERS

1 Observing other staff teaching.

2 Observing teachers in other schools – similar and different to yours.

3 Observing someone teach your class(es).

4 Observing someone teach a lesson that you have planned.

5 Observing how pupils of different ages learn.

6 Discussing lesson observations.

7 Tracking a pupil for a day to see teaching through their eyes.

8 Watching a colleague take an assembly.

9 Observing a visiting expert.

10 Shadowing a colleague.

11 Visiting and seeing other schools in action.

12 Observing and working with an artist in residence.

■ EXTENDING PROFESSIONAL EXPERIENCE

1 Leading school-based CPD.

2 Rotating roles/jobs.

3 Developing your professional profile.

4 Taking part in developing a learning community.

5 Posting comments to an online staffroom such as the *TES* staffroom.

6 Co-ordinating/managing a subject.

7 Assuming the role of leader for a special initiative in school.

8 Carrying out action research in the classroom/school.

9 Contributing to a professional publication.

10 Gaining experience of interviewing.

11 Acting as a performance reviewer.

12 Serving as a governor.

13 Contributing to courses.

14 Serving on professional committees/working parties and so on.

15 Becoming a union representative.

16 Leading/supervising non-professionals who work in the classroom.

17 Working on extracurricular activities.

18 Taking part in staff conferences on individual pupils.

19 Working with other professionals such as education psychologists.

20 Working with an exam board or marking examination papers.

21 Networking and sharing with a group of colleagues from another school.

22 Team teaching.

23 Learning through professional practice with others.

24 Developing use of ICT.

25 Counselling parents.

26 Collaborating with peripatetic staff.

27 Mentoring a trainee or NQT.

28 Organizing a display.

■ WORKING WITH PUPILS

1 Taking responsibility for a group of pupils on an off-site visit.

2 Developing teaching skills across a wide age and ability range.

3 Working with pupils on school councils.

4 Working with pupils to present an assembly, play, performance events.

5 Working with pupils preparing a school year book.

6 Integrating the use of pupil websites and online communities into teaching.

7 Using email/video conferencing between pupils.

8 Negotiating targets and evaluating work alongside pupils.

9 Mentoring and counselling pupils.

10 Helping pupils with peer mentoring.

GOOD VALUE CPD

There are many external providers of CPD: consultants, LAs and higher education institutions (HEIs). Some schools buy in external providers to deliver training within their building or join with some other schools. More typically schools send one or two people on courses and expect them to cascade information back. There are pros and cons to each approach. Courses may well not deliver in the way promised, and travel, parking and time finding the venue may reduce the effectiveness. In-house sessions usually do deliver what the staff need/want and people have less trouble with travel, parking, and so on.

The *Good Value CPD* document (DfEE, 2001b) has a code of practice delineating what schools and individuals can expect from people and organizations that provide professional development. The planning for CPD should begin with the identification of objectives emerging from the PM and school development processes and that from these 'it will be possible to identify needs, decide what development activity is required and how to provide it, and define the outcomes and how to measure them' (ibid.: 2). The provider of CPD, after a needs assessment analysis, should agree with the school or individual the needs to be addressed, the purposes of the development activity and the success criteria that will be deployed, including, where appropriate, the desired outcomes for pupils' learning and development. The provider should also set out clearly details of those individuals delivering the training as well as, where relevant, the research and inspection evidence that will be informing their input (ibid.: 2). Courses should indicate the target audience and give an outline of the overall aims of the activity, details of venue, accreditation and progression routes, and so on.

Providers should state in advance the delivery methods planned and the expectations of participants. Delivery should meet a number of criteria (for example, high-quality materials, differentiation of delivery, necessary expertise, high-quality venue, and so on). In addition, providers during the planning stage must establish success criteria to see the degree to which the provision has been successful in improving opportunities for pupils to succeed. The code of practice recognizes that not all of these outcomes will be easy to measure but does expect any assessment process to include a clear framework for considering the impact on pupils' learning. Participants must be given the opportunity to offer comments on the quality of the provision, whether needs have been met and what improvements might be made. Finally, it makes reference to monitoring processes, equal opportunities and health and safety.

LEARNING WITH AND FROM EACH OTHER

There is a big movement towards school-based professional development and 'learning with and from each other'. As someone on the *TES* staffroom says: 'Teachers are the most valuable resource we have for INSET. If more teachers exchanged ideas and shared good practice (cliché) on a regular informal basis, we would all be better off'. Some schools' staff are better at this sort of dialogue than others. You will really benefit if you are part of a networked learning community, as some schools are (see Chapter 2).

This is being carried out on the macro level as part of the 14–19 developments. There are funded learning visits to the organizations involved in the Pathfinder Programme at three levels:

a) a Focused Learning Visit (FLV) – typically a four-hour overview of a specific area of the Pathfinder work.

b) a 'Follow-Up' Service after the FLV to answer particular queries.

c) an introduction to the specific policy/practice delivered by the Pathfinder Programme in and for another area, consisting of a full day: half on an introduction to the Pathfinder replicable policy/practice; the other half on applying the policy/practice in their area, plus real action planning to help each area prioritize and plan.

We also know that training is often perceived as most effective when it is delivered by practitioners who are currently 'doing the job' often with the same kind of children as you have to teach! Credibility and pragmatism are key criteria. According to HMI:

> [O]ne of the most effective development activities was involvement in a well planned collaborative project designed to improve teaching and learning. Several schools, for example, had used external consultants to develop the staff's understanding of pupils' learning styles. Although there was little hard evidence of better teaching or higher standards, the staff had been enthused by the training and by the opportunities to discuss and develop their teaching with their colleagues. The benefits of this type of collaboration were also evident in well managed subject departments in secondary schools. (Ofsted, 2006: 13)

COACHING AND MENTORING

Having someone to talk to and help one reflect and develop is a fundamental form of professional development. Coaching fits in with what we know about how adults learn. It is generally agreed that adults learn best when they determine their own focus and that they learn through being asked questions and being given time to reflect. Coaching is a development tool that helps people move forward in their work, and can be used by line managers or people who help others decide their professional development priorities. Moss and Silk (2003) recommend that those acting as coaches/mentors ask searching questions to help staff find their own professional development needs. The power of the coaching model comes from the use of questions, rather than advice. The coach's expertise is in active listening on a number of levels, asking powerful questions and holding the member of staff accountable for the actions agreed.

Some of the tools used in a coaching conversation are:

- active listening (contextual to elicit meaning);
- rephrasing concisely;
- clarifying questions;
- asking permission;
- acknowledgement;
- accountability.

It is important that people feel ownership of their objectives. They should be jointly negotiated or at least the result of talking to someone, with the individual being proactive about identifying areas to develop, and how they can be achieved.

There is, however, considerable confusion about terms and definitions around coaching and mentoring. Mentoring is mainly about helping early professional learning and brokering access to a wide range of professional learning opportunities, including coaching. Coaching focuses on the development of specific skills, knowledge and the associated repertoire of teaching and learning or leadership strategies. Coaching seeks to empower a person to find their own solutions to their challenges, focusing on the present and the future and not dwelling on past events. Barrie Joy, from the Institute of Education's London Centre for Leadership in Learning, uses the term 'mentoring–coaching': mentoring focuses on who and where I am; coaching on where I need/want to be and how to get there (Joy, 2006).

There are different models of coaching such as STRIDE: **S** is for looking at people's strengths, **T** for identifying the target, **R** for what the real situation is, **I** for ideas, **D** for decisions and **E** for evaluating how well things have worked. The GROW model consists of the:

- Goal (for the session and/or project)
- Reality (the current state of play)
- Options (possible ways forward)
- Will (level of commitment to the planned action).

There is a national framework for coaching and mentoring (NCSL, 2005). This has ten principles that emphasize things like how much can be learnt from conversations and that there are benefits to acting as a coach as well as being coached. Coaching and mentoring form an integral part of many of their programmes (see Chapters 13 and 14).

Advanced Skills and Excellent Teachers are a superb resource and are usually skilled in coaching and mentoring. They are often responsible for the induction of newly qualified teachers, mentor colleagues, give demonstration lessons, help others with planning, preparation, and assessment, and help staff evaluate the impact of their teaching on pupils.

The most usual AST model is for individual ASTs to work one to one with other teachers to help improve their teaching skills. However, improvements in the work of individual teachers can be hard to sustain if they are not underpinned and supported by the overall ethos of the school. ASTs working together can produce rapid whole-school improvement, especially when working in multidisciplinary teams tackling issues which span schools. Research into ASTs working as a group (Robins, 2003) found that there was a critical mass effect. More teachers were exposed to ASTs at the same time and this prompted internal discussion about improvements in teaching and learning. The ASTs reinforced each other's understanding of the issues and solutions and they felt better able to put a case to, and influence senior management in the school.

OBSERVATION

Whatever role people have and whatever stage they are at in the profession, they will learn a great deal about their job from watching others doing it. Similarly, the more people watch children learning, and think about the problems that they have, the better their teaching will be. Newly qualified teachers find this the most useful of all induction activities (Totterdell et al., 2002).

Effective staff make the most of any opportunities to observe others, formally or just informally around the school. They watch a range of people. It is very cheering to see that everyone has similar problems and fascinating to study the different ways people manage them. Peer observation is stressful, so in a sense things get worse before they get better, but it is worth getting over initial discomfort or reluctance and shyness about being observed and sharing problems with colleagues.

However, observing so that one gets something out of it is not easy. People need to have a focus for observation because there is so much to see that they can end up getting overwhelmed. Observations need to be linked to something that people want to develop. For instance, someone who wants to improve pace in introductions, needs to notice the speed of the exposition, how many pupils answer questions and how the teacher manages to move them on, how instructions are given, resources distributed, and how off-task behaviour is dealt with.

It is essential to look at teaching in relation to learning. Always think about cause and effect. Why are the pupils behaving as they are? The cause is usually related to teaching. People should be encouraged to jot down things of interest, certain phrases that staff use to get attention, ways they organize tidying-up time, and so on. Forms with prompts can help observers focus by writing a few bullet points about what they have learned, and the ideas that could be implemented. It is valuable for staff to log who they have observed.

Staff may have an opportunity to take a sabbatical or a trip abroad, observing schools in other countries. The purpose of sabbaticals is to create opportunities for experienced teachers to take on a significant period of development to enhance their own learning and effectiveness, and to bring subsequent benefits to their pupils and their school. Government organizations, charities, unions and industries all have a history of supporting teacher involvement in educational research with the opportunities on offer changing from time to time. Advertisements for such things are often placed in the *TES* as well as in professional association journals. Advice on European Union funded initiatives is available from the Central Bureau, which is part of the British Council. The teachers' international professional development scheme enables people to learn from and contribute to educational ideas and good practice throughout the world.

CASE STUDY 5.1: TEACHERS' OBSERVATIONS FOR PROFESSIONAL DEVELOPMENT

Julian was interested in developing his explanations of mathematical concepts so that he could make things clearer and not get thrown by pupils' questions. With this clearly in mind, he chose to observe mathematics lessons where new topics were being started. He learned the benefits of rock-solid subject knowledge and scaffolding information. He also gained a broader repertoire of questioning techniques that he was able to try out in his own teaching.

Diana had problems with behaviour management, so observed a teacher with a good reputation for control. She gained some ideas, but found that much of this experienced teacher's control was 'invisible' – he just cleared his throat and the class became quiet. So, she observed a supply teacher, and someone with only a little more experience than herself. It was hard to persuade them to let her observe, but when they realized how fruitful the experience and the discussions afterwards would be, they accepted. These lessons, though not so perfectly controlled, gave Diana much more to think about and she learned lots of useful strategies. Both teachers found it useful to have Diana's views on the lesson, as a non-threatening observer, so they too gained from the experience.

Miranda wanted to improve how she shared learning intentions with pupils so she observed a teacher who was known to be good at this. She not only listened well to the teacher's explanation of what he wanted the pupils to achieve but saw that he wrote different lesson outcomes for each group under the headings 'What I'm looking for'. As well as focusing on the teacher, she watched the pupils carefully and spoke to them about their understanding of what they were doing and why. This gave her insight into children's learning and areas of confusion.

TEACHERS TV

Launched in February 2004 Teachers TV can be a great way to help teachers develop. It's on 24 hours a day on digital platforms and at www.teachers.tv. There are thousands of programmes lasting just 15 minutes covering these areas:

Training and Professional Development
1　Classroom-based CPD: observation, analysis, advice and tips.
2　Role-based CPD: support and advice for management, NQTs, TAs etc.
3　School improvement.

News and issues
4　News and current affairs.
5　Educational issues: information and discussion.
6　Career guidance and work/life balance.

Resources
7　Resource reviews.
8　Pupil programmes.
9　External resources: visits and working with institutions outside school.

It's a great source of professional development for all staff because the programmes reassure but spark new ideas. It's a window on the world of teaching and learning. The trouble is that some people see Teachers TV as 'Training being done on the cheap and in our own time'. This is a good point. Schools need to recognize the time that people spend watching – and notice the benefits of this way of learning by incorporating Teachers TV into their menu of professional development activities and arrange team discussions around a programme.

Teaching is a solitary business. This is the real advantage of Teachers TV: it gives people the opportunity to spy on and discuss lessons without having to intrude or disrupt. They can dismiss, damn, discuss or copy the ideas – and it's all safe.

COURSES

Although it is important to get away from a sole reliance on courses, there are clearly some great benefits to attending external input. The trouble is that there is so much to choose from. Penny Bentley, ex-head of Columbia Primary School says, 'I am sometimes amazed that I can go through a huge pile of post and most of it will be advertising for courses. Most of it I put straight in the bin' (Bentley, 2002/2003: 59). Indeed finding out what is worthwhile from this large offering is problematic and word of mouth, reputation, track record or recommendation is often used in making decisions about which providers to use. Some CPD co-ordinators collate all courses in an INSET bulletin and give it to all staff, but this is very time-consuming and may encourage demands that you simply do not have the budget to meet. Most schools build up a small bank of tried and tested providers whose courses they know will be successful. Outfits that cancel courses cause a huge problem especially if supply cover has been booked, money paid and expectations raised.

Universities and LAs generally charge less (especially if there is some sort of service-level agreement) than those courses held in hotels and organized by private consultancies. All that people in the hotel are getting extra is a pleasant venue and good food – and perhaps handouts in a folder rather than simply stapled. You also need to consider the timings, prices and environment – some LAs use poor quality venues, whereas others are based in swanky hotels (even if the training rooms are in the basement with no windows!). You will have to decide whether the extra money is worth the feel-good factor.

Course descriptions and target audience are very important to look at to ensure that training will meet needs. Schools are becoming more used to complaining when the course does not deliver what it promises, as in this case:

> Really the course was absolutely awful. It was advertised as a course for classroom practitioners and Sencos but basically it was an optician telling us about machines that can measure a

> child's perception … I got nothing from the course, certainly nothing practical for my children or anything which made me think about my work. (Hustler et al., 2003: 211)

Some people love going on courses: they seem to be professional course attenders. CPD co-ordinators need to have some system of making sure that courses are allocated fairly and that they relate to needs. Staff should keep a record of courses attended and their impact in their professional development portfolio. In this way, courses should be seen as more than a good day out.

MASTER'S COURSES AND FURTHER STUDY

Quite a few people consider doing some further study within five years of starting work as a teacher. Teachers, almost by definition, like learning. Some will be keen to improve their tennis and are adult education groupies, and a few like some rigorous intellectual stimulation. They get fed up with one-day professional development sessions, especially when so many of them reflect the school's or the government's agenda and not theirs! They want (and deserve) something more substantial. So, for many people the logical step is to do a higher degree and usually a Master's degree.

> I decided to do an MA as I was fed up with the very poor level of INSET available – nothing went deep enough into any area, and I wanted to understand teaching and learning a bit better. I prefer to pay for the course myself, because then I am not beholden to the school – I do not have to provide feedback from my research, and am not bound to research according to the 'party line'. Yes, it takes up a lot of time, but being able to think freely, to read widely and thereby make changes in your own personal practice makes it worthwhile! (From the *TES* staffroom)

An MA usually takes one year full time or two years part time. There are many to choose from. Within each Master's course you usually have some modules that are compulsory and others from which you can choose, so that you study what you like (for an example in the area of leadership see Chapter 14).

Some schools will pay for the Master's, or make a contribution towards the fees. Doing an MA or MBA is not easy but few regret doing so, and many are passionate, such as this evaluation from an MA student at the Institute of Education: 'It is difficult to write in a few lines the positive impact the course has had on my personal and professional life – I know that sounds a little melodramatic – but it is the case! It's been a thoroughly stimulating and enjoyable experience.'

LEARNING CONVERSATIONS – ONLINE

Schools can be lonely places where people don't have time to have professional learning conversations or share fantastic resources. But the posters on the *TES* website's staffroom (www.tes.co.uk) are the very opposite. Want some ideas for tomorrow's lesson? Ask and you'll get ten top tips in no time, as well as worksheets and links to websites. Fiona Duncan, Head of English at Longdean School in Hemel Hempstead, describes it as a real learning community, 'a kind of multi-coloured swap shop of ideas and resources' (Bubb, 2006). This has become formalized in the *TES* Resource Bank, an area where people can share materials and recommend resources and web pages.

The staffroom is freely available, 24/7 and 365 days a year. The *TES* staffroom is a massive place though it feels cosy, as if you're listening to real friends. Anyone can pop in and an astonishing 130,000 people do so each week, viewing 2.3 million pages. There are between 5,000 and 7,000 postings a day, with over 600 an hour at the peak times between 4 and 5pm and from 7pm to midnight. Registering is easy – the hardest part is choosing a witty username that hides your true identity. Some of the site's success must be down to the freedom that comes with this anonymity. People can ask the questions that they'd be too embarrassed to raise elsewhere.

There are over 50 virtual corners of the *TES* staffroom where people with the same interests hang out. As well as different forums for 19 subjects, there's a place for every type of school staff – not just teachers but trainees, admin, teaching assistants and governors as well. Scotland and Wales have their own patches. Bill Hicks who set up the staffroom considers, 'They're one of the few places where teachers and support staff can say what they need to say about their own jobs and the world beyond, where anyone in education with a problem can seek and usually find help from their peers or from experts, and where anyone with an educational axe to grind can get their 15 seconds of fame' (Bubb, 2006).

RUNNING TRAINING YOURSELF

Running training yourself has many advantages. It can ensure that input is tailor-made to the school context and its staff. It may be cheaper – but may not be if one adds up the many hours that you are likely to spend in planning it … and worrying about it! Teaching your colleagues is never an easy – or enviable – task. They may not listen to you as well as they would an outsider or a 'name'. Does this comment from a teacher on the *TES* virtual staffroom ring true?

> Next time you sit in a staff meeting you'll see all the behaviour present in a disruptive Year 9 class. How many teachers nail a pupil for being 'unmanageable' and then take a pride in behaving that same way with colleagues – being stroppy, self-centred and argumentative for the sake of it?

Teachers do not always make brilliant learners, especially at the end of an exhausting day, or in an INSET session when large numbers of your audience want to finish their packing or talk about their holiday. You are bound to have some people who do not want to be there, and others who delight in finding fault with your teaching strategies. Do not panic. You just need to prepare with the cunning of a battle strategist.

It is useful to think of a course (or part of one) that went well and consider the factors that led to its success. For instance:

- The trainer was motivating, had good knowledge of the topic, knew people's needs, had credibility and was confident.
- The group was correctly targeted, receptive and wanted to be there.
- The session was well planned and paced predicting issues but was flexible to needs and built in follow-up work in the school.
- The content was really useful and relevant.
- It was run at a quality time in a suitable venue.

Conversely analyse training that did not go well. For instance:

- There were too few or too many participants.
- People were tired; had unrealistic expectations; saw it as a day off; were not intellectually ready; had tunnel vision; arrived late and left early; one person dominated unhelpfully; there was an air of negativity.
- The course did not meet needs.
- The room was not big enough or was inappropriately arranged.
- There were problems with refreshments or technology.

- The tutor was tired, ill prepared, delivered training that people had done before, did not keep to time, or lacked detailed knowledge.

So, the secret is to copy elements that have worked well and avoid things that have not been successful. If only life were so easy! A good starting point is to think 'What do you want people to get out of the session?' As with any lesson, a focus on the learning objectives is key – but not very easy. You might want to refine it by asking yourself what you hope the new teacher, the deputy and the seen-it-all-before cynic will get out of it. Are your aims realistic for the time allocated? How are you going to achieve your intended outcomes? Few people like going to meetings, so how are you going make sure their time is spent well? Will they come prepared? Do you need an agenda? What snags can you foresee?

Take account of the audience's preferred learning styles and make your presentation appeal in visual, auditory and kinaesthetic ways. Think about what sort of meetings or courses you have enjoyed and got something from – the two do not necessarily go together. What were the elements? What sort of training do you not like? What has worked for your staff in the past? For instance, some people hate courses where they are expected to do an activity every five minutes. Nor do many people like hundreds of PowerPoint slides being flashed up, or speakers who recite every word of every slide. Most people like a bit of pace, a chance to talk through issues, and a trainer with personality and a lot of humour who can keep control of the group, especially that pain who keeps asking such stupid questions.

Think about seating and groupings. Plan the session to a tight schedule. Think of what will work best at the time of day you will be doing the training. What about handouts? If you have some, what will be on them and when will you give them out? As a participant, we want them stapled together, but as trainers we do not like people to read ahead. Are not these just the sorts of dilemmas you face when teaching classes? Yes, but unfortunately you cannot tell adults off when they misbehave, as you can children. They will think it strange when you give them a sticker, too! But you can think about how you will deal with mobile phones going off and people who are late and who wander off the point. Public humiliation is tempting, but remember that you have to work with the culprits.

Expect to be nervous. Being prepared and organized will help, but also give yourself a bit of quiet time before you start so you can focus on the task ahead. Practise your opening line. If you find the thought of everyone looking at you terrifying, get them to look at a screen or a flip chart. Give the group a clear purpose and outcome for the session, and the big picture – what is going to happen.

Make sure you explain any activities clearly – and why you are asking people to do them. Give people tight time limits so they get on with the job. Be selective in the amount of feedback you ask for, because it can take a lot of time and get repetitive. Keeping to time is tricky. Finishing early is never a problem. Over-running is a big no-no, so you will need strategies for moving things on. In your plan you might want to distinguish absolute must-dos from items that can be omitted if you run out of time. No matter how well you plan, you will have to think on your feet. One last tip: do not apologize for having no time for a certain activity – it will make that part appear highly attractive, and people will feel cheated. Pull the learning together in a slick way with a few minutes to spare and everyone will be happy.

CONCLUSION

Meeting needs, both of the school or college and its staff, in the most effective and cost-effective way is not easy. Staff will need to be encouraged constantly to evaluate whether the professional development activities are meeting needs appropriately and to change them if necessary. The impact of professional development is paramount, and it is to this that we now turn.

6

Monitoring and Evaluation: the Impact of CPD

♦ Monitoring

♦ Evaluating impact

♦ Models of evaluating impact

♦ Spreading the impact

♦ How schools have evaluated impact

The final stages in the staff development cycle are concerned with monitoring and evaluating the impact of professional development and training. Both are neglected areas. Monitoring activities are essentially about ensuring that things are going according to plan and, if they are not, taking appropriate action to ensure they do. Gauging the impact of CPD or evaluating its effectiveness – the sixth and last stage in the staff development cycle – is much more difficult. Few evaluation studies concerning CPD make any reference to its impact on teacher behaviour or pupil learning outcomes. However, evaluation is necessary to provide a sound basis for improving and upgrading programmes and processes but it needs to be relatively easy and inexpensive, otherwise it may be seen as diverting scarce resources away from other more important activities. Evaluation of training and development should be attended to but it often gets marginalized or forgotten.

Research has found that monitoring and evaluation are usually the responsibility of CPD co-ordinators who often felt that they had limited experience of evaluation methods and approaches. A DfES-funded national project concluded that most CPD leaders 'felt that they were generally not equipped with the skills and tools to adequately perform the evaluation role' (Goodall et al., 2005: 10). HMI too note that 'the weakest link in the (logical) chain was the way the schools evaluated the effectiveness of their professional development activities' (Ofsted, 2006:19), whilst adding that 'evaluation was effective when the professional development activity had a clear, pre-defined outcome and a suitable method for collecting evidence of its impact' (ibid.:19).

In this chapter we raise a number of important issues concerning monitoring and evaluating CPD, present several models of evaluation, consider cost effectiveness and value for money, and, finally consider what help is available to enable schools and CPD co-ordinators to become better at this necessary and important activity.

MONITORING

The monitoring of professional development at the most basic level importantly consists of checking that what has been planned has happened. This can be carried out in a wide range of ways: reminding people, asking for progress reports, and so on. The difficulty lies in finding a system that is manageable, efficient and that works. Writing progress notes on an action plan, on what has been learned through observing colleagues or going on courses are all valuable. However, measuring someone does not make them grow: it is simply the check that proper nourishment has had its natural effect. Time to talk with colleagues, for the exchange of expertise and the development of professional understanding, will have far greater and more beneficial effects.

EVALUATING IMPACT

Evaluating staff development for its impact is challenging as 'it involves checking the links of a long chain between a training programme for individual staff and beneficial results for the school' (Baxter and Chambers, 1998: 31). Investors in People has made schools much more aware of the need for systematic evaluation measures. A school's understanding of the impact of its investment in people on its performance is a fundamental aspect of the standard. Schools

> need to understand that staff development is the most powerful tool for change at their disposal. It is also the most expensive in terms of time, energy and money. It is for its contribution to ensuring that the benefits of this investment are achieved and sustained, that evaluation must now be considered an essential component of the staff development process. (ibid.: 32)

Evaluation needs to be thought about and planned for at the outset. HMI note that:

> evaluation was not good in schools which had failed to build it in at the planning stage. They had not defined the desired outcomes of professional development activities in terms of pupils' learning and achievement, still less agreed how achievement of these outcomes would be assessed. Consequently, their managers relied on subjective impressions for evidence of the impact of CPD. (Ofsted, 2006: 20)

Assertions and intentions are useful but CPD co-ordinators need to have evidence of the actual impact of professional development. Talking to staff about their development is important. Listening to what pupils say is becoming increasingly important. It is a key component of the school evaluation process and should, therefore, actively inform the school improvement plan and professional development. The most common forms and sources of evidence of impact are:

- Evaluation sheets.
- Discussion following training to CPD leader.
- Discussion at staff or subject area meeting.
- Written reports.
- Interviews, either formal or informal.
- Observing practice such as observing lessons, scrutinizing work.
- Performance data.
- The pupil voice.
- Self-evaluation/reflection.

These forms and sources of evidence are used occasionally:

- External review by, for instance, a university or consultant.
- Questionnaires.
- Learning journals.

- The views of parents and governors.

- Data such as staff absence, promotions, etc.

- Whole school measures such as Investors in People (CfBT/Lincs, 2006).

? **POINTS FOR REFLECTION**

What do you think of the impact of Mary's professional development described in case study 6.1?

CASE STUDY 6.1: A MUSIC TEACHER

Mary, a music teacher, got funding from the school to pay for her to learn a new instrument, but one that she was not going to teach so its contribution to her professional development was dubious. However, she asserted that she extended her knowledge about successful learning by becoming a learner herself and that this impacted on her teaching because she realized that she expected pupils to accept musical procedures without further questioning. As a learner, Mary needed to ask questions and be given specific answers; as a result, she modified her teaching methodology to include these aspects of learning. This professional development impacted directly on pupil learning and on the teacher–pupil relationship; it introduced a new paradigm of relationship that is 'learner-to-learner'.

She also spent professional development money on ICT hardware. This did not impact on her educational work in the same way as her music lessons. The new monitor and printer support Mary's desire to organize her administration efficiently, which is admirable but debatable in terms of being an educational use of developmental funding. Such requirements could have been noted on the department development plan.

Source: adapted from Minnis, 2003

MODELS OF EVALUATING IMPACT

Over the years a number of models to evaluate the impact of training and development have been devised. One of the first and perhaps the best known is the framework for evaluating training developed by Kirkpatrick and first published in 1959 in the *Journal of the American Society of Training Directors.* This has been adapted and developed over the years but Kirkpatrick's four-step framework remains the model or framework for evaluating most training programmes in business and commerce. As Bubb and Hoare (2001: 114) explain 'this is primarily because of the simplicity of the model, how it relates to the trainee and the workplace and the way in which it can readily be applied to almost every type of work situation and learning process'.

They go on to state that the Kirkpatrick model explores the relationship between training and the workplace at four levels: reactions, learning, behaviour and results. These are measured at suitable points during the training process. The first three are essentially trainee based, while the fourth changes emphasis and centres on the effectiveness of the training for the organization.

LEVEL 1: REACTIONS

By evaluating reactions, you find out if participants enjoyed the training, if the training environment was suitable and comfortable and if the trainers were capable and credible. In short, you are trying to learn what participants think and feel about the training.

■ LEVEL 2: LEARNING

By evaluating learning, you determine the extent to which trainees have done the following three things as a result of their training: changed their attitudes, improved their knowledge or increased their skills.

■ LEVEL 3: BEHAVIOUR

By evaluating behaviour, you determine if the trainees are using or transferring their newly learned knowledge, skills and behaviours back on the job. In other words, what behaviour changed because people took part in a training session?

■ LEVEL 4: RESULTS

By evaluating results, you determine if the training has affected school results or contributed to the achievement of an objective. This final evaluation which considers both personal evaluation and company benefit makes the Kirkpatrick model so suitable for so many types of training including in education (see Case Study 6.2) (Bubb and Hoare, 2001: 114–15).

CASE STUDY 6.2: THE LEVELS OF IMPACT OF JILL'S ONE-DAY INDUCTION TUTOR TRAINING COURSE

Level 1: reactions
Despite the day being well-organized and in pleasant surroundings, Jill did not enjoy the day because she had to sit next to and work with her ex-husband's second wife – the woman her husband left her for!

Level 2: learning
However, she gained much new knowledge and increased her skills. The handouts reminded her of her learning.

Level 3: behaviour
Jill used her newly learned knowledge, skills and behaviours in working with the two NQTs.

Level 4: results
The NQTs said that the school's induction was initially poor but improved after Jill attended the course. They really noticed a difference because of all the new systems and found their induction very effective. They felt well supported, and monitored and assessed fairly so that they were able to make good progress in their first year.

This impacted on their pupils who learned more and behaved better as a result of improved teaching by their inexperienced teachers.

Another American, Thomas Guskey, has developed and refined Kirkpatrick's model more specifically for education. He is clear that: 'We need to make evaluation an integral part of the professional development process … Systematically gathering and analysing evidence to inform our actions must become a central component in professional development technology' (Guskey, 2000: 92). The evaluation of CPD, in particular examining its impact and whether or not it meets individualized 'learning perspectives' so that the potential of training opportunities is realized, is very important. Professional development does not just happen – it has to be managed and led, and done so effectively ensuring it has a positive impact and represents good value for money. In Britain those schools that have sought Investors in People status have highlighted these issues and others.

Guskey talks in terms of five levels of evaluation of CPD with improved pupil outcomes being the desired result. These five levels, shown in Table 6.1, are:

1 participants' reactions;

2 participants' learning;

3 organization support and change;

4 participants' use of new knowledge and skills;

5 pupil learning outcomes.

Level 3 – organization support and change – is not found in the Kirkpatrick model and refers to the key role that the school can play in supporting or sabotaging any CPD efforts. The focus needs to be on the attributes and organizational features of the school that are necessary for success. Were changes at the individual level encouraged and supported at all levels? Were sufficient resources made available, including time for sharing and reflection? Were successes recognized and shared (Guskey, 2002: 47)?

Each level builds on those that come before:

> People must have a positive reaction to a professional development experience before we can expect them to learn anything from it. They need to gain specific knowledge and skills before we look to the organization for critical aspects of support or change. Organizational support is necessary to gain high quality implementation of new policies and practices. And appropriate implementation is a prerequisite to seeing improvements in student learning. Things can break down at any point along the way, and once they break down, the improvement process comes to a screeching halt. (Guskey, 2005: 12)

Reversing these five levels can be useful in professional development planning. So begin planning by asking, 'What improvements in pupils do we want and how will we know when they're achieved?' Then ask, 'If that's the impact we want, what needs to change?' Next, consider what types of organizational support or change are needed, and so forth (Guskey, 2005).

The other important contribution that Guskey has made is getting us to focus on 'the bottom line' and to think more broadly about what constitutes pupil outcomes (level 5). As can be seen in Table 6.1, he divides student outcomes into:

■ cognitive (performance and achievement);

■ affective (attitudes, beliefs and dispositions);

■ psychomotor (skills, behaviours and practices).

We might find the terms a bit off-putting but it is a useful classification. The cognitive is the most obvious – pupil attainment (the dreaded performance tables!) or knowledge and understanding. This might include examination results, grades, test scores – but we need to look at achievement in the round and think of the education of the whole child. The affective domain is crucially important and includes such things as pupil attitudes and dispositions. For example, has their attitude to school changed, their study habits improved and are they more predisposed towards the subject? Are they attending more regularly? And what about pupils' self-concepts? Do they have greater confidence in themselves as learners and do they accept more personal responsibility for their actions and behaviours?

Psychomotor outcomes or skills and behaviours might include such things as classroom behaviour, homework completion rates, participation in school activities including attendance at lunchtime and after-school clubs, and retention and drop-out rates. For example, have pupils adopted healthier eating habits and other desired practices, are they reading more outside of school time, are they more involved or active in their learning, do they engage more in classroom discussion?

POINTS FOR REFLECTION

How are all three of Guskey's student learning outcomes reflected in the *Every Child Matters* agenda and the evidence needed to inform the self-evaluation form?

All of this information about the impact of CPD – and, of course, some of it is easier to measure than others – can be used to guide improvements in the CPD cycle, including the design and implementation of training programmes and their follow-up. Guskey notes that in some cases information on pupil learning outcomes is used to estimate the cost-effectiveness of CPD, sometimes known as 'return on investment' (2002: 49).

TABLE 6.1 FIVE LEVELS OF PROFESSIONAL DEVELOPMENT EVALUATION

Evaluation level	What questions are addressed?	How will information be gathered?	What is measured or assessed?	How will information be used?
Participants' reactions	Did they like it? Was their time spent well? Did the material make sense? Will it be useful? Was the leader knowledgeable and helpful? Were the refreshments fresh and tasty? Was the room the right temperature? Were the chairs comfortable?	Questionnaires administered at the end of each session	Initial satisfaction with the experience	To improve programme design and delivery
Participants' learning	Did participants acquire the intended knowledge and skills?	Paper and pencil instruments Simulations Demonstrations Participant reflections (oral and/or written) Participant portfolios	New knowledge and skills of participants	To improve programme content, format, and organization
Organization support and change	Was implementation advocated, facilitated and supported? Was the support public and overt? Were the problems addressed quickly and efficiently? Were sufficient resources made available? What was the impact on the organization? Did it affect the organization's climate and procedures?	District (LA) and schools records Minutes from follow-up meetings Questionnaires Structured interviews with participants and district or school administrators Participant portfolios	The organization's advocacy, support, accommodation, facilitation, and recognition	To document and improve organization support To inform future change efforts
Participants' use of new knowledge and skills	Did participants effectively apply the new knowledge and skills?	Questionnaires Structured interviews with participants and their supervisors Participant reflections (oral and/or written) Participant portfolios Direct observations Video or audio tapes	Degree and quality of implementation	To document and improve implementation of programme content
Student learning outcomes	What was the impact on students? Did it affect student performance or achievement? Did it influence students' physical or emotional well-being? Are students more confident as learners? Is student attendance improving? Are dropouts decreasing?	Student records School records Questionnaires Structured interviews with students, parents, teachers and/or administrators Participant portfolios	Student learning outcomes Cognitive (performance and achievement) Affective (attitudes and dispositions) Psychomotor (skills and behaviours)	To focus and improve all aspects of programme design, implementation, and follow-up. To demonstrate the overall impact of professional development

Source: Guskey, 2002: 48

The Guskey model was used in a DfES national project to investigate how schools were evaluating the impact of CPD. It found that:

> the vast majority of evaluation takes account of participant reaction and learning. Organisational support and change was evaluated by only 41% of the schools in the fieldwork, and pupil learning outcomes were evaluated by only one in four schools. Even where the impact of CPD for teachers is evaluated in terms of student learning outcomes, the evaluation tends to be neither overly rigorous nor consistent. (Goodall, et al., 2005: 9)

The researchers also found that questionnaires were the main tool used for evaluation purposes, which were usually completed directly after the event. In most cases, the completion of the questionnaire was seen as an end in itself, and as the end of the evaluative process.

In England, David Frost and Judy Durrant (2003) have developed a framework to show how the process of development work culminates for the teacher in the transformation of professional knowledge. They argue that the outcomes of training or CPD can be seen not only in terms of professional development of individuals, but also in the extent to which there is an impact on pupils' learning, on colleagues' learning and on organizational learning. They suggest that staff may also be able to make a contribution beyond their school.

- *Impact on pupils' learning:*
    - attainment;
    - disposition;
    - meta-cognition.

- *Impact on staff:*
    - classroom practice;
    - personal capacity;
    - interpersonal capacity.

- *Impact on the school as an organization:*
    - structures and processes;
    - culture and capacity.

- *Impact beyond the school:*
    - critique and debate;
    - creation and transfer of professional knowledge;
    - improvements in social capital in the community.

This framework enables staff and schools to think beyond the effects of particular CPD provision or a training event and to focus more on their impact. In other words, the focus is on the actions of the staff and not so much on the development programmes and training events themselves. Causality is very difficult to establish, and the impact or effects of a particular programme or activity cannot be isolated. Frost and Durrant have designed tools and activities to enable staff themselves to plan, track and evaluate the impact of their activity and, rather than retrospectively evaluating the impact that has already taken place, the intention is to encourage staff to think more broadly about the influence they may have, thereby increasing impact as they adjust their planning accordingly. For example, they may be encouraged to introduce more collaborative working, they may offer to run a staff development session in their school and they may agree to contribute to a conference or run a session for another group on their specific area of expertise.

There are several 'tool-kits' or 'self-assessment' charts such as the DfES study's route map and self-assessment forms (Goodall et al., 2005); and *London's Learning* (DfES, 2005a). They raise a useful set of questions you might usefully ask as a means of ascertaining current practice in your school. You need to have some idea of where you and the school are now in order to plan a way forward. Both have divided schools into three levels of CPD development or progress towards becoming a learning community. Rather confusingly they use slightly different labels to describe these types; the former talks about 'emerging', 'establishing' and 'enhancing', whereas the latter refers to 'emerging', 'developing' and 'establishing'. Tables 6.2 and 6.3 illustrate how schools can evaluate their use of resources and the impact of CPD respectively.

TABLE 6.2 EFFECTIVE USE OF RESOURCES

EMERGING as a professional learning community	DEVELOPING as a professional learning community	ESTABLISHING a professional learning community
The school allocates central funds for individual training events.	The school allocates funding for teaching and some support staff opportunities.	Informed by a school framework, all staff are clear about those CPD opportunities which will be funded.
Time is allocated in response to requests from staff. The school is aware that more advance planning is required.	The school identifies time for some learning opportunities in advance although as yet there is no advance timetabling of activities.	Aspects of professional learning are timetabled. Time for CPD is identified on the calendar. The school has conducted an audit of time available for staff development and staff have a minimum time entitlement.
Professional training days involve teachers and whole staff activities with focus chosen by the school leadership team. Meetings are mostly concerned with business.	Professional training days focus on whole school improvement priorities with some choice for staff. TAs may attend. Interesting practice may be discussed in staff/team meetings.	The school uses professional training days flexibly and imaginatively in support of professional development to improve teaching and learning. Support staff are involved and lead sessions as appropriate.
Supply teachers are used to release teaching staff to attend training.	The school is beginning to use in-house staff to cover classes where necessary and is exploring imaginative approaches linked to the remodelling work.	Where appropriate, the school employs trained in-house staff such as HLTAs to release staff. Innovative and imaginative solutions release staff such as the use of IT suites for independent pupil learning.
Allocation of funding is done centrally by the leadership team. Teachers may bid for funds to support training.	Funding allocations are held and managed centrally by the CPD leader with some delegated funds to teams.	CPD leader has the overview of all allocations available to support professional learning from a range of sources, and delegates allocation as appropriate.
The school relies heavily on selected external expertise to offer professional development.	Staff are encouraged to contribute to the development of others. External expertise tends to focus on National Strategies and courses.	The CPD leader has an overview of the contributions that staff can make to the learning of others. When external expertise is selected it is explicitly linked to school based classroom practice.
The CPD leader holds all information about the costs of CPD.	Some team leaders are aware of the costs of the CPD.	All staff are aware of the real costs of CPD opportunities. 'Value for money' is built into the school's evaluation processes.

Source: DfES, 2005a

TABLE 6.3 EVALUATION OF THE IMPACT OF CPD

Evaluation	Evaluation of the impact of CPD not done	Evaluation of the impact of CPD dependent on a few means (observation, scrutiny of work, etc.)	Evaluation of impact of CPD done through a wide range of means
	Evaluation seen as quality control	Evaluation seen as quality control and dissemination	Evaluation of CPD seen as quality control, dissemination and as involving evidence of impact
Level of evaluation	Immediate evaluation of events is used	Immediate and interim evaluation are used	Immediate, interim and long term evaluation are used
	Participant reaction is only means of evaluation	Participant based evaluation (reaction, use of new knowledge and skills) used	All levels of evaluation used
		Some events are evaluated by a return to the immediate participant reaction (after a lapse of a set period of time)	All events are evaluated by a return to the immediate participant reaction (after a lapse of a set period of time)
		No or little linkage of evaluation to future planning (perhaps only in terms of 'not using' a provider or course again due to adverse feedback)	Evaluation of impact clearly feeds into future planning of CPD
			Evaluation of impact of CPD feeds into planning in other areas: SIP, etc.
			Outside sources used to evaluate impact of CPD: IIP, kite marks, charter marks, etc.
Planning	Evaluation of impact not built into planning of CPD	Evaluation of impact built into planning of whole school CPD	Evaluation of impact built into all planning of CPD
Reporting	Report of evaluation of CPD is confined to the participant	Report of evaluation of CPD sometimes forms part of meeting structures	Report of evaluation seen as part of team/department/school meeting structure
	Emerging	**Establishing**	**Enhancing**

Source: Goodall et al., 2005: 196

SPREADING THE IMPACT

The impact of any professional development is increased if other people within the school can benefit from it. Figure 6.1 illustrates that one person's professional development activity can benefit others and thereby more pupils if the school has systems to enable this to happen. This is known as 'cascading' and has been one of the key methods used in the national strategies. One person is trained at a local authority course and then delivers the training to staff at school. There are benefits to this model, particularly in terms of cost. However, much depends on the time available to cascade and the quality and confidence of the individual, and their perceived status in the school. Cascading happens at the start of new initiatives but the impact is reduced if there is no support or input later on. Her Majesty's Inspectorate found that 'schools on the whole failed to allow enough time to support effective professional development and to ensure that acquired knowledge and skills were consolidated, implemented and shared with other teachers' (Ofsted, 2002a: 3). They recommend that people should have half a day's non-contact time after each day's course to cascade and set up ways to implement new ideas.

There is much confusion in schools between dissemination and evaluation. Schools in the DfES study frequently responded to questions about evaluation of impact with examples of dissemination: cascade training, sharing new knowledge and skills. People were 'sharing the content of the CPD rather than gauging the impact of the CPD' (Goodall et al., 2005: 11).

For sustainability and impact, it's important to disseminate and log information and resources, such as in the staff library and website, so that everyone can benefit. Remember to have systems for recognizing unplanned learning and impact – there will always be some! Virtual learning environments, such as Moodle, can be very handy. Woodberry Down Primary in East London asks its staff to write blogs about their development (www.woodberrydown.org). Listing networks and contacts made can also be valuable to the whole school workforce. If dissemination is successful:

- people will know who to ask for advice;
- there will be greater awareness of resources;
- staff will start to see themselves as experts;
- the status of staff development will be raised;
- professional learning becomes infectious.

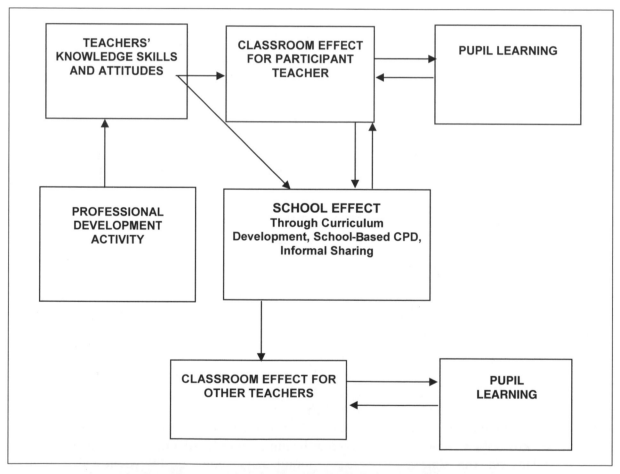

FIGURE 6.1 LOCAL EVALUATION OF INSET (ADAPTED FROM ERAUT ET AL., 1988)

HOW SCHOOLS HAVE EVALUATED IMPACT

This section has an example of how one school evaluated staff development. In Case Study 6.3, a questionnaire was devised in Cullompton Community College to see what activities had the greatest impact on the school.

CASE STUDY 6.3: CULLOMPTON COMMUNITY COLLEGE'S EVALUATION OF CPD

This case study of evaluation of CPD is based on an article by Davey published in **Professional Development Today** (Davey, 2000).

John Davey, the Vice-Principal of Cullompton Community College in Devon, wanted to devise a cost-effective way of evaluating staff development that was simple to administer and analyse, and would be sustainable. He wanted to know:

- how staff perceive the impact of developmental activities on their classroom practice and school improvement;

- which activities have the greatest impact on raising standards across the institution;

- which provided the best value for money, in order to ensure that limited budgets can be used to greatest effect.

'When we started to plan we became aware that there were two particular dimensions to staff development: those activities that took individuals forward in their professional practice and those activities designed to benefit the institution. These activities would have considerable overlap and in most cases both types of activity would assist in raising standards. An individual's personal development may not be used immediately within an institution but often constitutes a resource which could be drawn upon in the future to the benefit of the wider education service'. (ibid.: 34)

Recognizing this dual aspect to staff development led him to two key questions, one about how individuals had developed and one about how the institution had benefited. The key questions were:

- In what ways am I a better teacher than this time last year (in the classroom or in other roles)?

- How has this improved the experience of the pupils I teach and helped them raise their achievement?

A questionnaire was devised to be completed by staff that we have adapted in Figure 6.2. Davey found that the staff development activities perceived to have the greatest impact on teaching were those which 'took place within the school, had direct relevance to classroom practice and which provided a forum for sharing between professionals where there was an opportunity for participants to set at least part of the agenda' (p. 38).

While initially the school was mainly concerned with issues of cost effectiveness, the exercise led the leadership team to re-evaluate the importance attached to work-based and in-house activities and realize that they can have greater impact than those organized and run externally.

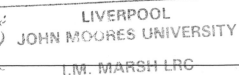

EVALUATION OF STAFF DEVELOPMENT

Name:..

In order to complete this evaluation you will need to set aside approximately 30 minutes. Some of this time will be for writing but thinking through your experiences during the year is at least as important.

The aim of this evaluation is:
- to document details of all the activities staff have been involved in this year
- to identify which activities have been of value
- to assess the impact staff development activities have had on teaching and learning
- to obtain details of the training needs perceived by staff.

1a. Please list the training activities you have been involved in during the year

Non Pupil Days (completed for you)

DATE	ISSUES COVERED	*
1&2/09	Target setting and getting. Examination analysis. Year team meetings.	
02/09	ICT training and departmental time.	
16/10	Ofsted preparation. Departmental work.	
04/01	Target setting, CATs work. Year team meetings. Departmental time.	
05/02	School improvement course. ICT training. Departmental work.	

Courses or other external activities:

	DATE	TITLE	ISSUE COVERED	*
1				
2				
3				

1b. Other activities that have contributed to your professional development (e.g. being observed, observing colleagues, mentoring, meetings, personal reading, etc.).

	DATE	TITLE	ISSUE COVERED	*
1				
2				
3				
4				

Of the activities listed above which <u>three</u> have had the greatest influence on your work? Please indicate by putting an asterisk in the last column.

FIGURE 6.2 EVALUATION OF STAFF DEVELOPMENT (ADAPTED FROM DAVEY, 2000)

1c. Insights or expertise gained during the year that you can share with other staff.

	TOPIC	EXPERTISE OR INSIGHTS OFFERED
1		
2		
3		

2. *Having considered the various staff development activities you have been involved in during the year please answer these questions:*

In what ways am I a better member of staff than this time last year (in the classroom or in other roles)?

How has this improved the experience of pupils I work with and helped them raise their achievement?

3. *What are your professional development needs now?*

	Topic	Specific needs
1		
2		
3		

Thank you for taking the time to think and write. Your help will assist us in making the most effective use of the limited funds available for staff development.

FIGURE 6.2 (CONTINUED)

CONCLUSION

We need to engage in some form of evaluation activity for both accountability and developmental reasons but we must also ensure that the activity itself does not become overly burdensome or costly for those staff and schools involved in the process. Evaluation of CPD, including devising measures of cost effectiveness and value for money, and for gaining insight into the impact of CPD on outcomes, are areas in which schools would welcome more advice and guidance. This is unsurprising as evaluating the impact of CPD at school, teacher or pupil level is often regarded as the most difficult part of the training and development cycle. As far as the 'logical chain' is concerned it is the weakest link! Schools are generally not skilled in evaluation processes and lacked experience and tools to consider the impact of CPD at different levels.

If the ultimate purpose of CPD for staff is to bring about improvement in the quality of teaching and learning in schools and classrooms – and thus impact positively on pupil outcomes – then it is important to have evaluation processes in place which give us some idea whether this is happening or not. We should be thinking about evaluation at the outset and not at the end of a professional development activity which is why the CPD form in Chapter 3 (Figure 3.4) could be so useful.

7

Collaboration and Enquiry: Sharing Practice

Graham Handscomb

♦ Collaboration

♦ Research – school staff doing it themselves

♦ The research-engaged school

♦ Developing staff for a new professional future

The road towards increased collaboration amongst teachers and between schools in which they work has been long and tortuous, but the signs are that the collaboration movement is beginning to gather pace and credibility. Recognition of the benefits of teacher collaboration and sharing of practice, combined with growing commitment to developing teachers as researchers of their own practice, has started to transform our understanding of what constitutes effective continuing professional development.

This chapter examines the dynamic relationship between collaboration, enquiry and CPD, along with the challenges involved in sharing expertise. Examples of effective approaches are offered for consideration.

COLLABORATION

Together the two ingredients of teacher collaboration and enquiry make a potent brew. In the context of the movement towards all schools becoming self-managing they have contributed to a reconceptualization of CPD in terms of processes owned and developed by teachers, with the school perceived as a reservoir of expertise and experience to be used. Thus a modern CPD agenda emerges which has the following features:

- tapping school expertise, not importing it;
- CPD focus on pedagogy and the 'craft of the classroom';
- the teacher is best placed to conduct classroom enquiry;
- developing, seeking out and sharing practice;
- developing communities of practice within and beyond the school;
- Local Authorities, government and others adopting a partnership role.

This emphasis on collaboration whilst specifying the school as the locus of CPD, reflects national drivers for change and poses certain challenges. The arrival of the era of collaboration, ironically, has occurred when there is a continuing commitment to school autonomy and diversity. Perhaps one of the greatest educational challenges facing government, Local Authorities and schools alike over the next few years is how to move forward on each of these three priorities.

This tension is also reflected in the *Code of Practice on LEA/Schools Relations* (DfEE, 2000), which establishes:

- the principle of school autonomy;
- the responsibility for school performance and improvement rest, in the first instance, with schools themselves;
- within this context is advocated the sharing of good practice within schools.

Therefore, placed alongside the Local Authority's core role to monitor, challenge and intervene in inverse proportion to success, is the role of promoting and facilitating the sharing of good practice. Effective schools are thus seen as those that manage autonomously but also share and seek out good practice within the wider educational community.

So the modernized school is not portrayed as ploughing its own furrow, perhaps to the detriment of others. True the diversity agenda is as strong as ever, and fears of divisiveness still persist. But the *Code of Practice on LEA/School Relations* makes it clear that 'autonomy does not mean isolation' (DfEE, 2000). Improvement, including the contribution of CPD, is now seen as essentially a collaborative exercise.

COLLABORATION AND PROFESSIONAL LEARNING

There is now a growing and authoritative consensus that the most effective professional learning is focused on teachers' classroom practice and is collaborative. The government's professional development strategy stressed the importance of 'learning together, learning from the best, and learning from what works' (DfEE, 2001a). Similarly the General Teaching Council's (England) *Teachers' Professional Learning Framework* (GTC, 2003) states that teaching has often been experienced as an isolated activity and that teacher development has consequently suffered from this. It claims that an increasing body of professional development work demonstrates 'the value of moving collegial learning from the margins of professional practice to the heart of it'. The GTC sees classroom teachers 'not only as classroom experts in a single school but also as members of the broader education community' (GTC, 2003).

So learning together is advocated because it tends to focus development on classroom practice. As Harris (2002) puts it: 'improvements in teaching are most likely to occur where there are opportunities to work together and to learn from each other'. She also identifies gains in terms of teachers' professionalism and wellbeing stating 'collaboration is important because it creates a collective professional confidence that allows teachers to interact more confidently and assertively' (ibid.). The NCSL's 'Networked Learning Communities' initiative (outlined in Chapter 2) strikes a similar note.

WHAT DOES COLLABORATION LOOK LIKE?

So given that there is now a considerable momentum towards collaborative professional learning in schools, what does this look like in practice and how is it achieved? The benefits of consortia working are:

- identifying joint problems and issues, and more effectively tackling them together;
- networking wide experience and expertise;

- economies of scale – effective and efficient joint training and sharing of resources;

- 'commissioning power' to secure CPD providers, LA facilitators and higher education partnerships;

- establishing and developing research communities;

- keying into local, regional and national opportunities;

- building a body of new professional knowledge within the consortium.

Fostering effective collaboration, however, is not plain sailing and establishing the right culture is key. It is unlikely to develop or to be replenished without seeking out and sharing practice beyond the school. Here are some key things to think about when setting up a consortium:

- Be clear about why your schools want to consort; common features/agendas/developments.

- Get started on a specific project together; this will help to build relationships and explore consortium potential.

- Make arrangements for some monitoring of early work and development so that organizational issues are identified and logged.

- Then look at ways you need to organize yourselves to make the best use of time and have the most impact.

- Consider producing a consortium development plan, containing limited, ambitious but attainable priorities in a specified time.

- Check that your consortium is focused on improving classroom practice.

- Ensure the consortium is founded on practical opportunities for shared professional learning.

Case study 7.1 describes an established consortium of small rural primary schools.

A CONTINUUM OF PRACTICE

Despite, or perhaps because of, the increased momentum towards collaborative professional learning, there has been insufficient attention given to what is entailed in the identification and sharing of practice between teachers and between schools. On the one hand, it will involve promoting the sharing and exchange of interesting and innovative practice, whilst on the other, also helping to build a body of knowledge about effective and best practice. The big issue here is the casual ease with which people often talk of sharing best practice when actually what is being disseminated is untried, untested, interesting practice. Schools and organizations that support them, like LAs, have a role in both these areas. So there is a need to promote a dynamic environment that fosters practitioner creativity, whilst also ensuring clarity about what works, and whether practice is of a high standard and stands the test of time.

CASE STUDY 7.1: A PRIMARY SCHOOL CONSORTIUM

Four small rural schools within a primary schools consortium worked in partnership with the University of Cambridge Department for Education on a school improvement research initiative. The group of schools had established themselves into a consortium for some time. The success of the consortium was reflected in the investment each school made in terms of:

- consortium management – regular management meetings attended by all headteachers, robust consortium management procedures;

- development planning – all schools committed to specific actions to implement in the consortium development plan;

- finance – each school investing £1 per pupil into the consortium finances;

- professional development – common non-pupil days and common weekly staff meetings agreed across the consortium to enable joint professional development linked to the consortium development plan.

This research project arose out of several years' experience of working together for professional development purposes, including work with Cambridge University. At consortium management meetings the schools' headteachers consider the individual needs of schools and identify areas for shared INSET provision and school improvement projects.

The project focused on school-based enquiry. It was decided that three non-pupil days involving all (40) teaching staff at the above schools would be devoted to this project and two twilight sessions per term for staff. An accreditation outcome was the award of the Cambridge Certificate of Further Professional Study. Teachers would pursue some school-based enquiry using research methods to study aspects of 'Teaching and learning linked to monitoring and evaluation'. Theoretical aspects of teaching and learning and monitoring and evaluation linked to management (subject leader roles) and school-based enquiry were introduced on the two non-pupil days. Following practice in research techniques – carrying out interviews, questionnaires, observations – each school chose to focus on enquiries, which were relevant to their own school development. These were:

- the effectiveness of the ICT suite in supporting children's learning;

- improving writing (linking writing to motor skills at Key Stage 1 and strategies to improve spelling at Key Stage 2);

- investigating ways to improve children's ability to read and write for information;

- investigating the development of listening skills;

- developing thinking skills.

Whilst each school pursued its own lines of enquiry it used schools in the consortium to help with planning and testing out ideas and development. Assistance from the university staff with theory and research methodology enabled some rigour to the investigations.

The project involved staff from all schools engaging in research-based improvement. Originally a range of staff from each school participated. However, as the popularity of the project grew, many more took part and in some schools all the staff, including support staff, conducted a research project. This meant that there was a critical mass of research development in each school. Children and staff in each school have benefited from the research and that progress has been made in the development of the schools as learning communities. It is hoped that further developments will occur between schools so that the learning community is extended within the consortium. The LA has worked actively with the consortium to facilitate opportunities to disseminate outcomes within Essex and on national conferences.

In his analysis of the role of the LA in the promotion and analysis of school practice, David Woods makes the following helpful distinctions:

> In the literature on school improvement the terms 'best', 'good' and 'innovative' practice are used in a variety of ways. Good practice is generally used to mean practice which is professionally judged to be effective, but may require further evidence and validation; best practice is used to mean practice which is proven over time, backed by supporting evidence; innovative practice may highlight new and interesting ways of doing things, with early indications of success. (Woods, 2000)

This is perhaps most helpfully illustrated as a continuum (see Figure 7.1) ranging from creative practice, to good practice, to best practice. So, for example, a teacher who has developed a set of practices in her classroom that works well with her group of learners, might be characterized as being at the left-hand side of the continuum. As this is shared with other school colleagues, who adapt and apply it in their different settings, it gets tested against a range of teacher professionalism and might then be termed 'good practice'. Eventually it might be developed into school-wide approaches, shared in other school settings, benchmarked and validated by supporting evidence and proven over time – and thus merit the accolade 'best practice'. Clearly calibration and judgements made about such distinctions should be part and parcel of the professional discussion, debate and agreement amongst teachers, schools and other parties like HEIs and LAs, and all of these types of practice have a part to play in the quest for continuous professional development and school improvement.

Continuum of interesting, good and best practice

Interesting and innovative practice	Good practice	Best practice
Encouraging creativity, innovation and a sense of dynamism, 'A thousand flowers bloom.'	Effective practice. Ideas shared with others, adapted to new contexts and tried out. Learning communities. Sharing and trialling.	Best practice validated by supporting evidence and proven over time. Structured systems. Benchmarking. Monitoring and evaluation. Quality assurance. Formal dissemination.

FIGURE 7.1 A CONTINUUM OF PRACTICE (HANDSCOMB, 2002/3)

■ TO NETWORK OR NOT TO NETWORK?

Even with such clarity about the nature of best practice, the process of actually sharing expertise between practitioners is in itself problematic. In McIntyre's research on 'expert teachers' he concludes that it is often difficult to disseminate the practice of good teachers because, by their very nature they tend to be intuitive, and use tacit expertise and knowledge, and their work is usually particular to themselves and their immediate context (McIntyre, 2001). Hargreaves has given considerable thought to this problem of how to 'bottle' and share teacher practitioner knowledge:

> If one teacher tells another about a practice that he finds effective, the second teacher has merely acquired information, not personal knowledge. Transfer occurs only when the knowledge of the first becomes information for the second, who then works on that information in

such a way that it becomes part of his or her context of meaning and purpose and pre-existing knowledge and then is applied in action … Transfer is the conversion of information about one person's practice into another's know-how. (Hargreaves, 1998)

So ensuring the effective transference and application of practice to other classrooms as part of collaborative professional development is far from easy. The report of the sub-group of the National Education Research Forum (NERF), chaired by Hargreaves, showed this to be a highly complex process (NERF, 2001). Referring to the application of research to policy and practice, the report distinguishes between the key elements of knowledge production, dissemination and use, each of which in turn have specific processes that need to be addressed. Robust sharing of practice involves a process of producing, disseminating and using new knowledge.

Some would argue that the process is so difficult that it casts doubt on the feasibility of transference of practice between different schools. David Reynolds (2003) is adamant that there is little evidence of collaboration working or of transference of good practice between schools sticking. He advocates schools 'learning from their own best practice' (ibid.: 23). By contrast David Hopkins (2002) strongly endorses the effectiveness of networks. He acknowledges that collaborative networks need to guard against cosiness and be committed to 'quality, rigour and a focus on outcomes', but insists on their transforming power. For schools addressing the issues of sharing practice and networking it would be useful to consider where they stand regarding these two contrasting views.

RESEARCH – SCHOOL STAFF DOING IT THEMSELVES

The concern about 'soft' unproductive collaboration is resolved, in Alma Harris's view, if a strategic link is made with teacher enquiry and research: 'For teacher development … to occur, commitment to certain kinds of collaboration is centrally important. However, collaboration without reflection and enquiry is little more than working collegially. For collaboration to influence personal growth and development it has to be premised upon mutual enquiry and sharing' (Harris, 2002).

The image of educational research for many teachers is something done by others in academic institutions – complex, difficult to access, and of limited relevance. Unfortunately, some developments in educational research have suffered from these features. However, this is changing. Increasingly, classroom practitioners have discovered the merits of investigating an aspect of their work that directly contributes to improved practice and benefits the children they teach. For instance Case study 7.2 is about one school's action research in art and emotional literacy and Case study 7.3 is a an overview of how the culture of a infant and nursery school was transformed through pupils as well as staff becoming researchers.

A number of authorities are involved in leading school-focused research activities. Here is a selection of research projects that schools in Wiltshire are involved in:

- identification of pupils with poorly developed emotional literacy in order to provide opportunities for remediation;
- implementing an 'enrichment' curriculum for all pupils;
- improving student critical faculties in making judgements;
- exploring the impact of the mentoring system for gifted and talented pupils to further strengthen the scheme;
- improving attainment in Year 7 by stimulating pupils to become independent learners;
- investigating websites useful to those new as heads to devise an easy guide for suggested use (*Wiltshire Journal of Education*, 2003, available on www.wiltshire.gov.uk).

CASE STUDY 7.2: A SCHOOL PROJECT TO RAISE THE STATUS OF VISUAL ART AND DEVELOP EMOTIONAL LITERACY

Alderbury and West Grimstead School set up a project to raise the status of visual art and develop emotional literacy through creative approaches. Their aims were very specific:

- to raise the status of visual arts in school;
- to further develop emotional literacy through creative approaches to raise levels of attainment and behaviour;
- to encourage young professional artists to work in schools;
- to contribute to a Local Authority and national model;
- to create new community links;
- to address gender issues related to boys' attitudes and skills in the visual arts;
- to link with Local Authority Out of School Hours Learning Initiative (OSHLI) bid with which the school is intending to be associated;
- to link with the Local Authority seminars on Creativity – 21st Century Learning Initiative.

The project included three artists working with different age groups. One worked at weekends and holidays with pupils, to create tiles for the school pond area. This involved a group of children ranging in ability from those with special educational needs, including behavioural difficulties, to children with particular talents.

The school particularly aimed at including a group of boys who would otherwise not take part in such creative work as well as a group of girls whose self-esteem needed to be boosted. The aims of raising self-esteem were fully realized and a bonus has been sowing the seeds of future creative work amongst these children.

The work undertaken raised the self-esteem of all the children involved, and had a visible effect on their behaviour. Attainment was raised through achieving success in Art, which then had a knock-on effect on effort and achievement in other subjects. The involvement of a variety of professional artists proved inspirational for both children and staff. Work done with the 21st Century Learning Initiative has been fed back to staff and governors, and many of the initiative's recommendations have been implemented. The teachers now have more confidence to block-teach work in many subjects, instead of trying to fit each subject in the crowded curriculum into each week. They now feel that they have the freedom and support to 'think outside the box' when it comes to setting homework, to encourage far more wide-ranging talents and activities than purely academic skills.

Research underpinning the project included carrying out activities with pupils, evaluating pupil responses, attending Local Authority creativity sessions, associated reading and disseminating information to staff and governors.

■ TEACHERS TAKING HOLD OF RESEARCH

Most teachers would not readily engage with the notion of being a 'teacher–researcher'. A more helpful term, which describes the skills that are part of good teaching, is the teacher as enquirer. This alludes to teachers who are keen to reflect upon and critique their practices. They make good use of research and evidence to stimulate new ways of thinking and to try out new ideas, and then systematically to evaluate the impact of any subsequent change they have brought about.

CASE STUDY 7.3: CHANGING CULTURE THROUGH PRACTITIONER RESEARCH

Colmore Infant and Nursery is a three-form entry school on the outskirts of Birmingham, with about 270 children. Although staff had little previous experience of research, they all became involved in an action research project to improve the way they taught reading. Staff talked to colleagues in other schools about good practice, introduced different reading activities and recruited parents to help support children who were struggling with reading.

The school's research showed that its new approach to reading was having a positive effect on children, staff and parents. The research identified communication as an issue and so the staff invented a new 'book mark' scheme to improve communication with parents and helpers.

The experience of being research-engaged was so positive that it has become part of the school's identity. Several members of staff have gone on to use research as part of studies for professional qualifications, and the school is supporting a local research network among primary schools.

Research engagement has entered the culture of Colmore School. This has included the children who have carried out research and produced a DVD working with students from a neighbouring secondary school.

One teacher reflected that 'A research-engaged school is a dynamic institution. It is looking, questioning and trying to improve things all the time.'

The headteacher observed: 'A range of indicators suggest that we are progressing very well. In order to improve further, we must become focussed on how and why we do things. Research engagement offers the prospect of reinvigorating our collective professional identity and self esteem.' (Handscomb, 2007a)

Teachers have long been involved in examining their practice in this way to make further improvements. But when does such activity 'count' as research? What is the relationship between large-scale research conducted by a university department and a piece of evidence-informed practice carried out by a teacher within the classroom? And how is such evidence-informed practice any different from what good teachers do anyway in refining and honing their craft in day-to-day lesson preparation and evaluation?

One view is that evidence-informed practice typically involves the individual teacher, reflecting on her own classroom practice and sharing this with colleagues, whilst in contrast 'research' is seen as involving a larger-scale more systematic enquiry. Another view is that these two characterizations are not different in kind, but rather two ends of a continuum of practice in which 'evidence-informed practice' merges into 'research'. However, many have found this a difficult debate and would be uncomfortable about making too sharp a distinction between evidenced-informed practice and research. There are tensions between the world of academic research and teachers pursuing research as part of their professional learning and practice, but many have become convinced of the great potential of practitioner research to transform both the classroom and the teacher.

Schools in the modern age are required to be self-evaluating, open to scrutiny, evidence-based and data rich. Yet teachers and schools may not be empowered effectively to use the data in which they 'swim':

> schools are at the same time, often 'information poor'. This is, in part, because teachers feel no ownership of the data they are expected to use, nor is it necessarily data that they value. It is, nonetheless, high stakes, so teachers find themselves busy in 'implementation' rather than inquiry, lacking in self-confidence to convert what they know or believe into a form that provides robust counter-evidence, that speaks with conviction from teachers' own context and experiences. (Handscomb and MacBeath, 2003)

The increasing engagement of teachers in both using research and carrying out research is helping to instil new confidence and ownership, and empower the teacher to effect evidence-based change – but further progress is still needed. Over recent years the majority of schools have become self-evaluating; the challenge now is for these to develop as self-researching institutions.

THE RESEARCH-ENGAGED SCHOOL

'As things stand, it is difficult for researchers and teachers to find an area in which they can negotiate the agenda for research on teaching and learning. Teachers are in danger of being the passive objects of research rather than active partners who contribute to the creation and dissemination of new knowledge' (Hargreaves, 1998). There has been some positive movement since Hargreaves wrote these words and stimulated the helpful debate that followed, but more needs to be done to enable teachers to lay claim to the research agenda, as part of their professional development and practice. Cordingley (2003) reports a growing awareness of the power of teachers researching their own work in terms both of better classroom practice and professional learning. However, to be effective, teachers need to gain some understanding of what is already known in the area of practice they wish to investigate. Unfortunately, school-based consumers of research have considerable obstacles put in their way; research abstract summaries do little to aid practitioner access and at worst actually get in the way or mislead! Developments like the GTC 'Research of the Month' website are endeavouring to improve teacher access and skill development. These are some of the projects that have been written about:

- Making research accessible to teachers.
- Researching effective pedagogy in the early years.
- Effective pedagogy using ICT for literacy and numeracy.
- An investigation into gender differences in achievement.
- Inside the literacy hour – a study of classroom practice.

In such a 'research-engaged school', research and enquiry would permeate all aspects of its life, including teaching and learning, professional development, and school planning and decision-making. There is a gathering interest in exploring the extent to which schools are becoming research-engaged – are they 'emergent', 'established' or 'established embedded' (Ebbut, 2003)? At local level some Local Authorities are forming research forums of practitioners, officers and higher education representatives. The Essex Forum for Learning and Research Enquiry (FLARE) has identified and explored four dimensions of the research-engaged school:

- It has a 'research' rich pedagogy.
- It has a research orientation.
- It promotes research communities.
- It puts research at the heart of school policy and practice (Handscomb and MacBeath, 2003).

Implications for schools are posed in each of these dimensions, including some basic audit questions by which schools can begin to examine their outlook and practice (see Figure 7.2).

There is now a growing body of evidence to show that practitioner engagement in enquiry and research can make a difference, particularly to the professional development and enrichment of colleagues' practice (Furlong, Salisbury and Coombs, 2003.) A two year national investigation into the Research-Engaged School, exploring the FLARE dimensions given above, took place in five authorities. Staff undertook a range of research activity, including:

- addressing under-achievement and raising standards;
- improving teaching and learning;
- increased involvement of parents and families.

The research concluded that there were key cultural and professional development conditions for becoming a research-engaged school (Sharp et al., 2006):

- a culture that values openness, reflection and professional debate;
- a commitment to using evidence for school improvement;
- a commitment of resources to the project;
- access to sources of expertise and support;
- a desire for people to work collaboratively, regardless of role or status;
- a willingness to embed research activity into existing school systems such as staff development activities.

DEVELOPING STAFF FOR A NEW PROFESSIONAL FUTURE

The nature of professional development is poised to undergo further radical change as we move into the future. New demands are being made on the school workforce. One of these is the new focus on personalized learning. This is an approach to teaching and learning that concentrates on an individual child's potential and set of learning skills. It also entails the organization of learning experiences that extend beyond the school context into the local community. This in turn calls for staff with transformed approaches to the whole enterprise of learning and the teaching that effectively supports such learning.

Linked to this is the major development known as 'Every Child Matters' (DfES 2003). This emphasizes the needs of the whole child in terms of five key outcomes:

- Be healthy.
- Stay safe.
- Enjoy and achieve.
- Make a positive contribution.
- Achieve economic wellbeing.

Every Child Matters (ECM) presents one of the biggest challenges to the very nature of professional learning that will be fit for purpose for the modern age. It poses forthright questions about the need to re-think our whole approach to how education professionals are developed for a very different future. Such a future will be one in which increasingly they will be working alongside and in fundamental partnership with colleagues from health and social care. The DfES Green Paper (2003) that heralded ECM rightly emphasized 'ensuring that the people working with children are valued, rewarded and trained'. However, developing the school workforce for this new world of multi-agency, collaborative working is a major undertaking. Developing the workforce from different professional backgrounds – with their own outlooks, understanding and cultures – to operate together in delivering the outcomes of ECM effectively is no small task! A whole range of issues are raised not just about the appropriate 'content' of continuing professional development, but also about the mode in which it is conducted and the cultural sea change that will be required (Handscomb, 2007b).

THE NEW CPD?

The case for collaboration and for empowering teachers to research their own practice is convincing. As Harris (2002) observes:

> there is sufficient evaluation evidence to show that when teachers are engaged in dialogue with each other about their practice then meaningful reflection and teaching and learning occur … and … there is now a growing literature that demonstrates and endorses the importance of evidence-based research as the basis for improving teaching.

As a consequence, a new perspective on CPD can be fashioned, focused on school-based processes, inter-school collaboration and teacher enquiry. The ingredients of this new CPD are:

- school determined and led;
- focused on pedagogy and 'the craft of the classroom';
- equipping staff to enable personalized learning;
- tapping expertise already present, enriched by partnerships beyond the school;
- effective teacher learning is collaborative – within and beyond the school;
- teachers as leaders of learning in the broader educational community;
- schools sharing and seeking out good/best practice;
- school staff as enquirers and researchers of their own practice;
- just as schools have become self-evaluating they now need to become self-researching;
- the growing and developing school as a research-engaged school, involving both practitioners and children as researchers;
- professional learning alongside other health and social care professionals to deliver *Every Child Matters*.

However, although consortia working, collaboration and development of an enquiring research culture are becoming established features of the professional development and school improvement agendas, ensuring effective sharing of validated practice remains problematic. If schools are really to put collaboration to work then they need to give much more robust thought and analysis to processes involved in creating genuine communities of practice – within and beyond the school. Conversely, schools and their staff need to be supported as reflective practitioners and equipped to access and conduct research investigations that will help to transform their practice.

Example of Audit question

Do people have access to tools that help them challenge their practice?

100%	75%	50%	25%
Yes, the development of research and enquiry skills is built into the school's professional development planning and practice	Major projects are supported by the development of research and enquiry skills	Some individuals have taken an interest in using research and enquiry to challenge and improve their practice	There is little evidence of people having access to opportunities to develop research and enquiry skills apart from isolated cases
☐	☐	☐	☐

Please tick the appropriate box

FIGURE 7.2 THE RESEARCH-ENGAGED SCHOOL (HANDSCOMB AND MACBEATH, 2003)

POINTS FOR REFLECTION

Think of a network to which you belong (this can be a 'local' one involving meetings and activities, or a virtual on-line network). How would you describe the main features of this network to someone who knew little about it? What would you say you gained from this network? What aspects of the network are key factors in keeping it going?

POINTS FOR REFLECTION

Are there aspects of school practice that might be of interest to you as potential areas for investigation and enquiry? Consider who else might be involved in scoping this with you.

PART II:

LEADING AND MANAGING THE CPD OF SPECIFIC GROUPS

Support Staff

◆ Types and range of support staff

◆ Meeting needs – qualifications

◆ Teaching assistants

◆ Higher level teaching assistants

◆ Midday supervisors and catering staff

◆ Bursars and education business managers

◆ Teachers working with support staff

To provide the best possible outcomes for children, schools must create conditions that enable all staff to realize their potential: a culture where all staff are valued and enjoy high morale and job satisfaction. Support staff who are well trained, fairly rewarded, and clear about their distinctive contribution, can be instrumental in the work of raising standards and enriching the lives of children. The opportunities for support staff to develop their skills are broadening and becoming formalized: the school workforce development board (SWDB) is the sector-wide body chaired by the TDA, concerned with training and developing the wider workforce.

TABLE 8.1 FULL-TIME EQUIVALENT TEACHER AND SUPPORT STAFF NUMBERS (IN THOUSANDS) IN THE MAINTAINED SECTOR IN ENGLAND

Staff in schools (FTE)	1997	1998	1999	2000	2001	2002	2003	2004	2005	2006
Support staff	133.5	140.7	148.7	161.6	185.8	213.4	223.2	240.7	264.8	287.5
Teachers	412.8	410.8	415.3	421.3	429.8	437.1	438.4	442.1	447.0	448.4

Source: DfES, 2007a

Greater flexibility in school budgets and local management of schools (LMS) has meant the number and range of support staff working in schools have increased considerably over the last decade. Table 8.1 shows that the growth in the number of full-time equivalent support staff has outmatched the increase in teachers. The total number of full-time equivalent support staff reached 287,500 in 2006: there were 153,100 teaching assistants; 62,500 administrative staff; 23,000 technicians; and 48,900 'other' support staff (DfES, 2007). Increases have occurred in both the number and type of responsibility as can be seen in Table 8.2.

But what of their training and development needs? What are these, how are they identified and how can they best be met? What are the main challenges for teachers and their CPD needs as they are increasingly working with a group of what are sometimes referred to as associate staff or 'paraprofessionals'? We begin by looking at the various types of support staff increasingly found in schools, before looking at development opportunities and issues of specific groups.

TABLE 8.2 FULL-TIME EQUIVALENT SUPPORT STAFF (IN THOUSANDS) IN THE MAINTAINED SECTOR IN ENGLAND

	1997	1998	1999	2000	2001	2002	2003	2004	2005	2006
Teaching assistants										
Teaching assistants	34.8	38.0	38.6	44.5	54.8	56.3	72.4	83.2	96.5	102.9
Special needs support staff	24.5	26.0	29.5	32.4	37.7	46.6	46.3	46.4	48.0	47.5
Minority ethnic pupil support staff	1.2	1.5	1.5	2.1	2.5	2.4	2.5	2.5	2.5	2.7
Total	60.6	65.5	69.6	79.0	95.0	105.4	121.2	132.1	147.0	153.1
Administrative staff										
Secretaries	27.4	28.3	28.9	30.0	30.4	25.4	24.5	28.4	28.3	31.4
Bursars	4.0	4.2	4.4	4.7	5.0	4.8	5.1	5.6	6.3	6.8
Other admin/clerical staff	7.5	7.3	7.7	8.2	10.7	19.3	20.7	20.1	24.1	24.3
Total	38.9	39.8	41.0	42.9	46.0	49.5	50.3	54.2	58.7	62.5
Technicians										
Total	12.7	13.0	13.5	14.1	15.0	16.5	17.9	19.6	21.6	23.0
Other Support Staff										
Matrons/nurses/medical staff	1.0	1.0	1.0	1.0	1.0	1.6	1.5	1.6	1.7	1.7
Child care staff	1.7	1.7	1.7	1.6	1.5	1.3	0.1	1.3	1.8	1.6
Other education support staff	18.6	19.6	22.0	23.0	27.3	39.1	32.1	31.8	34.0	45.6
Total	21.3	22.3	24.7	25.5	29.8	42.0	33.8	34.8	37.5	48.9
Total support staff	133.5	140.7	148.7	161.6	185.8	213.4	223.2	240.7	264.8	287.5

Source: DfES, 2007a

TYPES AND RANGE OF SUPPORT STAFF

Traditionally, teachers and support staff have been treated differently within schools; for example, access to appraisal and performance management, training and development, and involvement in school decision-making processes have usually been the right of professional staff but not other paid employees. Other adults working in schools were often taken for granted, marginalized or, in some cases, totally ignored! Investors in People (see Chapter 3) has helped to rectify such a situation by insisting that organizations give due consideration to the training and development needs of all staff.

The label 'non-teaching' staff is less frequently used in schools today as we have come to realize that defining a person's job in terms of what they do not do is no longer acceptable, whilst 'paraprofessional' and 'school workforce' are gaining popularity in usage. 'Support staff' is the term we have chosen to use in this chapter and it includes all those people who undertake paid employment in schools, other than teachers and heads. With so many paid employees in schools performing a myriad of roles, it is helpful to group such activities into broader categories as can be seen in Table 8.2. Blatchford et al. have researched the impact of support staff and categorized them into seven groups:

1 TA equivalent (TA, LSA [SEN pupils], nursery nurse, therapist).

2 Pupil welfare (Connexions personal advisor, education welfare officer, home–school liaison officer, learning mentor, nurse and welfare assistant).

3 Technical and specialist staff (ICT network manager, ICT technician, librarian, science technician and technology technician).

4 Other pupil support (bilingual support officer, cover supervisor, escort, exam invigilator, language assistant, midday assistant and midday supervisor).

5 Facilities staff (cleaner, cook, and other catering staff).

6   Administrative staff (administrator/clerk, bursar, finance officer, office manager, secretary, attendance officer, data manager, examination officer, and PA to the headteacher).

7   Site staff (caretaker and premises manager) (Blatchford et al., 2006: iv).

MEETING NEEDS – QUALIFICATIONS

Blatchford and colleagues' large scale research for the DfES found that two thirds of support staff didn't need specific qualifications and just over half (56 per cent) didn't need to have previous experience in order to be appointed to their post (Blatchford et al., 2006). This puts a great deal of responsibility on schools and colleges to train people on the job. There is a growing knowledge base about the training and development needs of the various categories of support staff through, for instance, the work of Trevor Kerry (2001) who has written about working with support staff, Ann Watkinson (2003) on teaching assistants and David Naylor (1999) on midday assistants.

The TDA has produced many materials for support staff and an interactive qualifications site so that people can see what qualifications would suit them best. The TDA has developed three broad career progression routes for support staff, described as the 'pedagogical', 'behaviour and guidance', and 'administration and organization'. The pedagogical route serves those supporting pupils and teachers in the learning process and would include the higher level teaching assistant role. The behaviour and guidance route involves all those helping schools with pastoral, attendance and discipline issues, including learning mentors who support individual pupils. The administration and organization route covers school administration and could lead to a higher-level bursar role.

As part of the *Every Child Matters* agenda, the government wants a single framework of qualifications for everyone who works with children, young people and families. The common core of skills and knowledge for the children's workforce sets out the basic skills and knowledge that everyone working with children, young people and families should have, under the following headings:

1   Effective communication and engagement.

2   Child and young person development – physical, emotional, intellectual, linguistic and social development.

3   Safeguarding and promoting the welfare of the child.

4   Supporting transitions.

5   Multi-agency working.

6   Sharing information (DfES, 2005b).

All relevant national occupational standards (NOS) should incorporate the common core and they can also help people:

- define the coverage and focus of their role;

- assess how well they are performing;

- identify training and development needs;

- select qualifications that match the role;

- make the links between the role and the school's overall aims and objectives.

The National Association of Professional Teaching Assistants (www.napta.org.uk) has developed systems to profile and analyse the workforce development requirements of support staff and advise on sources of funding beyond local authority budgets. The resources help identify individual development needs, offer institutional guidance and act as reference and self-study sources. It is provided in digital formats on CD-Rom using standard web browsers over a school network or on standalone computers. The 'Meeting Individual Needs' section has detailed structured resources closely mapped to the National Occupational Standards for Teaching/Classroom Assistants.

Where different awarding bodies offer vocational qualifications with the same titles – such as the CACHE certificate for teaching assistants and the Edexcel certificate for teaching assistants – the qualifications often have a very different content and focus but NVQs with the same title and level will have the same content and focus regardless of the awarding body. However, there may be some differences in evidence requirements and assessment so when choosing a qualification it is important to look at:

- whether it is accredited to the national qualifications framework or validated by a recognized higher education institution (HEI);
- whether it is based on national occupational standards;
- how well it covers recent changes in working practice, legislation, regulation and technology;
- how well it matches the job role and the context the person works in.

Training and development is not only about qualifications, though. When choosing any training and development activity people should also look at:

- how well it matches learning needs;
- how well it equips you to do your current role more effectively and/or widens your career options;
- how well it develops the knowledge, skills and understanding needed for your role;
- how well it relates to school circumstances and development priorities;
- how well it builds on your previous experience and qualifications, including opportunities for accreditation of prior learning;
- whether it supports you to progress within your own role or move into another role;
- whether there are any restrictions on access – for example, do you need prior qualifications?;
- whether it is consistent with any requirement for statutory qualifications such as first aid;
- how to manage practical issues such as location, timing and travel;
- how well the school can support you, e.g. by providing a mentor, access to workplace learning and assessment, or time and facilities for private study;
- the cost (direct and indirect) to the school and you;
- the availability of funding;
- whether it is available or can be arranged locally – some providers may not offer a particular qualification because of lack of demand. If a local provider doesn't offer the qualification you're interested in, let them know that you're interested anyway. This will help them monitor and respond to local needs.

TEACHING ASSISTANTS

Anne Watkinson reminds us that the induction and development of TAs can be time-consuming. Managers must ensure TAs know all the emergency, health and safety, confidentiality and child protection procedures as well as SEN, relevant curriculum and behaviour policies. 'A mentor, and clear line management needs to be established, the former particularly if there is any external course involvement such as the DfES Induction training' (2003: 30). She argues that TAs must be included in relevant school-based INSET and meetings, and must plan with teachers and feedback to them. It is important that staff are paid for the time spent in such activities, including travel and child-care costs of attending off-site training. Also, as Watkinson notes:

> They also need time, resources and facilities to prepare just like teachers, which may well include access to ICT. They can have hidden skills and talents which need cherishing, they need training to do a job properly; they should be monitored and evaluated … They need a voice, recognition and valuing. (2003: 30)

It is good practice to include all staff in whole-school training. Managing discipline is often acknowledged as a key issue where joint training is especially valuable. Training together can lead to a shared perspective, helps to reduce anxiety and it demonstrates that those in authority are showing an interest in the work that TAs do. Research (for example, Swann and Loxley, 1998) has shown that training TAs on their own is unlikely to have much of an impact or be successful because of their relatively low status as a group. Frustration can result if TAs feel that teachers are not listening to them or making full use of their experience and expertise.

It is important to ask the question with TAs – indeed with all staff – is training targeted at their needs? If it is not then it can be a missed opportunity and perceived as 'a waste of time'. Are mechanisms in place in school to enable this to happen? Training must be supported by the SMT and the support staff member's line manager and, whenever possible, followed up. Relevant CPD improves perceptions of self-worth, generates a feeling of being valued by the school and improves relationships with teachers and with pupils. They see themselves more clearly as part of the team, reducing any 'them' and 'us' feelings. Giving support staff opportunities to take part in whole-school meetings and INSET training has been shown to lead to greater confidence in the performance of their roles in school (Kendall et al., 2000: 31). An example of one school's teacher assistant CPD project is briefly outlined in Case study 8.1.

There are specialist courses available to classroom assistants to work towards qualified teacher status. Those who complete a specialist teacher assistant (STA) course can use these for credit towards a higher-level qualification such as a Certificate of Higher Education, a Diploma of Higher Education or a foundation degree. Nationally, there is a wide range of training available for TAs but the main opportunities for qualifications are:

- DfES induction training (basic training available to all TAs after starting the job).
- National strategy training, such as Further Literacy Support.
- NVQs level 2 and 3.
- Higher level teaching assistant.
- Foundation degrees.
- The Graduate and Registered Teacher Programme for those who want to qualify as teachers.

Knowledge about training and accreditation options and availability is important as the lack of such information makes career progression and development planning for support staff difficult.

HIGHER LEVEL TEACHING ASSISTANTS

It's long been recognized that teaching assistants (TA) are unsung heroes deserving of a career structure. The higher level teaching assistant (HLTA) enables people to cover classes for teachers. The only entry requirement is English and maths at the equivalent of GCSE C grade. There are tried and tested qualifications that teaching assistants take such as the specialist teaching assistant course and numerous NVQs but none of these count. Applicants are assessed on the HLTA standards which can be seen in Figure 8.1.

The 31 standards are organized in three sections:

1   Professional values and practice.

2   Knowledge and understanding.

3   Teaching and learning activities.

Not only are there a lot of them but they're made up of several components. For instance, for standard 1.1 HLTAs must 'have high expectations of all pupils; respect their social, cultural, linguistic, religious and ethnic backgrounds; and are committed to raising their educational achievement'. How on earth do they prove all those seven bits?

Professional values and practice

1.1   They have high expectations of all pupils; respect their social, cultural, linguistic, religious and ethnic backgrounds; and are committed to raising their educational achievement.
1.2   They build and maintain successful relationships with pupils, treat them consistently, with respect and consideration, and are concerned for their development as learners.
1.3   They demonstrate and promote the positive values, attitudes and behaviour they expect from the pupils with whom they work.
1.4   They work collaboratively with colleagues, and carry out their roles effectively, knowing when to seek help and advice.
1.5   They are able to liaise sensitively and effectively with parents and carers, recognizing their roles in pupils' learning.
1.6   They are able to improve their own practice, including through observation, evaluation and discussion with colleagues.

Knowledge and understanding

2.1   They have sufficient understanding of their specialist area to support pupils' learning, and are able to acquire further knowledge to contribute effectively and with confidence to the classes in which they are involved.
2.2   They are familiar with the school curriculum, the age-related expectations of pupils, the main teaching methods and the testing/examination frameworks in the subjects and age ranges in which they are involved.
2.3   They understand the aims, content, teaching strategies and intended outcomes for the lessons in which they are involved, and understand the place of these in the related teaching programme.
2.4   They know how to use ICT to advance pupils' learning, and can use common ICT tools for their own and pupils' benefit.
2.5   They know the key factors that can affect the way pupils learn.
2.6   They have achieved a qualification in English/literacy and mathematics/numeracy, equivalent to at least level 2 of the national qualifications framework.
2.7   They are aware of the statutory frameworks relevant to their role.
2.8   They know the legal definition of special educational needs (SEN), and are familiar with the guidance about meeting SEN given in the SEN code of practice.
2.9   They know a range of strategies to establish a purposeful learning environment and to promote good behaviour.

Teaching and learning activities – Planning and expectations

3.1.1   They contribute effectively to teachers' planning and preparation of lessons.
3.1.2   Working within a framework set by the teacher, they plan their role in lessons including how they will provide feedback to pupils and colleagues on pupils' learning and behaviour.

FIGURE 8.1 PROFESSIONAL STANDARDS FOR HLTA STATUS (TTA, 2003)

3.1.3   They contribute effectively to the selection and preparation of teaching resources that meet the diversity of pupils' needs and interests.

3.1.4   They are able to contribute to the planning of opportunities for pupils to learn in out-of-school contexts, in accordance with school policies and procedures.

Teaching and learning activities – Monitoring and assessment

3.2.1   They are able to support teachers in evaluating pupils' progress through a range of assessment activities.

3.2.2   They monitor pupils' responses to learning tasks and modify their approach accordingly.

3.2.3   They monitor pupils' participation and progress, providing feedback to teachers, and giving constructive support to pupils as they learn.

3.2.4   They contribute to maintaining and analysing records of pupils' progress.

Teaching and learning activities

3.3.1   Using clearly structured teaching and learning activities, they interest and motivate pupils, and advance their learning.

3.3.2   They communicate effectively and sensitively with pupils to support their learning.

3.3.3   They promote and support the inclusion of all pupils in the learning activities in which they are involved.

3.3.4   They use behaviour management strategies, in line with the school's policy and procedures, which contribute to a purposeful learning environment.

3.3.5   They advance pupils' learning in a range of classroom settings, including working with individuals, small groups and whole classes where the assigned teacher is not present.

3.3.6   They are able, where relevant, to guide the work of other adults supporting teaching and learning in the classroom.

3.3.7   They recognize and respond effectively to equal opportunities issues as they arise, including by challenging stereotyped views, and by challenging bullying or harassment, following relevant policies and procedures.

3.3.8   They organize and manage safely the learning activities, the physical teaching space and the resources for which they are given responsibility.

FIGURE 8.1 (continued)

Another unrealistic expectation is that HLTAs must understand the curriculum, the expectations required of pupils, the main teaching methods and the testing/examination frameworks in the subjects and age ranges in which they are involved. How is someone working in a primary school, across Year 1 to Year 6 going to be able to do that? In working with individuals, groups and whole classes they have to demonstrate skills in planning, monitoring, assessment and class management. However, in many schools TAs are not required to plan or assess because that is the teacher's role. In the age-old chicken and egg dilemma, teaching assistants are rarely on their own with a whole class – covering classes is one of the intended roles of a HLTA, not of a TA. So, what are they to write about? The five minutes they were left in charge of the class watching a video while the teacher nipped out? Thus Standard 3.3.5 'They advance pupils' learning in a range of classroom settings, including working with individuals, small groups and whole classes where the assigned teacher is not present' becomes a significant challenge. Advancing pupils' learning – that's a tall order! Although it's a reasonable expectation, it isn't even one of the standards for trainee or newly qualified teachers.

The handbook of guidance explains the standards further and has examples of the types of evidence people have used but there is little indication of what is good enough. For instance, to meet standard 1.6 – 'They are able to improve their own practice, including through observation, evaluation and discussion with colleagues' – examples from the TDA website include:

'I was impressed when I saw the way that teachers and pupils in the school used signing to include pupils with speech and language difficulties more fully in school life. I discussed with colleagues how to improve my performance in this area and I'm now attending a signing course.'

'I found the performance management process – being observed by a colleague and the subsequent discussions – really useful in helping me to reflect upon my own practice. I found the SMART targets that we set helped me focus on areas where I could improve. My latest targets relate to aspects of physical science as I have recently started to support one class in physics. I have attended a training course and am working closely with a science teacher to make sure that I have the necessary up-to-date knowledge to support and reinforce learning in each lesson.' (www.tda.gov.uk)

How do you think someone assesses HLTAs? Being observed in the classroom would seem sensible, but that isn't the case. They're assessed on four written tasks through which they have to show that they are meeting all 31 HLTA standards. They have to write about specific lessons and incidents with an individual, group and whole class. Obviously, this will be easier for those people who are good at writing in a certain style because assessors don't want a stream of consciousness or a simple recount of what happened but a concise analytical account that gives evidence for each and every standard. People who are excellent at supporting pupils but who find writing hard may not get through. On the other hand there may be people who can write about it but not do it. Who would you prefer to work with?

If the writing wasn't enough to try the patience of the most saintly TA, this is followed by a half-day visit to the school by an assessor who reviews all the evidence the candidate has provided and discusses it with them. They also meet the headteacher and a teacher who works with the candidate. Mary Jones, a special needs assistant at Langley Park Boys School in Bromley, says that she can't see why anyone would want to apply. 'If you're going to put all that effort in you may as well train to be a teacher'.

Assessors aren't allowed to go and watch them in action with the children. This seems odd. Most TAs wouldn't mind being observed – they're used to it, and would much prefer it to writing. Jill Staley, director of the support staff development group at the TDA says, 'Observation in school by an external assessor would necessarily only provide a snapshot of a candidate's work, may not take place on a typical working day for them, and would be unlikely to provide the candidate with opportunities to demonstrate all of the standards'. Hmmm, that doesn't marry up with the assessments for excellent and advanced skills teachers where a key component is observation. The snapshot works for them – and Ofsted too!

All this is being expected of people who are grossly underpaid. Many are only paid by the hour and not for holidays. But surely HLTAs will have better pay and conditions? No, getting HLTA status doesn't automatically mean being on a higher salary scale. Union officials say that the Workforce Agreement gives TAs more 'status'. This has vexed many on the *TES* online teaching assistant forum (www.tes.co.uk/staffroom). One says

'The very title "Higher Level Teaching Assistant" instantly devalues bog standard ordinary ones! I don't want 'status' as a poxy babyminder (sorry, 'cover supervisor') or halfbaked teacher (sorry, HLTA). I would just like some recognition for the unique job that hundreds of us do, and to not be devalued because we only work in class and not IN FRONT of a class.'

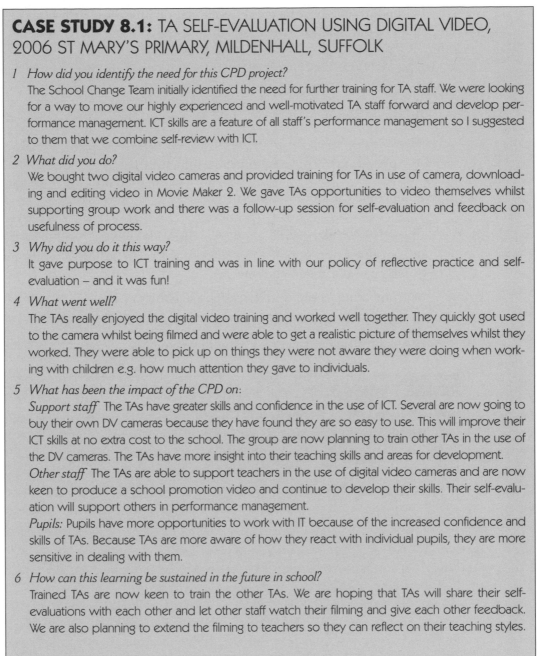

CASE STUDY 8.1: TA SELF-EVALUATION USING DIGITAL VIDEO, 2006 ST MARY'S PRIMARY, MILDENHALL, SUFFOLK

1 How did you identify the need for this CPD project?

The School Change Team initially identified the need for further training for TA staff. We were looking for a way to move our highly experienced and well-motivated TA staff forward and develop performance management. ICT skills are a feature of all staff's performance management so I suggested to them that we combine self-review with ICT.

2 What did you do?

We bought two digital video cameras and provided training for TAs in use of camera, downloading and editing video in Movie Maker 2. We gave TAs opportunities to video themselves whilst supporting group work and there was a follow-up session for self-evaluation and feedback on usefulness of process.

3 Why did you do it this way?

It gave purpose to ICT training and was in line with our policy of reflective practice and self-evaluation – and it was fun!

4 What went well?

The TAs really enjoyed the digital video training and worked well together. They quickly got used to the camera whilst being filmed and were able to get a realistic picture of themselves whilst they worked. They were able to pick up on things they were not aware they were doing when working with children e.g. how much attention they gave to individuals.

5 What has been the impact of the CPD on:

Support staff The TAs have greater skills and confidence in the use of ICT. Several are now going to buy their own DV cameras because they have found they are so easy to use. This will improve their ICT skills at no extra cost to the school. The group are now planning to train other TAs in the use of the DV cameras. The TAs have more insight into their teaching skills and areas for development.

Other staff The TAs are able to support teachers in the use of digital video cameras and are now keen to produce a school promotion video and continue to develop their skills. Their self-evaluation will support others in performance management.

Pupils: Pupils have more opportunities to work with IT because of the increased confidence and skills of TAs. Because TAs are more aware of how they react with individual pupils, they are more sensitive in dealing with them.

6 How can this learning be sustained in the future in school?

Trained TAs are now keen to train the other TAs. We are hoping that TAs will share their self-evaluations with each other and let other staff watch their filming and give each other feedback. We are also planning to extend the filming to teachers so they can reflect on their teaching styles.

Source: Support Staff Conference, Suffolk, 2006

MIDDAY SUPERVISORS AND CATERING STAFF

Little is known about midday supervisors and catering staff, and their training needs. We do know, however, that they have infrequently been offered training opportunities and rarely trained in what might be described as a core skill – group and behaviour management. As the *Elton Report* (DfEE, 1989) noted years ago, many midday supervisors rely entirely on their status as adults as a source of authority. Naylor (1999), one of very few to have investigated (and provided for) their training needs, makes reference to such things as games organization and encouraging appropriate social behaviour in pupils. He found midday supervisors rarely talked about behaviour management in terms of school behaviour policy, suggesting a real need for training to link to the schools' expectations of their pupils. Also how can midday supervisors help children to develop friendships at break times? Several guides are available to help schools with the training and support of midday supervisors. Henry Maynard Infants School in Walthamstow has given their midday assistants ICT and behaviour management training, and some have enrolled on an accredited national vocational qualification (NVQ level 2) course with the school in partnership with a local sixth form college (Kabra, 2002). Case study 8.2 outlines a project of training for midday supervisors.

There are NVQs for catering staff. There are two compulsory units with options at level 2 in:

- maintaining food safety when storing, holding and serving food;
- maintaining food safety when storing, preparing and cooking food;
- preparing to cook and finish healthier dishes.

At level 3 people can opt for units such as:

- maintaining food safety when storing, preparing and cooking food;
- ensuring appropriate food safety practices are followed whilst food is prepared, cooked and served;
- preparing, cooking and finishing healthier dishes;
- contributing to the development of recipes and menus;
- controlling practices for handling payments.

CASE STUDY 8.2: TRAINING MIDDAY SUPERVISORS TO WORK WITH CHILDREN DURING PHYSICAL ACTIVITIES, WOODHALL COMMUNITY PRIMARY, SUFFOLK

1 How did you identify the need for this CPD project?
Problems with children's lunchtime behaviour and their poor attitude towards the authority of midday supervisors. The need to fit in more PE time.

2 What did you do?
The LA PE advisor gave all midday supervisors and two teachers a morning's training. The Headteacher trained midday supervisors one hour per week. We purchased lots of playground equipment for children to use. There was supply cover for the lead teacher to set up and monitor the scheme.

3 Why did you do it this way?
We felt that much of the poor behaviour at lunchtime was directly linked to the low status of the midday supervisors. We wanted to raise their status and profile. We also felt that by providing lots of things to do at lunchtime, the children would be busier and there would therefore be fewer problems to sort out.

4 How did it go?
Regular meetings with MDS, lead teacher and headteacher have helped to sort out problems as they have arisen. Children are very much enjoying the activities.

5 What did you learn?
You have to keep working at it until all the problems are sorted. It would have been better if the midday supervisors had been more involved at an earlier stage. Some members of the midday supervisor staff felt at times that it was being done to them rather than with them.

6 What has been the impact of the CPD on:
a Support staff? The status of midday supervisors has been raised.
b Other staff? Fewer problems to deal with after lunch.
c Pupils? Much more is now going on at lunchtimes. The children are more active and have fewer arguments. We feel that we are in step with the government's PE initiatives.

Source: Support Staff Conference, Suffolk, 2006

BURSARS AND EDUCATION BUSINESS MANAGERS

Bursars and business managers can play a significant part in school management, bringing their expertise to bear on the planning and management of resources, as well as taking some of the management load off headteachers. Bursars are taking on more diverse functions and need greater degrees of support and training. In addition to financial duties, management and leadership roles are increasing in importance. The Bursar Development Programme developed by NCSL includes the Certificate of School Business Management (CSBM) followed by a higher level qualification, the Diploma of School Business Management (DSBM).

The CSBM aims to assist school business managers in developing their expertise through a range of different learning techniques. It covers eight subject areas:

- school business management;
- facilities management;
- risk management;
- financial management;
- office systems management;
- ICT management;
- human resource management;
- environmental management (sustainable development).

The DSBM is at a higher level and has three subject areas:

- strategic management;
- change management;
- managing school improvement.

Some universities offer Bachelor and Master's degrees in school business management and administration. The Institute of Education, University of London, runs an MBA for school business managers in conjunction with other school leaders.

Geoff Southworth, NCSL Deputy Director, believes that the Certificate and Diploma have already helped School Business Managers – and their schools – at three levels.

1 *At the level of the individual.* It is a real joy to see how individual participants have developed. How, in particular, their self-confidence has improved and there is an increased willingness to share information and participate in discussion – these courses are having a major and positive impact.

2 *At school level.* We have lost count of cases where funds have either been saved, or found, and new ideas and processes introduced as a result of candidates using their learning and of course sharing problems and ideas through the talk2learn online community.

3 *At the level of the profession as whole and across the education sector.* If the profession is to flourish, then we need all School Business Managers to promote their role and the work they do. Inevitably some individual stakeholders will be resistant to the expanded role of School Business Managers. However this mustn't deflect all school managers from the central key message that effective school business management skills are required in each and every one of our schools (Southworth, 2005: 2).

Support staff, like any other staff members within the school, have to be managed. Extended schools have a much larger and more diverse staff, which need managing all year. Case study 8.3 illustrates how one school has organized this. Appointment and management procedures create extra work for school leaders and managers, but teaching assistants also increase the workload of all teachers as they have to plan for and recognize the effects of additional adults in classrooms. The standards for qualified teacher status and induction (TDA, 2007) acknowledge this.

CASE STUDY 8.3: AN EXTENDED SCHOOL

South Hunsley Comprehensive School in Yorkshire offers a wide range of extended services to its community and the cluster of eight primary schools that it leads. It is open all year round from 7am until 10pm on weekdays, from 7am until 5pm on Saturdays and from 8am to 5pm on Sundays. An extensive range of clubs and activities are offered from 4pm until 6pm. The school's catering facilities now make a profit from providing food for events.

The school has completely reorganized its management and staffing structures, with non-teaching staff taking on many roles – including senior management positions – to ensure that teachers could concentrate on teaching and learning. 'We had to radically look at the management structure when we moved to operating for 52 weeks a year,' says headteacher Chris Abbott, 'because some of the school's staff are only available in term time. Everything has changed from the model we had. We now have a full-time finance manager and assistant finance manager, because the school is fully operational during the summer, and we also have full-time staff in sports, catering and premises.'

At South Hunsley the scale of its year round operation is such that associate staff – 140 in all including cleaners – now outnumber the 100 members of the teaching staff. 'Associate staff play a very important role in the school,' says Chris Abbott. 'As we set about developing extended services we went through a workforce remodelling process and the decision we took was that teachers should be free to teach, and that we should use a range of other professionals and support staff to make this possible.'

The decision caused a radical re-structuring of the senior management. 'We moved to one deputy head, three assistant heads and three key stage directors for KS3, KS4 and KS5, as well as appointing a director of extended services. In addition, we appointed heads of year that were associates or non-teaching staff, plus a range of other associate staff dealing with various aspects of the core teaching and learning function.'

The school has appointed a training manager to be in charge of CPD for all staff. 'This person has a training rather than a teaching background. We did this because it's not just teachers getting training it's everyone in the whole institution,' says Chris Abbott. 'The training manager also sets up training for the consortium of secondary schools we belong to, as well as external training events that include the hire of facilities – such as the LA training events we host. It's organizing these that helps to pay for her salary.' (From www.tda.gov.uk)

Teachers may well have to be trained in the management of additional adults and attitudes may need to change if support staff are to be considered as equal members of the school community and their contribution valued. Teachers' perception of support staff is sometimes negative (Kerry, 2003). Figure 8.2 gives an indication of some of the issues and possible solutions that may need consideration in any training aimed at teachers working with support staff and particularly teaching assistants (Bubb, 2003b).

It might be helpful to ask support staff if they can devise a similar list from their own perspective. Similarly, Kerry (2003) who has researched support staff's needs, suggests we ask two key questions:

1   What do you do in your school to ensure that teachers are trained to manage the work of support staff effectively?

2   What do these teachers do that marks them out as successful managers of support staff?

Issue	Ideas/solutions
Being unsure of the additional adult's role	Find out exactly what they are paid to do; some are funded to work with individual SEN pupils.
Not sure when they are going to be in the class	Find out exactly when they're coming and make sure they know that you're expecting them.
Not wanting to ask them to do menial tasks	Again, look at their job description. Most are happy to help out.
Some do too much for the children and encourage over-dependence	Model the sort of teaching you want. Don't be afraid to mention concerns – they haven't benefited from training like yours and so are usually more than pleased to be given advice.
Some have little control over the children	Again, model how to manage behaviour. Speak to their line manager if it's a big problem.
Some can take over the class	This is very tricky. Speak to them about the need to establish yourself as the teacher, but otherwise get advice on how to deal with this.
Some talk when the teacher has asked for everyone's attention	Theatrically or humorously emphasize that you need *everyone's* attention.
Some don't do quite what you've asked them to	Explain, model, write instructions; speak to them about your concern.
Some are stuck in their ways and do not like new ideas and practices	Tricky. Try to get them on your side by asking for their advice, their patience in trying things out.
Planning for them, but they do not turn up.	Make sure they and others know how much you depend on and value them. Make a fuss if they're taken away too often.
They have poor literacy skills and spell wrongly	Deploy them to avoid them needing to write
They don't use initiative	Thank them and encourage them when they do use initiative, making them realize that it's ok.

Source: DfES, 2007

FIGURE 8.2 ISSUES WITH TEACHING ASSISTANTS (BUBB, 2005a: 90)

He suggests that teachers need to be made aware of how to manage support staff, and to be trained in the skills of management. There is no shortage of literature offering advice and guidance and practical strategies for effective classroom support (for example, see Balshaw and Farrell, 2002; Kay, 2002; Watkinson, 2002) and these would be useful additions to any school's staff development library.

CONCLUSION

Creating the right school climate where teachers and support staff work in partnership, and feel part of a team, is going to be facilitated by staff development for professional and paraprofessional staff, both individually and, at times, together. The CPD needs of both groups of staff need to be recognized, including those relating to working effectively with each other. A whole school approach to CPD with joint planning and, where appropriate, joint training is to be recommended.

Much is happening or proposed but research by a support staff union has shown that the quality of training varies considerably and support staff pay is often poor. Four in ten schools do not pay teaching assistants during school holidays and many work extra hours for no additional pay, and one in five teaching assistants needs a second job to make ends meet. Obviously, many of these issues are beyond the control of schools and CPD co-ordinators. Some, however, are not and this chapter has highlighted the importance of attending to the training and development needs of support staff. The training and development of support staff have improved and are likely to continue to improve. Schools with Investors in People status have been shown to have managed support staff more effectively than those without this status (Ofsted, 2002c). Support staff have much to contribute to schools, and those heads and CPD co-ordinators who ignore them are doing their pupils a grave disservice.

9

Initial Teacher Training – the CPD Needs and Benefits

- ◆ Different ways to be involved
- ◆ ITT partnership – pros and cons
- ◆ CPD needs of mentors

There are many benefits to be gained by schools and their staff from engaging in initial teacher training, particularly its effect as a catalyst for continuing professional development. It can help the development of reflection and learning-centred communities with wider links to higher education and other schools.

DIFFERENT WAYS TO BE INVOLVED

Many schools are involved in initial teacher training in a variety of different ways. There are three main routes to qualified teacher status, which are compared in Figure 9.1:

- The undergraduate route – people combine subject studies with professional training over three or four years and are awarded a BA (QTS) or a BEd.

- The postgraduate route – which is offered full-time for one year, part-time or through a flexible programme and gives a post-graduate certificate in education (PGCE) with QTS, unless the PGCE is for the post-compulsory sector.

- Employment-based routes (England and Wales) – the Graduate Teacher Programme which is for people with a degree, and the Registered Teacher Programme for people without a degree but with two years' higher education such as an HND. Both courses give qualified teacher status, but trainees have to be over 24 years old.

Many changes have happened in ITT in the past few years and acronyms abound, which may leave people confused. The BA (QTS) or BEd is a teaching qualification and a degree, and normally takes three years. Just under half of all primary school trainees are on undergraduate courses, whereas the PGCE outnumbers the BA QTS/BEd in secondary by about 12:1 as can be seen in Figure 9.1.

Most people do a PGCE based at an ITT provider. Postgraduate certificate in education courses last for about 38 weeks but involve a great deal of time in school, usually in six-week blocks starting with observing teaching and learning, then working with small groups, then team teaching and finally taking whole classes independently. Primary PGCEs spend at least 18 weeks in school, and secondary PGCEs at least 24 weeks – over half of the course. When at college, learning takes place in lectures, seminars, workshops and tutorials. The PGCE combines theory and practice and trainees will have written assignments to do as well as planning for school experience. There are 'flexible routes' for people who cannot do a full-time PGCE. Many PGCEs carry Master's level credits so they will leave training with a third or a half of an MA. In order to gain an MA they will need to undertake two-thirds or half of an MA programme within five years. This has significant implications for CPD leaders.

	BEd, BA (QTS)	PGCE	GTP
Entry requirements	Eng & maths GCSE C, science C for primary people born after 1.9.79	Eng & maths GCSE C, science C for primary people born after 1.9.79; degree	Eng & maths GCSE C, science C for primary people born after 1.9.79; degree; 24+ years old
Apply through	UCAS	GTTR	A DRB
Time spent in school	32 weeks for 4 year courses and 24 weeks for 3 year courses	24 weeks for secondary and 18 weeks for primary	All
Funding for trainee	none	Bursary + free training	Salary + possible training grant
Golden Hello	no	Secondary shortage subjects	no
Secondary numbers 2007	1,170	15,870	2,650
Primary numbers 2007	6,830	8,780	1,550

FIGURE 9.1 COMPARING ROUTES INTO TEACHING

School-centred initial teacher training (SCITT) is run by groups of schools, with some input from outside. All courses lead to qualified teacher status and may also lead to a PGCE validated by a higher education institution.

The Graduate Teacher Programme (GTP) is growing fast and gives people with a first degree who want to train on the job in England or Wales qualified teacher status, but not a PGCE. It suits people who have already got a good amount of school experience. Entry to what are called Designated Recommending Bodies (DRB) is competitive, with places going to the best applications in priority funding categories. The GTP requires a big commitment from schools because most learning is on the job. Inspection has found that trainees show greater skills in classroom management than their PGCE peers but are less able to apply their subject knowledge to teaching and assessment of pupils. Ofsted commented that: 'Trainees gain considerably from on-the-job training. However, there is still work to be done to further improve the quality of their teaching, particularly to ensure that secondary trainees are given a good grounding in teaching their specialist subject' (Ofsted, 2007b: 3).

The snag with the GTP is that schools have to employ an unqualified teacher before they know that the person will have a place on the programme. Places are very competitive and experiences have been mixed, with a fair number of people getting turned down or, if accepted, feeling that they were left to sink or swim. School-based training via the GTP route can be isolating for both trainees and mentors. It was originally thought that people on the GTP would be supernumerary but in most cases they have full responsibility from the start. To obtain QTS people have to have teaching experience in two schools and at two consecutive key stages – clearly this is a problem for a school that is employing one as a class teacher. The GTP requires a big commitment from schools because most learning is on the job:

> GTP trainees are in school full time apart from occasional central training days. This has implications for their training and our professional development in that we have been able

> to develop a programme of in-house training customized to the needs of the individual and working to the strengths of our staff. We have also been able to organize some of the training to coincide with the PGCE block practices and in some instances we have opened up the invitation to GTP trainees in other schools in the borough.
>
> (Kabra, 2002: 33)

Teach First started in 2003. This is the business and government-backed organization that provides teacher and business training to attract talented graduates to schools facing teacher shortages. After a short but intensive training at an ITT institution, Teach First places participants in inner city secondary schools that have at least one-third of pupils eligible for free school meals, are not in Special Measures, and which can provide the necessary support.

Many schools have trainees on teaching practice but a small number are designated as Training Schools because they demonstrate excellent practice across the range of teacher training activities, especially in initial teacher training and the continuing training of the whole school workforce. The difference between being a school that mentors beginning teachers and being a training school is an increase in funding so that roles and responsibilities within a HEI partnership are expanded. Drawing on the experience of the existing 240 Training Schools, the following ten characteristics (based on information from the DfES) epitomize those which have been most effective:

i) Corporate responsibility

- A Training School policy clearly identifying the school's role and whole-school community responsibility for outcomes.
- Structured mentor/school based tutor training provided for all staff.
- All curriculum areas and subject departments contributing to stated Training School objectives.

ii) Vibrant partnerships

- Frequent and effective ITT consultation and planning with HEI partners and with School-Centred Initial Teacher Training (SCITT) consortium partners.
- Input to wider HEI professional studies activity and materials by in-school experts.
- School involvement in action research activity with a variety of partners.
- Strong working links with an LA enabling the Training School to act as a hub for local and regional training activities.
- Direct in-service training provision for partner schools.
- Cross-phase mentoring/school based tutoring.
- Complementary partnership with other Training Schools.

iii) Clarity of management aims and objectives

- The existence of a Training School Policy incorporating an ITT policy.
- The integration of the Training School 4-year development plan with the School Improvement Plan.
- Co-ordination/management responsibilities vested in senior staff.
- Plans which incorporate sustainability and are not person-dependent.

- Clear operational planning which adequately resources all training activities.
- Pro-active recruitment strategies.
- A clear framework for periodic evaluation relating outcomes to aims and objectives.

iv) Increased throughput of ITT trainees

- Effective dissemination of information about access routes and taster courses.
- Breadth of access routes supported, e.g.:
  – Teaching Assistant or equivalent (LSA) entry and training.
  – TA progression to foundation degree courses.
  – PGCE/BA QTS placements.

v) A training continuum from ITT through middle management into leadership

- An established 'Investors in People' culture.
- A framework of coherent career development pathways for all staff.
- Development and promotion of ASTs as an internal training resource.
- Training courses for potential TAs/LSAs.
- NQT induction and training courses.
- Professional support courses for teachers in the early years of teaching.
- A focus on staff retention strategies.
- An entitlement CPD programme for all staff, clearly linked to performance management process.
- Advanced mentor training as a pre-requisite for middle management posts.

vi) Extensive outreach activity

- A high throughput of trainees at all levels.
- Liaison with other networks to provide a 'training hub' for NQTs and other specialist groups.
- Sharing of expertise through in-service training for other schools.
- Hosting of specialist training courses at the Training School.
- Sharing of expertise in areas of national priority.
- Provision of cross-phase experience and mentoring for trainees.
- Promotion of networking to support curriculum, teaching and learning expertise.
- Dissemination through networks, conferences, and use of websites.

vii) Innovation

- The use of Observatory Classrooms as a training tool.
- The application of new technologies in training.
- The development of 'classrooms of the future'.
- The promotion of team teaching, paired teaching and support staff.
- The promotion of new pedagogical approaches.

- Value added elements to ITT programmes.

viii) Enhanced resources for trainees
Manifested by:

- Dedicated training centres to support Training School activity.
- Regular access to video observatory facilities.
- Provision of recorded 'demo' lessons demonstrating excellence of practice.
- Facility for use of video-conferencing linking trainees to HEI tutors.
- Access to an organic library of text, audio and video resources for trainees.
- Provision of laptop computers and access to online resources for trainees.
- Provision of adequate protected time for mentor–trainee interaction.

ix) A culture of research and innovation

- Practical teacher-led research and experimental projects.
- Supported school-based action research activity.
- Support for staff engaged in research degree study.
- Development of working parties involving trainees, e.g. workforce remodelling, vocational provision and assessment, etc.
- Involvement of pupils as feedback mentors for trainees.

x) Active dissemination

- Hosting of dedicated training conferences.
- Provision of management training.
- Publication of research papers.
- Publication and distribution of training materials, including CD, DVD and video.
- Effective use of online and interactive websites.
- Involvement in local and regional training networks.

ITT PARTNERSHIP – PROS AND CONS

As the outline above indicates, the TDA is shifting responsibility for training teachers away from ITT providers, into a 'partnership' with schools. This means that for the GTP, schools are practically on their own and even those linked to PGCEs have half of the responsibility for making sure that the trainee is successful. So ITT partnership has mixed blessings.

NEGATIVE ASPECTS

Training someone for the new generation of teachers is a great responsibility. How do you know that you will do it right? It is a complex skill and one in which ITT providers are very experienced. At least one person on your staff will need to have the specialist skills to train beginning teachers and to share their knowledge with others involved. They will need specific CPD and support in handling tricky situations. They will need to understand the QTS standards fully (TDA, 2007) and know what is required to meet them.

Trainees need good teachers as role models, but maybe your school has a limited number of people you would put in that category. This can cause bad feeling in the staffroom where having a trainee on teaching practice is seen as a bit of an 'easy ride'. Many teachers find letting go of their classes difficult. They do not want to see their routines and so on changed. They are very controlling and find it hard to let trainees develop and learn from mistakes. On the other hand, a few teachers see having a trainee as a chance to have a rest, to abdicate responsibility for their class, to get other things done.

Unless you are heavily involved in an SCITT or have someone on the GTP, you will get the trainee that you are given. Most are great but occasionally there are nightmares: people with a very different pedagogical philosophy from you who cause no end of difficulty for all concerned. Trainees are learning to be teachers so it is unlikely (but not impossible) that they will be as effective as experienced colleagues. Typically this will affect the behaviour and learning of pupils. This needs to be managed well to limit damage.

Being in partnership means having to rely on others and may mean compromising on judgements. Your school may think that a trainee should not qualify but others think otherwise, for instance.

And then there are the pragmatics. You will have lots of new people in the school. More is usually better – but not always. They will need somewhere to sit in the staffroom. What do you do about confidential matters? Are there any staff meetings that trainees should not attend?

POSITIVE ASPECTS

There are clear benefits to being involved in ITT. There is the philanthropic buzz that comes from the influence practising teachers have upon the quality of future entrants to the profession. On a more pragmatic level it means being able to hand pick your new teachers – many trainees obtain jobs in schools they do a teaching practice in. It increases the adult to pupil ratio, which means that children get more attention and teachers should be less stretched. Kathryn Kabra believes:

> The children gain so much more adult contact in an average school day, experience so many different teaching styles that there has to be something to meet every learning need and they're guaranteed a teacher in front of them rather than the uncertainties of staff shortages and supply availability. It's a win–win situation for everybody. (Kabra, 2002: 36)

? POINTS FOR REFLECTION

What do you think are the benefits and disadvantages to you and the school of being involved in initial training?

CASE STUDY 9.1: A TRAINING SCHOOL

Kathryn Kabra describes the opportunities that her school has been offered through gaining training school status, and the many ways in which it has made a difference.

Having had a regular stream of PGCE trainees passing through our doors over the last decade many staff had already received quality mentor training from our HEI partner, and had experienced the highs and lows of mentor life and trainee morale boosting. We were, as a staff, very aware of what was to be gained from contact with enthusiastic, innovative individuals who implicitly demand that we draw upon the strengths of our own experience and re-acquaint ourselves with those convictions which first drew us into teaching. To rediscover the extent of our expertise and find that it is recognized and valued is no small spin off for a workforce, which can feel jaded and finely tuned to criticism. So raised morale and self-affirmation have had a significant impact on the energy generated within the school. Being selected to be a training school was a powerful recognition of the quality and value of the mentoring that staff have provided over the years.

The reflective practice that mentoring and modelling good practice entails, and the opportunity to disseminate their skills and knowledge through leading INSET both in school and at the HEI, have made significant contributions both to their professional portfolios and to a general 'can-do' culture. Four people have applied for assessment this term as advanced skills teachers (ASTs). We are hoping to set up two research projects during the next academic year, one to evaluate innovations to the organization of Foundation Stage classes and the other as part of a wider research project looking at the educational needs of children of Pakistani origin. Two of the staff have acted as professional tutors for the HEI and have been involved with supporting mentors of PGCE trainees in other schools. Through this an incidental effect has been the formation of closer links with neighbouring schools and an opportunity to learn from other teachers.

Training school status has brought together many of the school's on-going developmental initiatives under one umbrella and made economies of scale possible. In the best practice of good teaching and learning we have been able to step back from an activity led training curriculum into a cycle of needs analysis, target audience identification, identification of the best person for the job, identification of the best method of presentation and evaluation of its effectiveness, leading to modification and improvement. A training school co-ordinator post was created, and a second member of staff appointed to tutor PGCE trainees in this and other HEI partnership schools for one day a week. The training school, like Jack's beanstalk, is growing and reaching for the sky! (Kabra, 2002: 33–5)

Having lots of enthusiastic beginning teachers around gives schools a buzz and may influence those experienced colleagues who might be described as 'professionally stagnant' (Child and Merrill, 2002). Trainee teachers bring to schools the benefits of up to date subject and pedagogical knowledge.

Data from the *Becoming a Teacher* research project, which is tracking people's development from 2003 to 2009, suggest that mentors who were considered helpful by trainees provided a range of forms of assistance including:

1 provision of ideas and techniques for teaching;

2 providing encouragement and boosting trainees' confidence;

3 direct intervention in trainees' relationships with pupils;

4 'being there';

5 allowing trainees to have an input into the kinds of early activities they would be involved in.

A significant minority of case study trainees (n=13) reported that relations with their mentors and/or other school staff had a negative impact on their early experiences in schools (Hobson et al., 2005: ix).

Effective mentoring is at the heart of ITT. In supporting and assessing trainees, mentors have to reflect on their own performance and often become better teachers themselves as a result. This is recognized in advanced skills teachers for ITT who are recognized as successful mentors/trainers. A major benefit for schools involved in ITT is the transferability of mentoring skills to other aspects of the school's life and work, specifically in working with NQTs and performance management. Mentoring trainees is good practice for working with other teachers – ones who are perhaps less willing to develop! Two schoolteachers (Butler and Geeson, 2002) seconded to work on PGCE courses state, 'mentoring has become an increasingly significant mode of professional development'. They continue: 'where mentoring has been an integral part of the school's ethos, there is likely to be greater collaboration amongst staff in sharing ideas, schemes of work and practice'.

Teachers who have a trainee working with them will eventually be able to leave the classroom, enabling them to support others. In Child and Merrill's research only three out of 53 mentors thought that ITT took up too much teacher time: just over a quarter claimed that trainees taking classes generated meaningful 'free' time for teachers, whereas two-thirds took the view that they created 'quality' time for other staff. They conclude that 'free time is considered an inappropriate phrase as it implies some kind of shirking of responsibility; quality time is redolent of something professional, a time in which CPD might be occurring' (Child and Merrill, 2002: 20).

CPD NEEDS OF MENTORS

It is important to ask mentors what they need. Common areas are understanding the QTS standards and observation skills. The standards for QTS have changed three times in the last 10 years, which makes for confusion: Figure 9.2 shows the 2007 standards.

---

1 Professional attributes
Those recommended for the award of QTS should:

Relationships with children and young people
Q1 Have high expectations of children and young people including a commitment to ensuring that they can achieve their full educational potential and to establishing fair, respectful, trusting, supportive and constructive relationships with them.
Q2 Demonstrate the positive values, attitudes and behaviour they expect from children and young people.

Frameworks
Q3 (a) Be aware of the professional duties of teachers and the statutory framework within which they work.
(b) Be aware of the policies and practices of the workplace and share in collective responsibility for their implementation.

Communicating and working with others
Q4 Communicate effectively with children, young people, colleagues, parents and carers.
Q5 Recognize and respect the contribution that colleagues, parents and carers can make to the development and wellbeing of children and young people and to raising their levels of attainment.
Q6 Have a commitment to collaboration and co-operative working.

Personal professional development
Q7 (a) Reflect on and improve their practice, and take responsibility for identifying and meeting their developing professional needs.
(b) Identify priorities for their early professional development in the context of induction.
Q8 Have a creative and constructively critical approach towards innovation, being prepared to adapt their practice where benefits and improvements are identified.
Q9 Act upon advice and feedback and be open to coaching and mentoring.

2 Professional knowledge and understanding
Those recommended for the award of QTS should:

Teaching and learning
Q10 Have a knowledge and understanding of a range of teaching, learning and behaviour management strategies and know how to use and adapt them, including how to personalize learning and provide opportunities for all learners to achieve their potential.

Assessment and monitoring
Q11 Know the assessment requirements and arrangements for the subjects/curriculum areas in the age ranges they are trained to teach, including those relating to public examinations and qualifications.
Q12 Know a range of approaches to assessment, including the importance of formative assessment.
Q13 Know how to use local and national statistical information to evaluate the effectiveness of their teaching, to monitor the progress of those they teach and to raise levels of attainment.

Subjects and curriculum
Q14 Have a secure knowledge and understanding of their subjects/curriculum areas and related pedagogy to enable them to teach effectively across the age and ability range for which they are trained.
Q15 Know and understand the relevant statutory and non-statutory curricula, frameworks, including those provided through the National Strategies, for their subjects/curriculum areas, and other relevant initiatives applicable to the age and ability range for which they are trained.

Literacy, numeracy and ICT
Q16 Have passed the professional skills tests in numeracy, literacy and information and communication technology (ICT).

FIGURE 9.2 PROFESSIONAL STANDARDS FOR QUALIFIED TEACHER STATUS (TDA, 2007)

Q17 Know how to use skills in literacy, numeracy and ICT to support their teaching and wider professional activities.

Achievement and diversity

Q18 Understand how children and young people develop and that the progress and wellbeing of learners are affected by a range of developmental, social, religious, ethnic, cultural and linguistic influences.

Q19 Know how to make effective personalized provision for those they teach, including those for whom English is an additional language or who have special educational needs or disabilities, and how to take practical account of diversity and promote equality and inclusion in their teaching.

Q20 Know and understand the roles of colleagues with specific responsibilities, including those with responsibility for learners with special educational needs and disabilities and other individual learning needs.

Health and wellbeing

Q21 (a) Be aware of current legal requirements, national policies and guidance on the safeguarding and promotion of the wellbeing of children and young people.

(b) Know how to identify and support children and young people whose progress, development or wellbeing is affected by changes or difficulties in their personal circumstances, and when to refer them to colleagues for specialist support.

3 Professional skills

Those recommended for the award of QTS (Q) should:

Planning

Q22 Plan for progression across the age and ability range for which they are trained, designing effective learning sequences within lessons and across series of lessons and demonstrating secure subject/curriculum knowledge.

Q23 Design opportunities for learners to develop their literacy, numeracy and ICT skills.

Q24 Plan homework or other out-of-class work to sustain learners' progress and to extend and consolidate their learning.

Teaching

Q25 Teach lessons and sequences of lessons across the age and ability range for which they are trained in which they:

(a) use a range of teaching strategies and resources, including e-learning, taking practical account of diversity and promoting equality and inclusion;

(b) build on prior knowledge, develop concepts and processes, enable learners to apply new knowledge, understanding and skills and meet learning objectives;

(c) adapt their language to suit the learners they teach, introducing new ideas and concepts clearly, and using explanations, questions, discussions and plenaries effectively;

(d) manage the learning of individuals, groups and whole classes, modifying their teaching to suit the stage of the lesson.

Assessing, monitoring and giving feedback

Q26 (a) Make effective use of a range of assessment, monitoring and recording strategies.

(b) Assess the learning needs of those they teach in order to set challenging learning objectives.

Q27 Provide timely, accurate and constructive feedback on learners' attainment, progress and areas for development.

Q28 Support and guide learners to reflect on their learning, identify the progress they have made and identify their emerging learning needs.

Reviewing teaching and learning

Q29 Evaluate the impact of their teaching on the progress of all learners, and modify their planning and classroom practice where necessary.

Learning environment

Q30 Establish a purposeful and safe learning environment conducive to learning and identify opportunities for learners to learn in out-of-school contexts.

Q31 Establish a clear framework for classroom discipline to manage learners' behaviour constructively and promote their self-control and independence.

Team working and collaboration

Q32 Work as a team member and identify opportunities for working with colleagues, sharing the development of effective practice with them.

Q33 Ensure that colleagues working with them are appropriately involved in supporting learning and understand the roles they are expected to fulfil.

FIGURE 9.2 (CONTINUED)

■ OBSERVATION – GENERAL POINTS

Mentors may find observing stressful, because they feel inexperienced and uncertain of the best way to go about it. The year group and area of the curriculum to be taught may not be familiar. They may feel that their observation and feedback will compare unfavourably to that of the university supervisor. As the person responsible for the trainee, they will also be mindful of the need to move them forward while maintaining a good relationship. This can lead people to be too kind, and to not bite the bullet. Trainees sometimes feel that they are not being sufficiently challenged. This is particularly true of the most successful ones, but they too need to be helped to develop professionally.

Observation and giving feedback are very complex skills, for which training and practice are required. The important thing to remember is that the whole process needs to be useful for the trainee. It is for their benefit that it is being done. To this end it is essential that mentors, ITT and induction tutors consider the context of the observation. This includes:

- the stage of the trainee (is this an early or final teaching practice?);
- how they are feeling;
- their previous experiences of being observed;
- the state of the mentor's relationship with the trainee or NQT;
- what part of the school year, week and day it happens in;
- the disposition of the class.

Mentors also need to recognize their own values, beliefs and moods. This is why it is important to concentrate on the progress the children make before judging the effectiveness of the teaching. The more we observe other teachers, the more convinced we are that there is no one way to teach.

■ BEFORE THE OBSERVATION

It is useful if not essential to have a focus – something the trainee is trying to get better at. This will not exclude you from noticing and commenting on other things but will ensure that you have information on the key area that you are working on. Discuss ground rules such as how your presence is to be explained to the class, what you are going to do, where you should sit, your exact time of arrival, what you will need before or at the beginning of the observation, such as the lesson plan and access to the planning file. Agree a time and place to discuss the lesson, giving yourself time to reflect and write notes, within 24 hours of the observation.

■ DURING THE OBSERVATION

It is essential to look at teaching in relation to learning. One must always be thinking about cause and effect. Why are the pupils behaving as they are? The cause is often related to teaching. Thus, the observer needs to look carefully at what both the teacher and the pupils are doing. Read the lesson plan, paying particular attention to the learning objective. If you have a photocopy it is useful to annotate the plan, for instance showing what parts went well, when pace slowed, and so forth. Look at the planning file and pupils' work to see what the lesson is building on.

If the student teacher has not given you a place to sit, choose one which is outside the direct line of the teacher's vision, but where you can see the pupils and what the teacher is doing. When the pupils are doing activities, move around to ascertain the effectiveness of the teacher's explanation, organization and choice of task. Look at different groups (girls and boys; high, average and low attainers; and students with English as an additional language or special needs) to see whether everyone's needs are being met.

Make notes about what actually happens, focusing on the agreed areas but keeping your eyes open to everything. Make clear judgements as you gather evidence. Refer to the criteria you agreed to use – have a copy with you. Try to tell 'the story' of the lesson, by noting causes and effect. For instance, what was it about the teacher's delivery that caused students' rapt attention or fidgeting? Think about the pupils' learning and what it is about the teaching that is helping or hindering it. Note what they actually achieve. Trainees are not always aware that some students have only managed to write the date and that others have exceeded expectations, for instance. Look through books to get a feel for their progress and marking.

WRITTEN NOTES

Before you write observation notes you need to remind yourself of their purpose and audience. Are they aiming to develop someone or be brutally honest? Some things are easier to approach orally or in an oblique way. There are two sorts of writing from an observation: the notes you make during the lesson and the summary of strengths and areas for development for feedback. We think both should be used. That way the observer can make informal jottings during the lesson knowing that they will be pulled together in a tidy summary afterwards.

Written feedback should contain praise and acknowledgement of success, identify strengths and weaknesses or areas to develop, which will be useful in future lessons. There is a range of sorts of comments in observation feedback:

- Descriptive – what happens but without any evaluation. This is not very helpful.

- Questioning/reflective – there are two sorts of questions:
  - those designed to stimulate thought and get people thinking about an area that could be improved, for example, 'How could you have avoided the arguments over pencils?'
  - genuine questions for clarification – for example, 'Why are you ignoring Paul's behaviour?'

- Evaluative – judging, for example, 'very well planned'; 'shouting simply raises the noise and emotional level'.

- Advisory – suggestions, for example, 'Dean and Wayne might behave better if they were separated'.

AFTER THE OBSERVATION – DISCUSSING THE LESSON

Take some time to reflect. Think about the teaching and learning you have seen, focusing on strengths and a few areas for development. Be clear about your main message – this will take some thinking about. There is no point listing every little thing that went wrong. You need to have 'the big picture' in your mind in order to convey it to the beginning teacher. Remember it needs to be useful to them – aim to help them develop. You want to avoid the extremes of crushing them or giving the impression that things are better than they really are. It is a very fine line to tread, but your knowledge of the context and the person will help you.

Good feedback is:

- prompt – takes places as soon as possible after the lesson observation;

- accurate – based only on specific, observations/evidence which can be readily shared with the teacher;

- balanced – the positive emphasized and points for development related to the focus chosen as an objective;

- respectful to the teacher's perspective – allows for input from the teacher;
- related to objectives set for review and directly actionable by the teacher;
- conducted in a quiet and private space.

Be aware of your body language and notice the teacher's. A large proportion of communication is non-verbal. Try to ask questions to guide the trainee's thinking, but not in a way that intimidates or implies criticism. Encourage reflection and listen well by asking open-ended questions, such as:

- How do you think the lesson went?
- What were you most pleased with? Why?
- What were you trying to achieve?
- What did the pupils learn?
- What did the lower attaining pupils learn?
- What did the higher attaining pupils learn?
- Why do you think the lesson went the way it did?
- Why did you choose that activity?
- Were there any surprises?
- When you did … the pupils reacted by … Why do you think that happened?
- Help me understand what you took into account when you were planning?
- If you taught that lesson again, what, if anything, would you do differently?
- What will you do in the follow-up lesson?

Be aware of what you say, and how you say it. Focus on the teaching and learning that took place, using specific examples of what pupils said and did. Avoid talking about yourself or other teachers you have seen, unless this will be useful to the trainee. Comments such as 'I wouldn't have done that' or 'I would have …' are inappropriate and can irritate and alienate the beginning teacher.

Aim for the beginning teacher to do most of the talking and thinking. Paraphrase and summarize what the person says. It involves reflecting back your interpretation of what you have heard, which can be very useful for the teacher. Use phrases such as 'So what you mean is …' 'In other words …' Be positive and upbeat throughout. Be sensitive to how the trainee is taking your feedback, and ease off if necessary.

CONCLUSION

Involvement in initial teacher training can bring many benefits to the school and can help to develop that all-important learning and development culture, but it should not be entered into lightly. This chapter has highlighted some of the pros and cons of such involvement and tried to throw some light on what is for many a complex and confusing situation regarding the routes to achieving qualified teacher status. It has also concentrated on the training needs of tutors and school-based mentors, focusing particularly on observation and feedback skills. Many of these skills are, of course, generic and can be used for both performance management and for the induction of newly qualified teachers – the subject of our next chapter.

10

Newly Qualified Teachers and their Induction

♦ The induction entitlement

♦ How schools organize induction

♦ Induction programmes

There is much interest throughout the world in the value and impact of professional development for new teachers, especially in relation to its ability to contribute to raising standards and improve retention rates. Research on induction from around the world (see for example: Villar and Strong, 2007) has found that carefully constructed and managed induction programmes – designed on the basis of outcome-based objectives for the participants and monitored for progress against staged targets for achieving the specified outcomes – achieve their goals. However, the relationship between government policy initiatives and grassroots implementation is key.

Most people would agree with the aims of England's policy – that induction should ensure that the future professional and career development of individual teachers is built upon a firm foundation. It helps develop informed professionalism by providing newly qualified teachers (NQTs) with significant opportunities to: show their potential; make rapid advancement towards excellence in teaching; and begin to make a real impact on their school's development (DfES, 2003b: 4).

The induction year is arguably the most formative period in a teacher's career. So we need to set high expectations and standards at this time of greatest receptiveness and willingness to learn and develop. However, support is crucial if new teachers are to develop the competencies, confidence and attitudes that will keep them happy in the job and serve as the basis for on-going professional development.

However, some school leaders have a sink or swim attitude to new teachers – a form of hazing like the initiation rites that gangs or clubs like Hell's Angels or American fraternities make their new members go through to prove their worth. Some teachers are put into the least survivable situations and face impossible challenges, but professional development that could really help is denied them. Newly qualified teachers in England are meant to be protected from unreasonable demands by law since 1999 but in some schools the best resources, timetables and classrooms are reserved for those who have served their time. If new teachers fail in such contexts they're deemed to be not much good, if they complain they're 'unprofessional' and if they survive they're a 'real' teacher. Such cultures become self-perpetuating as one NQT on the *TES* forum wrote:

> 'Schools can be dog eat dog places. Established teachers take the best resources, the best class-rooms, the best classes so that they can get by. NQTs get the crap. Once these guys leave, the NQTs become the established ones and so it goes on...'
>
> (cited in Bubb and Earley, 2006)

Many new teachers work in schools in challenging circumstances. By definition most vacancies will be in places with a high staff turnover and that more experienced teachers shy away from. Some schools employ more new teachers than they can possibly support: schools where a third of the staffroom are newly qualified, another third have only up to five years' experience and the other third are close to retirement. Such schools simply don't have enough people with sufficient expertise to support inexperienced teachers.

THE INDUCTION ENTITLEMENT

All parts of Great Britain now have statutory induction arrangements. They are different, albeit similar, as illustrated in Figure 10.1. Induction arrangements should be an incentive to a career in teaching. Newly qualified teachers should feel that they will be well supported especially when things do not go smoothly. Induction should be a carrot. Indeed, many aspects of England's induction policy are clearly attractive to new teachers. It is statutory so that they know that all schools by law have to comply with it, and they have the following entitlement:

1   A 10 per cent lighter teaching timetable than other teachers in the school.

2   A job description that does not make unreasonable demands, such as unduly difficult classes.

3   Meetings with a school 'induction tutor', including half termly reviews of progress.

4   An individualized programme of support.

5   Objectives with action plans (see Figure 10.2), informed by strengths and areas for development identified in the career entry and development profile, to help them meet the Induction Standards.

6   At least one observation of their teaching each half term with oral and written feedback.

7   Procedures to air grievances at school and local authority level.

This entitlement should give NQTs protection against the worst of experiences that others have encountered during their first year.

However, England has built into its induction policy a rigorous assessment and monitoring system. This is seen by some NQTs as beneficial in that they like to be told that they are doing well and to know that if there are concerns they will be raised. For many, however, the assessment component of induction is a stick to threaten and potentially beat them with. Formal assessment reports are written at the end of each of the three terms, placing considerable demands on the headteacher and induction tutor as well as the teacher (see Case study 10.1 for an extract from a termly report). Newly qualified teachers are judged on whether they meet the demanding standards for the end of the induction year. They have to demonstrate that they meet all the core Standards (www.tda.gov.uk). These standards are demanding and the consequences of not meeting them severe. Unless they are successful on appeal, those failing to meet the standards will not be able to teach in a maintained school or non-maintained special school, despite still having qualified teacher status. These teachers would still keep QTS but are de-registered from the General Teaching Council. Thus, the only teaching they could do is in an independent school, as a private tutor or abroad. They cannot repeat induction or their initial training.

CASE STUDY 10.1: AN EXTRACT FROM THE END OF TERM 1 ASSESSMENT REPORT

Professional Knowledge

Miranda is making good progress in this area and has good subject knowledge. She uses ICT extremely well to enhance learning, including the use of music, film and photography as well as competent use of the IWB. Miranda is very reflective and quickly identifies her own areas for improvement and actively seeks support to improve. She quickly acts upon advice and strategies observed during demonstration lessons. For example she felt the children were becoming restless during the afternoon sessions so, following an observation in a reception class, she altered her timetable to allow for activity based afternoons where a variety of activities are available for the children to choose from. She also included more regular brain breaks to increase energy levels and focus.

She manages the space within the classroom extremely well and is willing to carry out a variety of adventurous activities despite space restrictions (whole class bread making!). She is aware of the SEN Code of Practice and works closely with the SEN co-ordinator and TA support within class to ensure that the needs of every child are met. The IEPs written are of a high standard with clear and manageable targets and strategies in place to support children in meeting these targets. She is developing a range of assessment strategies – both summative and formative and is able to record these systematically. She uses AfL well and has a good understanding of prior learning which she uses to support future needs.

Although good progress has already been made in this area, Miranda continues to refine and improve methods of assessment. This is supported in school with guidance on whole school assessment procedures and the opportunity for Miranda to review good practice already in use across the school.

POINTS FOR REFLECTION

What do you think of this report? How does it make clear how well the new teacher is doing and what level of support and monitoring she has had?

	England	Scotland	Wales
First year called	Induction	Probation	Induction
New teacher known as a	NQT	New teacher	NQT
Arrangements started	May 1999	Aug 2002	Sept 2003
Lead organization	General Teaching Council for England	General Teaching Council for Scotland	General Teaching Council for Wales
Timetable reduction	10%	30%	10%
Looked after by	Induction tutor	Supporter	Induction tutor
Time for their job	None	0.1	None
Judged against	Core standards	The Standard for Full Registration	The End of Induction Standard
Assessment	3 times	2 times	3 times
How to get a job	New teacher finds it	New teacher placed in a school	New teacher finds it
Time limit between QTS and induction	None	Should do probation straight away	5 years

FIGURE 10.1 THE FIRST YEAR – DIFFERENCES BETWEEN ENGLAND, SCOTLAND AND WALES

HOW SCHOOLS ORGANIZE INDUCTION

Professional support is key to the success of the induction year. Newly qualified teachers may need colleagues to take a range of roles:

Planning partner	Helper	Expert practitioner
Colleague	Disciplinarian of pupils	Organizer
Friend	Adviser	Monitor of progress
Supporter	Critical friend	Trainer
Counsellor	Facilitator	Protector
Assessor	Motivator	Parent

Clearly, an induction tutor could not and should not take on all these roles. The whole staff is responsible for inducting a new teacher, and often people will take on certain roles naturally. Figure 10.3 shows how different schools have arranged induction support. Problems may arise when key roles are not taken by someone in the NQT's life. Equally problematic is when one person takes on too many roles or when people assume erroneously that someone else is taking a role.

Induction tutors have a crucial role. The DfES considers these to be their roles and responsibilities:

■ Provide, or co-ordinate, guidance and effective support for the NQT's professional development.

■ Have the necessary skills, expertise and knowledge to work effectively in this role. In particular, you should be able to make rigorous and fair judgements about the NQT's progress in relation to the requirements for satisfactory completion of the induction period.

■ Play a key role in providing assessment throughout the NQT's induction programme. The support and assessment functions may be split between two or more teachers where this suits the structures and systems of the school. In such circumstances, responsibilities should be clearly specified at the beginning of induction and arrangements should be put in place to ensure that monitoring and assessments are based on, and informed by, the NQT's teaching and professional development.

■ Undertake most of the observations of the NQT's teaching. Professional reviews of progress, based on discussions between the NQT and the induction tutor, should take place at intervals throughout their induction support programme.

■ Keep a dated copy of all reports on observations, review meetings and objectives until the Appropriate Body has decided whether the NQT has completed their induction support programme satisfactorily and any appeal has been determined. A note should be kept of the other evidence used. The NQT should receive copies of all such written records and the Appropriate Body should have access to them (from DfES, 2003b: 24).

Thus induction tutors, like mentors of trainees, will have specific professional development needs. Local authorities, HEIs and consultancies run varying degrees of training, and some of the longer and more in-depth courses are accredited. Many of the skills required of ITT mentors and induction tutors are the same – observation, feedback, coaching, report writing. However, the similarities can disguise the differences, and a lot is at stake for NQTs who do not meet the standards so it is important that induction tutors have the necessary skills, expertise and knowledge.

	Name	Date	Date obective met
Objective: Write annual reports to parents that give a clear picture of children's progress and achievements.			

Success criteria	Actions	When	Progress
You have an evidence base – i.e. you know what each child can do.	Collate assessment information so that you know what each child can do in the key aspects of every subject. Gather information from other teachers if necessary. Fill gaps in knowledge of what class can do. Give pupils a self-assessment so that you have insight into what they think they've learnt and their greatest achievements.		
You know what the school expects.	Find out the school system for writing reports – speak to the assessment co-ordinator. Read some examples that have been identified as being good. Note stylistic features and key phrases.		
You have written one report to an acceptable standard.	Read the children's previous year's report. Write one child's report in draft. Give to the headteacher for comment.		
You have a timetable that will enable you to meet the deadline.	Set up the system for reports (i.e. computer format). Draw up a timetable of when you're going to write the reports, allowing about two hours for first five, one hour for next twenty, three quarters for last five, one-third over half term. Liaise with other teachers who are contributing to the reports.		
You meet the deadline.	Write the reports. Give them to the headteacher for checking and signing. Celebrate!		

Review:

FIGURE 10.2 AN ACTION PLAN TO MEET AN OBJECTIVE: REPORTS

More than anything, NQTs value someone who can give them time. This is a very precious resource. Induction tutors often have many other time-consuming roles and their time spent on induction is rarely funded. As ever, much has to be done on goodwill or it does not happen. Induction tutors should want to do the job and be suited to it, otherwise the NQT will suffer. Here are positive comments that a group of NQTs made about their induction tutors.

1 They were always available for advice.

2 They gave me a regular meeting time, even though they were busy.

3 They were genuinely interested in how I was doing.

Primary School 1 (mono-support)
Induction tutor: Member of the senior management team.

Primary School 2 (mono-support)
Induction tutor: Headteacher.

Primary School 3 (bi-support)
Induction tutor: Member of the senior management team.
Mentor: The parallel class teacher.

Primary School 4 (tri-support)
Induction co-ordinator: Member of the senior management team.
Induction tutor: Year group leader.
Buddy mentor: A recently qualified teacher.

Secondary School 1 (mono-support)
Induction tutor: Senior member of staff.

Secondary School 2 (bi-support)
Induction co-ordinator: Senior member of staff in charge of all NQTs in the
                                        school.
Induction tutor: The head of department.

Secondary School 3 (tri-support)
Induction co-ordinator: Senior member of staff in charge of all NQTs in the
                                        school.
Induction tutor: The head of department.
Buddy mentor: A recently qualified teacher.

Secondary School 4 (tri-support)
Induction tutor/co-ordinator: A senior teacher who organizes the induction
                                        programme, meetings, assessment reports, etc.
Academic mentor: The head of department who advises on all subject
                                        related matters.
Pastoral mentor: A head of year who gives guidance on behaviour
                                        management and pastoral issues.

Secondary School 5 (multi-support)
Staff Development Officer: In charge of co-ordinating the induction programme for
                                        all NQTs and organizes contracts, job descriptions, staff
                                        handbook and the pre-induction visits before the NQTs
                                        start work.
Subject mentor: Head of the department that the NQT works in:
                                        supervises planning and teaching and gives subject
                                        specific input.
Pastoral mentor: A head of year who gives guidance on behaviour
                                        management and pastoral issues.
Buddy mentor group: A group of recently qualified teachers who provide a
                                        shoulder to cry on.

FIGURE 10.3 ORGANIZATION OF INDUCTION PERSONNEL (BUBB et al., 2002: 29)

4 They were honest and open, which encouraged trust.

5 They listened to me – and did not impose their own views.

6 They made practical suggestions.

7 They shared their expertise, ideas and resources.

8 They were encouraging and optimistic – they made me feel good.

9 They stopped me working myself into the ground by setting realistic objectives.

10 They were not perfect themselves, which was reassuring!

11 They looked after me, keeping parents and the head off my back.

12 Their feedback after observations was useful. Good to get some praise and ideas for improvements.

13 They were well organized, and if they said they would do something they did it. (Bubb, 2000: 14)

■ VARIABILITY OF INDUCTION EXPERIENCE

There is still variability of new teachers' experiences in spite of statutory regulations. One of the benefits of England's induction policy is that it should help standardize the provision that new teachers receive across and within schools. Though induction provision appears to have improved, there are still too many NQTs (20 per cent) who do not get their ten per cent reduced timetable (Totterdell et al., 2002). This reduction is a crucial part of induction without which other elements, such as observing other colleagues, cannot be achieved. Schools' interpretation of what is a 'good enough' meeting of the induction standards varies and this is felt to be unfair by NQTs. It seems a flaw in the system that decisions are made so subjectively by induction tutors and headteachers with only limited input from LA, university or Ofsted specialists in this field.

There needs to be a balance between support, monitoring and assessment as indicated in Figure 10.4. Although the induction circular makes clear that NQTs are responsible for raising concerns with their school and Appropriate Body, this is hard to do in practice. Complaining is always uncomfortable, and NQTs are in a particularly tricky situation, since the headteacher is responsible for recommending whether they pass or not. As one NQT wrote:

> It is very difficult to discuss problems. I want to pass my induction year and, if this means keeping my head down and mouth shut, that's what I'll do. The alternative is to highlight problems with my support and then have to face awkward times with my induction tutor or head, with the implications that might have on whether they pass or fail me.
>
> (Bubb, 2001: 19)

■ SCHOOL INDUCTION POLICY

If schools have an induction policy, everyone will know about procedures, rights and responsibilities. The most effective policies we found were those in which there had been input from the people they affect, and which were regularly updated in the light of experience.

School policies should be based on an understanding of good practice, to ensure that procedures can be followed quickly, consistently and effectively by reference to agreed practices and principles. A school induction policy should serve to ensure that a structured induction programme is followed; individuals involved in induction are aware of their role and responsibilities; individuals are aware of each other's roles and responsibilities, and NQTs are treated fairly and consistently. So a school policy on induction should cover three main areas:

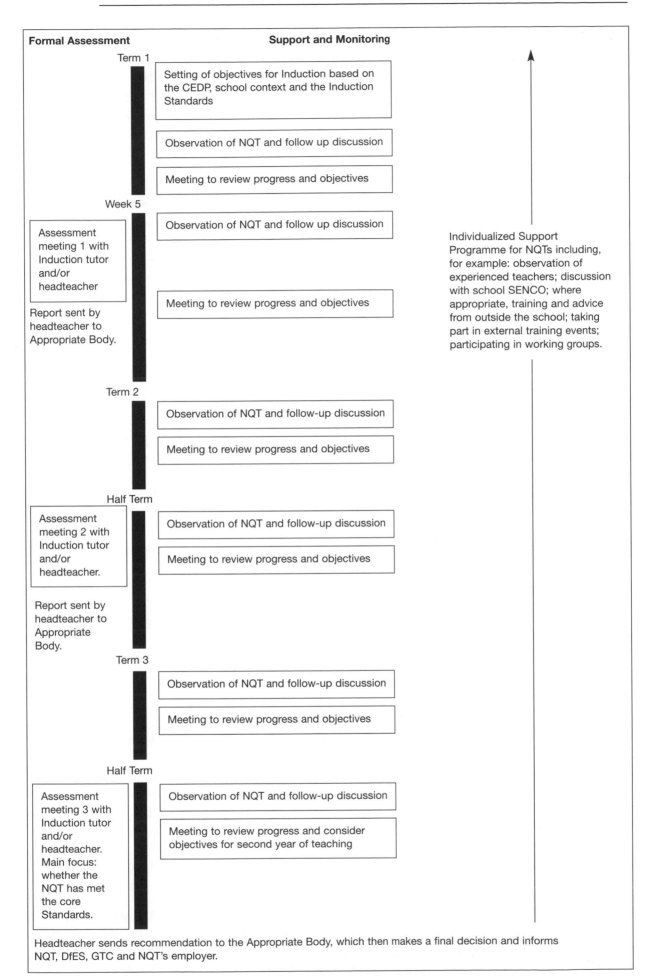

Formal Assessment

Support and Monitoring

Term 1

Setting of objectives for Induction based on the CEDP, school context and the Induction Standards

Observation of NQT and follow up discussion

Meeting to review progress and objectives

Week 5

Assessment meeting 1 with Induction tutor and/or headteacher

Report sent by headteacher to Appropriate Body.

Observation of NQT and follow up discussion

Meeting to review progress and objectives

Individualized Support Programme for NQTs including, for example: observation of experienced teachers; discussion with school SENCO; where appropriate, training and advice from outside the school; taking part in external training events; participating in working groups.

Term 2

Observation of NQT and follow-up discussion

Meeting to review progress and objectives

Half Term

Assessment meeting 2 with Induction tutor and/or headteacher.

Observation of NQT and follow-up discussion

Meeting to review progress and objectives

Report sent by headteacher to Appropriate Body.

Term 3

Observation of NQT and follow-up discussion

Meeting to review progress and objectives

Half Term

Assessment meeting 3 with Induction tutor and/or headteacher. Main focus: whether the NQT has met the core Standards.

Observation of NQT and follow-up discussion

Meeting to review progress and consider objectives for second year of teaching

Headteacher sends recommendation to the Appropriate Body, which then makes a final decision and informs NQT, DfES, GTC and NQT's employer.

FIGURE 10.4 OVERVIEW OF THE INDUCTION PROCESS (www.tda.gov.uk)

- why the senior management team regards induction as beneficial for the school;

- the procedures staff should follow in order to support, monitor and assess NQTs;

- how NQTs can make best use of opportunities offered to them (Bleach, 2000: 100).

Procedures that staff should follow can be outlined in induction policies through describing the roles and responsibilities of individuals involved including headteacher, induction tutor, induction manager if appropriate, other people involved in induction, the governing body and LA staff; the induction programme which will be provided; and guidance for the assessment and monitoring of NQTs. A procedure for review should also be included in the policy, to ensure that the school's intentions and procedures continue to be effective. Figure 10.5 is an example of an induction policy for the first term.

Your Induction Year: Who does what and when in the first term

The school will:

By the end of the first month:
- Negotiate an agreed Individual Action Plan with you, identifying objectives for professional development for the first term based on the Career Entry and Development Profile.
- Ensure that the induction tutor observes you.
- Provide an appropriate weekly support programme for you.

During the term:
- Ensure that the induction tutor maintains a written record of all support;
- Monitoring and assessment evidence carried out in relation to your progress;
- Ensure that half-termly review sessions take place between your induction tutor and you.

By the end of the term:
- Ensure that the induction tutor carries out a formal assessment of your progress according to national guidelines and criteria;
- Ensure that the induction tutor conducts the first formal assessment meeting with you, providing well-founded feedback on your progress;
- Return the Assessment Report to the LA Induction team.

You will:

By the end of the first month:
- Negotiate an agreed Individual Action Plan with the induction tutor.
- Attend the weekly NQT meeting (Tuesdays, 3.30pm–4.00pm).

During the remainder of the term:
- Develop your professional practice to meet the objectives agreed in your Individual Action Plan.
- Respond to feedback from lesson observations.
- Keep a written record of all support, monitoring and assessment.
- Meet each half term with your induction tutor to review progress.
- Attend the first LA conference for NQTs.

FIGURE 10.5 INDUCTION POLICY FOR TERM ONE (BUBB et al., 2002: 25)

INDUCTION PROGRAMMES

The DfES guidance says that schools must, 'provide a programme of monitoring, guidance and support which is tailored to individual needs and will help the NQT meet the requirements for satisfactory completion of induction' (DfES, 2003b: 6). This is easier said than done. Schools need to be prepared to cater for the full range of people who go under the NQT umbrella. The ease with which teachers settle into their first job will depend on:

- how well they met the QTS standards during training;
- the type and calibre of their initial teacher training and school placements;
- their motivation;
- the new context of the school and class;
- how reflective they are in completing the Career Entry and Development Profile;
- the quality of the school's induction programme.

For those who only just scraped through their teaching qualification, a deficit model of induction is just what they need – an opportunity to develop from a low base. However, schools may be grateful for the protection of the assessment system to weed out people whose flaws identified during training turn out to have a detrimental effect on pupils' learning when tested in the workplace.

At the other extreme, there are NQTs who are highly effective early on in their first year. Induction should meet their needs too. The Fast Track programme, which those who meet the rigorous entry requirements can join in the first few years of teaching, does just that. It is an accelerated development programme towards leadership positions that enables teachers to work with a particular remit in addition to class teaching. This should be a worthwhile task that moves the school on and which provides an appropriate challenge to the teacher. The entry requirements are high. People need a strong academic record and they have a computer-based and residential assessment.

Schools need to treat NQTs in a professional manner and to provide a high-quality induction from which people will benefit not only in the first year of teaching, but which will form a foundation for future professional development. Everything known about effective professional development needs to be considered carefully when drawing up induction programmes, that should be individualized but which exploit opportunities for NQTs to work together. A clear picture of the NQT's strengths and development needs at the end of their initial training course is an essential foundation stone. This picture comes from the Career Entry and Development Profile and discussions with the NQT about their experiences, strengths and needs.

In relation to planning and reviewing the NQT support programme, induction tutors need:

- full access to, and knowledge of, the school's policies and procedure, and a clear picture of how induction fits into the wider context of teachers' professional development;
- to be familiar with the standards for the award of qualified teacher status;
- a thorough understanding of the core Standards and the requirements for satisfactory completion of induction;
- an ability to work with the NQT to set, use and review appropriate development objectives;
- a knowledge of the resources available to support NQTs both within and beyond the school (DfES, 2003b).

A primary induction tutor, for instance, planned the programme from her analysis of NQTs' initial needs. She made sure she covered the important areas relating to the induction standards. Courses were identified and the NQTs met with all the curriculum co-ordinators, the SENCO and staff from outside services. The NQTs also undertook observations of experienced teachers modelling good practice, in their own school and then others. There were meetings on parents' evenings, classroom management and with the link inspector. Figures 10.6 and 10.7 give examples of an induction programme for a secondary school and an individual primary NQT programme.

A secondary induction tutor reported on working with one of her ex-NQTs for input into what makes a programme work from the NQTs' point of view. 'I want to find out for next term what they want from the course. They might have individual needs or they might collectively choose something' (Bubb et al., 2002: 74). She offers them a menu of possible activities such as classroom management, working with the industry links co-ordinator, the SENCO, the primary–secondary liaison officer.

PRE-EMPLOYMENT INDUCTION

An induction visit, before starting work, is very valuable. Some schools organize an unpaid or paid induction day or week in July for all new teachers, including those who are newly qualified. (Some also get paid over the summer holidays!) One school that paid for new staff to be put up in a local hotel felt that the expense was justified in terms of the valuable bonding that took place. It also helped to prepare new staff adequately for the start of the new year. One NQT said: 'It was good to met people properly, spend some time with the head of department, get schemes of work' (Bubb et al., 2002: 70). Another NQT said: 'We got all the information and had a couple of months to go away and mull it over and work out what it all meant' (Ibid, 2002: 70).

REGULAR MEETINGS WITH INDIVIDUAL NQTs

The majority of induction tutors in the national research project for the DfES (Totterdell et al., 2002) said that they held meetings lasting 30 minutes or more with an NQT at least fortnightly – 27 per cent held them weekly, 26 per cent fortnightly and 37 per cent half termly. However, NQTs thought that meetings were taking place less regularly than did the induction tutors. We believe there is a lesson to be learnt here about clear communication over the programme of activities, and sticking to an agreed schedule. Publishing the schedule in advance is good practice.

Most NQTs have scheduled weekly or fortnightly meetings to discuss issues and progress. The most common topics of these meetings were:

- feedback after lesson observation;
- behaviour management;
- the curriculum;
- schemes of work and lesson planning;
- school development;
- parents' evenings.

It is useful to record key points from meetings with NQTs, particularly those for the half-termly reviews. They provide a useful record and focus discussion and reflection – and provide evidence that procedures had been fully followed. Figure 10.8 is an example of notes from a half termly review meeting.

GROUP MEETINGS FOR ALL THE NQTs

Where there are several NQTs in a school, it is useful to hold group meetings on topics of interest to all. Figure 10.6 shows one secondary school's general programme, which co-ordinated with the LA's induction programme. An induction manager explains:

> One night a week for the first term we look at issues that are pertinent to school, then in the second and the third term we just do it a bit more ad hoc and look at various issues as they come up. For example, this week it's their very first parents' evening. But they meet as a group because then they can also say, 'I had a terrible time this week' and I can help them or they can help each other, which is very important.
>
> (Bubb et al., 2002: 71)

Date	Topic
Sep 5	Welcome to the school
Sep 12	NQT information session and get together
Sep 19	Settling in – what you can expect
Sep 26	Pastoral care – working with parents – LA
Oct 10	First half-term review
Oct 17	SEN and student support for learning and behaviour – LA
Nov 7	A pro-active approach to classroom management
Nov 14	Gifted and talented initiative
Dec 5	Raising the attainment of girls
Dec 12	End of term review
Jan 16	Assessment: serving learning
Jan 23	EAL/Partnership teaching – LA
Feb 13	End of half-term review
Mar 6	Literacy and numeracy strategies – LA
Mar 27	Accessing and using school data
Apr 2	End of term review
May 1	ICT across the curriculum – strategies – LA
May 8	To be decided by NQTs
May 22	End of half-term review
Jun 12	To be decided by NQTs
Jul 3	Evaluation session and congratulations social
Jul 10	End of year review: what's next?

FIGURE 10.6 AN EXAMPLE OF A SECONDARY SCHOOL GROUP INDUCTION PROGRAMME (BUBB et al., 2002: 72)

Objectives:	To write clear and informative reports for parents
	To conduct parents' evening confidently
	To plan an outing

Week beginning… Observation of NQT	NQT release time for induction	Induction tutor meetings	Staff meetings and INSET
5 June	Observe Y4. Written reflection	Plan the induction programme	Report writing formats, tips and agreed procedures
12 June Observation by induction tutor	Observe Y1 & Y2 in Beacon school, focussing on good practice. Written reflection	Feedback from observation Reading reports	Moderation of science investigations for Years 1–6.
19 June	LA induction course: professional development – being a curriculum co-ordinator		School trips and outings – health and safety procedures including risk analysis
26 June Observation by headteacher	Preliminary visit to farm to prepare for class trip – risk assessment	Feedback from observation	Mathematics – the mental and oral starter
3 July	Prepare for class trip, using school policies	Discuss planning for the outing	Mathematics – purposeful plenary ideas
10 July Final assessment meeting	Gathering evidence for the final assessment meeting	Final assessment meeting Sports Day arrangements	
17 July	Looking at new class and their records		Planning for next year

FIGURE 10.7 A PRIMARY NQT'S INDIVIDUAL INDUCTION PROGRAMME – 2ND HALF OF SUMMER TERM (BUBB et al., 2002: 73)

Professional review meeting

Date and time:

Agenda

Things that are going well

Things to improve

Progress on current objectives

Date of next meeting

FIGURE 10.8 PROFESSIONAL REVIEW MEETING

Newly qualified teachers need support of a very practical nature to deal with issues such as behaviour management. It seems to be the most common reason why teachers leave the profession in their first year and so must be addressed early on in any induction programme.

INFORMAL MEETINGS

Informal meetings are also important. Over 80 per cent of induction tutors said they met informally and often daily with their NQTs, initiated by either party and covering a wide range of immediate concerns.

WHOLE-SCHOOL INSET

Staff meetings and INSET days make a valuable contribution to NQTs' development. Figure 10.8 shows how this can be recorded alongside other more individual activities.

INDUCTION PROVISION FROM OUTSIDE THE SCHOOL

Although the school is a valuable source of specific support for NQTs, outside help brings expertise and fresh perspectives. Local education authorities, universities and private consultancy firms run NQT courses and conferences. Newly qualified teachers value the opportunity to meet with other NQTs outside their school. Peer group support plays a key role in validating NQTs' experiences and helps them to succeed in the induction year: 'It's lovely when you speak to other reception teachers and they say exactly the same things and you think, that's super, because I know it's not just my children, it's not just me' (Bubb et al., 2002: 71). Some schools involve LA induction staff or outside consultants in reviewing objectives, observing NQTs and conducting formal assessment.

CONCLUSION

Newly qualified teachers are a precious resource who have invested much time and effort into getting where they are – and the government has invested heavily in their training. They need to be treated well. They are agents of change and the profession's new generation – millions of children's teachers and the school leaders of the future. Their early experiences and the foundation that is laid in the all-important first year have important consequences, not only for the rest of the NQTs' career in teaching but also for staff retention, motivation and morale. We ignore them at our peril!

? POINTS FOR REFLECTION

Think of an example of good classroom practice that you have experienced or led. If you were describing this to a colleague what would be the criteria that you would use to persuade the colleague that this was good practice? What would need to be considered before your colleague was able to apply this practice in her own classroom?

11

Supply and Overseas-Trained Teachers

♦ Why temporary teachers need CPD

♦ Analysing needs

♦ Meeting needs

♦ Professional development – getting QTS

This chapter looks at CPD and supply/temporary teachers, and issues around their induction, as well as the intricacies of helping those who trained overseas gain qualified teacher status in England and Wales. It starts by stating why supply teachers need CPD before presenting a case for meeting their training needs. It is argued that schools should be prepared to devote some of their limited CPD funds to temporary and overseas-trained teachers (OTTs), especially as the cost of employing temporary teachers is not insignificant.

WHY TEMPORARY TEACHERS NEED CPD

England's GTC 2006 large scale survey found that supply teachers were the least likely of all to feel that their professional development needs had been met or to have participated in CPD activities in the last year. Less than half considered that their needs were satisfied to any extent. The least satisfied group of all were the supply teachers who were newly qualified. They had participated in very little professional development activity, and were anxious to have more (Hutchings et al., 2006). Temporary or supply teachers need CPD not only because they form a 'vital and substantial component of the teaching workforce' (Hallgarten, 2002) but also because:

- their teaching is not always effective;

- they cost schools a lot;

- many professional development opportunities involve supply teachers taking regular teachers' classes, so it is important that pupils are taught well;

- many people who come on supply stay with the school;

- CPD is a good way to retain supply teachers.

The cost of employing temporary teachers is a significant element in the budget of schools. The DfES Value for Money Unit calculated that schools in 2001 spent on average £43.00 per pupil from their budget on supply teachers (£50.78 for primary schools and £32.80 for secondary schools) (DfES, 2002c). One recruitment analyst estimated that schools spent more than £600 million annually on supply teachers, including both agency and non-agency teachers. If this estimate is accurate, it would amount to 3.4 per cent of the entire expenditure of maintained schools in England, 5.3 per cent of the entire expenditure on teachers and twice the amount spent by schools on ICT for teaching and learning in 2000 (Hallgarten, 2002). Data from almost 3,000 schools inspected in 2000–01 show that on average primary schools had spent a yearly 3.4 per cent of their budgets, while the average in inner London was 4.6 per cent (Ofsted, 2003d). On average, secondary schools spend 2.2 per cent of their budgets with the average of inner London schools again higher at 4.3 per cent. London schools have a greater reliance on supply teachers than England as a whole – 5.6 per cent of London's teaching workforce is made up of supply, while in England the figure is 4.6 per cent (DfES, 2002c). Naturally, these difficulties are more pronounced in some schools than others and for the worst-hit, their development has been severely inhibited by the time-consuming tasks of recruiting and inducting new teachers.

The Ofsted report, *Schools' Use of Temporary Teachers*, found that temporary teachers required to teach unfamiliar classes after only very limited briefing by the school are faced with a very challenging task. As a result, they teach a higher proportion of unsatisfactory or poor lessons than permanent teachers. Inspectors found that the quality of some pupils' work had declined in approximately half of the secondary schools surveyed, as a result of being taught by temporary teachers for a significant period of time. Impact on behaviour was also significant. In just over half the secondary schools, and about one-quarter of the primary schools, pupils' attitudes to their work and their behaviour were of a lower standard to those in lessons taught by permanent teachers (Ofsted, 2003d).

Unfamiliarity with schools and pupils and having to teach age groups and subjects for which they have not been trained are common problems for temporary teachers. A lack of understanding of the National Curriculum or examination syllabuses, along with a lack of continuity and poor briefing on teaching programmes, impact on standards.

Joe Hallgarten of IPPR believes that improvements in the quality, professionalism and retention of the permanent teaching profession need to be extended to supply teachers so that they are not seen as 'expensive babysitters'. They would also benefit from the extension of CPD opportunities. 'The increase in the use of supply teachers seems here to stay and progressive policies, based on thorough research, are necessary to take account of that change'. Professional development would help the status of supply teaching. Hallgarten (2002) suggests that this should be two-way, with supply teachers giving advice on behaviour management.

Schools appreciate the need for training supply teachers but no schools felt that they could allocate their own training budget towards supply teachers. However, long-term supply teachers were often treated as permanent staff for training purposes (DfES, 2002c). Supply teachers may end up staying longer than some of the 'permanent' staff they have worked alongside. It is not unusual for someone recruited to fill a week's absence to remain at the school for two years. The introduction of workforce remodelling has also meant schools have had to look carefully at how they provide cover during planning, preparation and assessment (PPA) time. Supply teacher usage has been re-evaluated and many schools have chosen instead to train up teaching assistants and cover managers to fill the gaps. This is a measure that has led some, most noticeably the teacher associations, to talk about the dilution of teaching as a profession.

ANALYSING NEEDS

Current practices for identifying and meeting CPD needs are not constructed in a way that takes account of supply teachers. For example, the national arrangements for performance management do not have to include supply teachers. This leaves a significant proportion of the teaching workforce untouched.

Definitions of supply teachers are confused: occasional, temporary, floating, emergency cover and others terms are used interchangeably. A whole range of different people with very different professional development needs are employed as supply teachers:

- newly qualified teachers who can't find a full-time job, or are having a taste of several schools before committing themselves;

- people with young families who are returning to teaching after a career break. They may be 'testing the water' before finding a full-time job or may just wish to have flexible part-time work;

- teachers (often very experienced and knowledgeable) who have taken early retirement;

- overseas-trained teachers – from a range of countries but mainly South Africa, Australia, New Zealand, Canada and the West Indies.

Teachers who are new to the country can provide a particular challenge to CPD co-ordinators. Their experiences are variable which leads to them having a spiky profile of strengths and weaknesses. For instance, an Australian OTT may have excellent rapport with students and adapt easily to manage challenging classroom behaviour whereas Caribbean and African teachers may be well trained in discipline and a methodical teaching style. Margaret Craig, headteacher of an inner London secondary school, considers: 'No teacher who has joined the school from overseas has been able to achieve their own potential performance level without a markedly greater degree of support than would be given to a British trained newly qualified teacher' (Craig, 2002: 29).

CASE STUDY 11.1: AN OVERSEAS-TRAINED TEACHER

Sadia Tufiq, who has an MA and an MSc in Economics, trained and taught in Pakistan. She came to England in 2002 and her story is on www.teachernet.gov.uk/teachinginengland:

The education system in England is totally different to that in Pakistan. In England it is more structured and planned. In Pakistan the teaching specialism is subject based, whereas in England it is both age and subject based. It took me a while to get used to the curriculum and the teaching practices. I was very fortunate to have supportive colleagues at work and a school committed to the career progression of its staff.

In April 2003 the school agreed to train me to obtain QTS. Before I started my training I had to contact The National Academic Recognition Information Centre (NARIC), which is an organization that compares international qualifications against UK standards. I had to take GCSE level Maths and English examinations, as recommended by NARIC, in order to be able to teach in the UK. I was given the post of an unqualified teacher to teach Reception as I chose to specialize in the 3–7 age range. The training for QTS involves a lot of hard work. There is a considerable amount of paperwork that took up extra hours, in addition to my normal teaching work.

The CPD needs of supply teachers and the amount of additional support required is difficult to predict. Certainly overseas-trained teachers' needs can be hard to gauge. Those from English-speaking countries with similar educational systems will normally need less CPD than those from other contexts. Most schools consider, however, that a disproportionate allocation of CPD and other resources needs to be put into programmes for new staff, and that this is only worthwhile if the people stay. A key to the success for all appears to relate to the adaptability of the individual.

Common needs include:

- up-to-date information about the education system as a whole;

- teachers' legal liabilities and responsibilities;

- understanding provision for pupils with special needs;

- subject knowledge – for instance the primary history curriculum has proved difficult for OTTs who do not know about life in Victorian England;

- curriculum – schemes of work need to be very detailed and easy to understand;

- pedagogical philosophy – it is easy to underestimate the importance of this;

- planning – many OTTs are not accustomed to planning in the detail required in schools, and so expectations have to be clear and monitored;

- health and safety – conforming to recognized good practice;

- teaching strategies – many of the strategies that are taken for granted in England nowadays may not be in the repertoire of supply teachers. For instance, Margaret Craig noted a tendency for OTTs to tell students answers rather than draw out knowledge from them;

- behaviour management – some supply teachers are very skilled but others have a limited range of strategies for dealing with difficult behaviour. Cultural differences need to be understood. Some pupils are 'in your face' and OTTs may interpret their forthrightness as lack of respect. Pupils become bewildered by inconsistency of expectation across classrooms;

- differentiation – meeting the needs of all, including the highest and lowest attaining pupils;

- assessment procedures – it is often only when assessments are analysed that misunderstandings and gaps in subject knowledge become apparent;

- communication problems – these include not understanding pupils' vernacular language (for example, 'wicked', 'hot'), pupils not fully understanding OTTs' accents and style of speech, and the grammatical and spelling differences of people from different countries. This is true even of English-speaking countries.

This may seem like an intimidating list but there is 'great benefit for students of attracting and retaining a culturally diverse staff, many of whom provide role models of success over difficulty' (Craig, 2002: 30).

MEETING NEEDS

KNOWLEDGE OF THE EDUCATION SYSTEM

All supply teachers but especially newly arrived overseas teachers need quick and easy access to information about the English education system and the 'big picture' of the curriculum, such as how the strategies map onto the National Curriculum. The website, www.teachernet.gov.uk/teachinginengland/, is very useful. People who have not had an introduction to the big picture of the education system find that they have gaps and misunderstandings in knowledge that are hard to address once embedded. Explanations of the many abbreviations and acronyms used in education are very useful – and not just for OTTs!

Certain concepts that are taken for granted within our education system may be problematic for those brought up in cultures with different sets of values. For instance, some OTTs find the notion of the inclusion of pupils with special needs difficult. 'Why aren't they kept down a year?' they ask. Socialization into a country's education culture can be difficult. Some schools have an induction for all new staff before they start teaching.

■ TRAINING BY SUPPLY AGENCIES

The government, the GTC and Ofsted have all called for further professional development for supply teachers, while the unions have produced a charter calling for supply teacher parity with permanent staff members. Some supply agencies offer free training on Saturdays, during holidays or as twilight sessions to ensure paid work does not have to be missed. Capita, for instance, promises:

- In-depth subject coverage, specifically designed to aid supply teachers to improve teaching and learning in the classroom.

- Trainers providing contact details to ensure post-course support is available.

- Free training support notes, reading lists and, if appropriate to the course, CD Roms containing worksheets and resources for classroom use.

- Advice and support on developing a CPD profile.

There is an Advanced Professional Certificate in Effective Supply Teaching. The Edexcel accredited course will offer supply teachers the chance to achieve a Business and Technology Education Council (BTEC) Professional Development qualification. As the qualification is funded by the Learning and Skills Council (LSC) and Hays Education Personnel, supply teachers can embark on a CPD programme without having the financial burden normally associated with it. The certificate not only enables teachers to enhance their classroom practice and education knowledge, but also allows them to produce clear evidence of continuous professional development. This portfolio can be used to support their future career, in interviews for permanent posts or as evidence for Performance Management and Threshold Assessment. The certificate takes two years to complete during which teachers will need to attend ten one-day courses, five each year.

■ INDUCTION INTO THE SCHOOL

In 2003, Her Majesty's Chief Inspector (HMCI), said:

> There is a need for careful induction of temporary teachers into schools. Supplying necessary information about pupils' abilities and curriculum targets will enable the temporary teacher to focus on providing an adequate challenge to learners. It is also essential that schools provide temporary teachers with clear and simple information that defines teaching expectations … Schools should provide the guidance and support of a senior mentor especially with regard to managing classes and maintaining discipline. (Ofsted, 2003c)

Furze Platt Senior School in Maidenhead does just this. A senior teacher is responsible for supply teachers. She gives them a folder containing key information in an accessible, concise way. Figure 11.1 shows the Contents page. The DfES suggests that schools make sure that supply teachers are clear as to what has to be done.

As we explained in Chapter 6, monitoring and evaluation are key aspects of any training and development process. Thus, it is useful for schools to get feedback on supply teachers' experiences so that systems can be refined.

Contents

Welcome
Management Structure
Internal telephone extensions
1. Cover requirements (example sheet) – loose sheets will be provided daily
2. Pupil school day
3. Useful information in brief
4. Furze Platt Senior School aims
5. Some particular expectations
6. Registers of attendance
8. Pupil code of conduct
9. School rules
10. School uniform and dress codes
11. First aid information
15. Protection of children from child abuse
16. Reward, punishment and discipline
17. Pupil record books/common marking scheme
18. Assemblies and collective worship
21. Referrals of difficulties – heads of department should always be contacted in the first instance. Please report any problems to Mrs W at the end of the day
22. Pupil incident report forms and detention forms
25. Health and safety in school
26. Fire extinguisher information
27. Fire notices and procedures
28. Fire assembly points
29. Map of the school
30. Sample form for LA supply teachers
31. Sample evaluation sheets (a loose sheet will be provided for you to complete).

FIGURE 11.1 FURZE PLATT'S FOLDER FOR SUPPLY TEACHERS

PROFESSIONAL DEVELOPMENT – GETTING QTS

One of the best forms of professional development for overseas-trained teachers is to get qualified teacher status. Overseas-trained teachers do not need to be qualified here in order to work – they can teach for four years without QTS and many are understandably resentful when they realize that the qualification from their own country does not fully qualify them to teach in England. However, people become more effective teachers in English schools through gaining QTS (Bubb, 2003d), and it gives them a focus for their professional development – and another qualification for their CV. They can also be assessed for exemption from induction at the same time as for QTS, if they have been teaching for more than two years in this country or elsewhere.

Unless people are qualified to teach in a country that is part of the European Economic Area, they will need to get QTS here in order to be classed as fully qualified – and to be paid accordingly. Headteachers usually pay them on the unqualified teacher pay scale. Those lucky enough to be on the qualified teacher pay scale (often working in schools which do not fully understand the regulations) find that they cannot apply to cross the threshold without QTS.

However, there is much more to getting QTS than being a good teacher. The initial step is to contact the Teaching Information Line (0845 6000 991) who will send a pack of useful materials and the application form. *How to Qualify as a Teacher in England* (TTA, 2005) contains all the necessary information, but needs careful reading. The steps are summarized here:

1 Check their command of spoken and written English, and their qualifications and experience.

2 Carry out police and medical checks.

3 Request OTT pack.

4 Find out whether the OTT wants to get QTS – when they have looked at the information in the pack so that they understand what is involved.

5 Make contact with someone listed in the OTT pack that can act as a designated recommending body (DRB).

6 Check eligibility – degree, English and mathematics GCSE, standard English.

7 Complete the pages on the application form that refer to the school and to the OTT's qualifications and experience and send to the DRB.

8 Collect original certificates for DRB to see.

9 The DRB will draw up a training plan so that the OTT is helped to meet the standards. The application form needs the headteacher's and chair of governors' signatures.

10 OTT applies for, takes and passes the literacy, numeracy and ICT skills tests, having practised online.

11 When the DRB is convinced that the standards are met they recommend the OTT for QTS.

12 QTS is awarded by the DfES and then they must register with the General Teaching Council.

■ ENTRY REQUIREMENTS

The first thing to check is qualifications. The TDA insists that all people applying for QTS need to provide their original – not photocopied – proof of qualifications. It would make sense for schools to insist on seeing original certificates and to check their equivalence with the National Academic Recognition Information Centre (NARIC) before contracts are signed. Many schools find out too late that employees they assumed were well qualified do not, in fact, even meet the QTS entry requirements. Degrees from other countries are not always equivalent. Beware, for instance, the New Zealand diploma in education – only the higher diploma is equivalent to a UK degree.

To be eligible to apply for QTS, OTTs need to meet the same criteria as any home-grown prospective teacher:

- A qualification equivalent to a UK degree. NARIC (01242 260 010) can provide information on the comparability of qualifications to UK qualifications.

- Secondary OTTs need to be at degree standard in the subject they are being awarded QTS in by the time they are assessed – not when they apply. However, if their degree bears little relationship to the subject they are teaching they will need to study to gain additional knowledge.

- The equivalent to a GCSE pass at grade C or above in English and mathematics and, if they were born after 1 September 1979 and wish to teach the primary age range, science. If they do not have suitable qualifications they will need to take the GCSE or an equivalence test at an ITT provider.

- To communicate clearly in spoken and written standard English. You can get a feel for this by asking for them to handwrite you a letter of application and talking to them over the phone. Look out for grammatical errors, especially tenses and plurals.

Many fall at this first hurdle, as you can imagine, but if you know these requirements problems can be avoided. They also need experience of teaching in at least two schools and at two consecutive key stages.

ASSESSMENT

Like anyone training to be a teacher nowadays, OTTs must pass the infamous online skills tests in numeracy, literacy and ICT as well as all the other QTS standards (which can be seen in Figure 9.2). To have other qualifications in these subjects is not enough. The TDA website (www.tda.gov.uk) has downloadable practice tests, links to the registration and test booking pages, and email advice lines to help with specific areas of knowledge. Once applications have been approved, OTTs are sent a registration number and can apply to take the tests at one of the designated centres. Those whose mother tongue is not English can apply for a 25 per cent extension to the time limit. They will also need evidence of knowledge and teaching experience in two consecutive key stages and in two schools.

CONCLUSION

Schools get frustrated when supply teachers, in whom they have invested a great deal of professional development time and money, leave. This issue is an important one to address but training and development are vital if the whole school workforce is to be more effective. It is also a significant factor in the retention of staff as we shall see in the next chapter which focuses on teachers in the first five years of their career.

12

Early Professional Development

- ◆ Why is it important?
- ◆ Learning from the EPD pilots
- ◆ EPD activities
- ◆ Chartered London Teacher status
- ◆ Threshold assessment
- ◆ Advanced skills teachers

This chapter focuses attention on teachers in their first five years of teaching (29 per cent of teachers nationally), traditionally a time when many feel a little lost and neglected after the intensity of the training and induction years. Early professional development (EPD) is a term which because of the EPD pilots, which had earmarked government funding, has become associated with the second and third years of a teacher's career. However, our use of 'early' professional development is broader, covering the first four years after induction. After considering why EPD is important we will look at the lessons learned from the EPD pilots. Then we will examine a scheme for teachers in London, Chartered London Teacher status, which although open to all teachers has most relevance for those in their first five years. Finally we will consider the CPD implications of people wishing to cross the threshold and those who decide to apply to be advanced skills teachers.

WHY IS IT IMPORTANT?

So why do teachers in their first five years need help with their professional development? Ofsted's reports (2003c) say that because the quality of training has improved schools now have the best NQTs ever. Excellent! However, not all who train end up working as teachers. As Table 12.1 shows, only 87 per cent of those who are on a training course get QTS and of those only 81 per cent are teaching within six months – and this percentage includes those working abroad, in the independent sector and on supply.

But the picture gets worse. Smithers and Robinson's research (2003) into why teachers leave the profession found that it is the very newest teachers who are leaving. Only about 70 per cent of teachers stay in the profession for more than five years. So of the 100 people who start a PGCE primary course, only 49 are teaching after five years. What a waste!

Teachers have often felt a little at sea in the years immediately after induction. They get lots of attention (or should do) when training and during induction, and then it suddenly stops. They are meant to be experienced and know what they are doing, and no longer have allowances made for them. But in reality learning to teach confidently takes years so having early professional development can be a bit like being able to drive with P plates on – it is a safety net. Teachers also feel that they are in CPD limbo: neither entitled to NQT courses nor ready for leadership and management type development. They are no longer observed regularly and do not get stimulated. As a result some teachers go off the boil. A typical pattern emerges: if they do not get a tonic they do not teach so well, then they do not enjoy the job so much, so they leave.

TABLE 12.1 NUMBERS AND PERCENTAGES OF PEOPLE GAINING QTS AND IN EMPLOYMENT IN TEACHING WITHIN SIX MONTHS 2004–05 (www.dataprovision.tda.gov.uk)

PHASE AND LEVEL OF TRAINING		NUMBER OF FINAL YEAR TRAINEES	TRAINEES AWARDED QTS (INCL. EBR)		TRAINEES AWARDED QTS IN TEACHING EMPLOYMENT (EXCL. EBR)	
		(a)	(b)	as a % of (a)	%	
Primary	**Total**	**17127**	**15259**	**89%**	**9920**	**78%**
	Undergrad	5338	4686	88%	3569	78%
	Postgrad	11789	10573	90%	6351	78%
Secondary	**Total**	**20717**	**17865**	**86%**	**11578**	**83%**
	Undergrad	868	714	82%	539	83%
	Postgrad	19849	17151	86%	11039	83%
Key stage 2/3	**Total**	**730**	**626**	**86%**	**465**	**81%**
	Undergrad	182	161	88%	136	84%
	Postgrad	548	465	85%	329	79%
ITT Total		**38574**	**33750**	**87%**	**21963**	**81%**

Although many people have long seen the need for giving teachers special support after induction, it is fairly new as a formal notion. It was first mentioned in England's *Learning and Teaching: A Strategy for Professional Development* (DfEE, 2001a). However, Northern Ireland has recognized it for some time and in Wales induction is seen as the first year of a three-year long EPD, but in Scotland there is no named period of EPD as such.

The Ofsted report (2003b) on teachers' early professional development found little differentiation in the CPD offered to second- and third-year teachers in at least half of the schools inspected, so that their particular needs remained unrecognized and, consequently, were not addressed. In the schools where EPD was effective, Ofsted found a raft of benefits including stronger teaching, a clear contribution of second- and third-year teachers to the work of their colleagues, and more commitment to a career in teaching. The NFER evaluation (Moor et al., 2005) of the EPD pilots found that teachers reported that they had more confidence, had implemented new teaching strategies, were able to pursue career paths and were happier in their job.

LEARNING FROM THE EPD PILOTS

In response to the sorts of concerns above, the DfES and GTC (England) set up a pilot project of early professional development for teachers in their second and third years of teaching. The pilot programmes ran from 2001 to 2004 in 12 LAs at a cost of £25 million. There was to be a national roll-out of funds for EPD but that has been cancelled due to the funding crisis of 2003. England is now lagging behind its neighbours. Northern Ireland has recognized teachers' need for help in second and third years for some time and in Wales induction is seen as the first year of a three-year long EPD. Carol Adams of England's GTC speaks for many in airing her disappointment at the government's u-turn when she said, 'Today's new teachers are the education leaders of the future and we should be prepared to invest long-term in the early stages of their careers'.

The DfES (2002b) aims for teachers involved in EPD were:

- to have made significant progress towards the threshold standards – increasing their pedagogical skills and their ability to apply them effectively to a wide range of children and a wider range of situations;
- to have strengthened their ability to learn from the knowledge base in schools, professional networks, research and enquiry;

- to have increased the ability to contribute, as professionals, to immediate colleagues, their school and the wider education community;

- to be more strongly committed to teaching as a career.

The NFER evaluation considered the pilot successful and analysed key factors. Classroom observations and being mentored by an experienced colleague were rated highly by second-year teachers. Teachers were also more positive if they had chosen their mentor and their own training programme. The more involvement teachers had in selecting their EPD programme, the more likely they were to feel their professional development needs had been met, and record higher ratings for the effects of EPD on their teaching practice and professional attitudes.

In Wakefield, one of the pilot LAs, teachers appreciated having a bursary to support professional development. They emphasized the importance of having quality time with a mentor to discuss professional and career development because this 'focuses on asking the right questions about what I need to do' (Thompson, 2002: 24). They liked the opportunity to network with teachers from other schools but overall the real benefit was that professional development was a clear priority.

However Minnis (2003) in her small-scale research into EPD in one secondary school in another pilot LA, considered that only two teachers out of the group of ten made 'significant' progress towards threshold standards because their EPD was linked to performance management targets. Because the mentoring system broke down, the remaining eight teachers did activities that bore little relationship to what they needed to get better at in the classroom. Some spent their funds on computers, printers and software which may have made their job easier but did not really make them better teachers. Others made visits or went on courses to develop extracurricular activities such as school trips and clubs. This made them happier but did not make them any better at or more committed to teaching.

EPD ACTIVITIES

Teachers have done a wide range of things with their EPD funds. Teachers were encouraged to 'be creative' with their EPD funding, and some have considered career moves to alternative forms of educational provision as a result. One such example is a drama teacher who attended a course on drama and movement therapy with her third-year money, and is now considering specializing in drama therapy in education, a long-term goal:

> The EPD fund gave me an opportunity to get this plan into action and let me know that I hadn't been forgotten. My needs are as important as the students' but we often forget this as teachers. When I feel creative and inspired, as I certainly did after this course, it has an effect on students and colleagues. (*TES*, 2003: 8)

Someone posted this on the *TES* staffroom website:

> I'm hoping to spend mine on a MPhil programme with the aim of getting out of the classroom and developing a career in research and uni work. Not sure if this is realistic (and it's the opposite of what the government have set the scheme up for) but I can't go on as I am. (www.tes.co.uk)

One mainstream secondary school teacher wanted to work with children with emotional and behavioural problems. So she went on behaviour management courses, visited another school's unit, studied inner-city schools in New York state, and now wants to shadow a youth offending team and visit local special schools. It all helped prepare her for her current post, as second in charge of her school's social inclusion unit.

Someone else wanted to work on pastoral issues and is now acting head of Year 9. Her EPD fund went on training, working with a head of year, buying resources and developing a project on attendance. She was delighted: 'I have friends teaching in other boroughs who feel they haven't progressed as they would have liked to, yet I have gone through the roof. It's motivated me because I was able to get extra training in areas I was interested in' (*TES*, 2003).

There also used to be 'professional bursaries' for teachers in their fourth and fifth years. These were worth £500 per year, which is not a lot but some people have used these very well. Some teachers spent the money on professional development directly related to their current post and teaching. Others put it towards the fees for a higher degree, to further their own subject knowledge or to explore places to take pupils on educational visits. Others did things that seem a little self-indulgent such as the English teacher who is buying guitar lessons on the grounds that it is a good stress buster and that he will run a guitar club.

Overall, the most successful EPD activities have had the same constituents as any effective form of CPD (see Chapter 2). They have taken into account preferred learning styles, had a great deal of autonomy and addressed areas that have been carefully considered with someone in a mentoring role. However, teachers need to be accountable for their EPD activities to ensure that authentic teacher development impacts on pupils' learning. The use of CPD portfolios during EPD is a basis for establishing teachers' adoption of a philosophy of career-long learning – and it also helps teachers prepare for passing the threshold and career development.

There are several ways for teachers to gain 'chartered' status. Scotland's Chartered Teacher (McMahon and Forde, 2005) involves study at Master's level and there are subject qualifications such as the Chartered Science Teacher. The largest scheme is Chartered London Teacher status, and it is to this that we shall now turn.

CHARTERED LONDON TEACHER STATUS

Chartered London Teacher (CLT) status was set up in September 2004 by London Challenge to recognize and reward the skills and expertise of teachers who work to raise the achievements of all pupils. More than one in five pupils in London are taught by someone with less than three years' experience so working towards CLT can be particularly beneficial to those in the early stages of their career. As well as having the prestige of being a Chartered London Teacher, when people achieve the award they receive Fellowship of the College of Teachers and a one off payment of £1,000 from their school budget. As London schools commissioner Tim Brighouse says: 'Chartered London Teacher status creates the habits of intellectual curiosity and learning which combine to energise teachers and the schools they work in' (DfES, 2006c).

Teacher recruitment, retention, mobility, experience and quality are considerable challenges. The DfES School Workforce Statistics (DfES, 2007a) show that teachers in London have less teaching experience than those in England as a whole: a fifth of inner London teachers have less than three years' and 37 per cent have less than six years' service (cf 15 per cent and 29 per cent of teachers in England). Inner London has a young teaching workforce with nearly half of teachers under 40, compared to England as a whole (42 per cent). London schools have a higher teacher vacancy rate (1.2 per cent) than the rest of the country (0.6 per cent). There are higher turnover and wastage rates for teachers in London (23 per cent and 12 per cent respectively) than England (19 per cent and 10 per cent). Nearly 40 per cent of teachers leaving schools in London are aged under 30 – much higher than the 25 per cent leaving nationally. There are 63,000 (full-time equivalent) teachers in London, an increase of 11 per cent since 1997 compared to 8.1 per cent in England (ibid.). Communicating with them is a challenge as they work in over 2,600 schools organized into 33 different local authorities without any overarching London body to unite them (Bubb and Porritt, 2006).

Managing the CLT process should fit in with day-to-day work, self-evaluation, performance management and professional development, as the guidance material shows (DfES, 2007b). To help, a virtual learning environment has been set up at www.lcll.org.uk. It's easy to slot working towards the CLT standards (Figure 12.2) into the school's performance management systems and professional development opportunities. The CLT development cycle is illustrated in Figure 12.1. Evidence of how someone is doing could include:

- Planning – short, medium and long term, that shows how different pupils' needs are met and which draw on the range of resources and experiences in London.

- Monitoring of teaching through observation, work sampling, etc.

- Pupil targets, assessments, reports and records.

- Analysis of relevant data.

- Observations of others.

- Communication with parents.

- Records/certificates of qualifications and professional development activities.

- Notes made from visits to schools and other organizations.

- Contributions to relevant associations, committees, networks and working groups.

- Leadership responsibilities and collaboration.

- Mentoring, coaching and leading professional development activities.

- Knowledge of communities, cultures and sub-cultures.

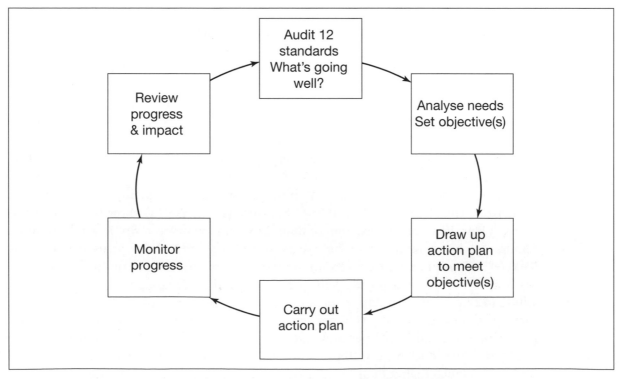

FIGURE 12.1 THE CHARTERED LONDON TEACHER DEVELOPMENT CYCLE (DfES, 2007b)

Pedagogy and pupil learning

1 Create and manage a classroom environment to ensure a secure and supportive achievement culture and behaviour strategy to meet the needs of London's diverse and mobile pupil population.

2 Apply a wide range of teaching and learning strategies to reduce individual barriers to learning and to meet the variety of pupil needs in London.

3 Develop and implement inclusive practices in a range of learning settings appropriate to the diversity of pupils in London and the complexity of their personal learning, including support for Special Education Needs, to raise pupils' achievements.

4 Progress partnerships within and beyond the classroom with support staff, teachers, other professionals, agencies and community resources, to promote pupils' achievements, learning, development and wellbeing.

5 Analyse and use relevant data to inform and promote the highest possible aspirations for pupils and to target expectations and actions to raise pupil achievements.

Subject, specialism and/or phase knowledge

6 Demonstrate on-going development and application of subject, specialism and/or phase knowledge and expertise, drawing on opportunities and resources in London to enrich the learning experience.

7 Identify and use the knowledge and experiences that pupils, their families and other communities bring from outside the school to enrich curriculum development and teaching practices.

Whole school issues

8 Contribute to the development and application of whole school policies and activities, to extend opportunities for pupil and school achievements in London.

9 Promote and apply shared professional learning and other forms of support and development for teachers to learn and work together, taking account of teacher mobility, to strengthen collective knowledge and expertise across teachers in London.

Diversity, communities and cultures

10 Build on, extend and apply knowledge of the range of communities, cultures and sub-cultures in London, to inform and promote individual pupils learning.

11 Promote and implement policies and practices that encourage mutual tolerance and respect for diversity, challenge discrimination and widen pupils' understanding of their contribution to society.

12 Demonstrate a capacity to deal constructively and sensitively with conflicting community and cultural values in classrooms and schools.

FIGURE 12.2 CHARTERED LONDON TEACHER STANDARDS (DfES, 2007b)

When the areas for development have been analysed and prioritized, objectives can be set. There are many professional development opportunities that would help teachers meet the standards (see Chapter 5).

Teachers also need to demonstrate *professional reflection*. People reflect on teaching and learning all the time but what is required for CLT is a reflection on a specific activity or piece of work, which:

- is grounded in day-to-day practice, addressing something that needs to be improved or analyses why something successful works well;

- relates to at least one CLT standard;

- is shared as widely as is relevant within and across schools, so that other people benefit;

- makes a difference, in that it contributes to improved teaching and learning.

It shouldn't be onerous because it should be based on something teachers are doing anyway, such as reviewing how well a policy is working in practice or investigating how to integrate new arrivals.

Teachers will be able to make the Chartered London Teacher status submission through the school's performance management system at one point in the year, when they:

- have taught in London state schools for four years;
- are on the upper, AST, excellent teacher or leadership pay scales (not the main pay scale);
- have completed the two year minimum CLT registration period;
- meet the 12 CLT standards (and have completed a professional reflection).

Headteachers are ultimately responsible for deciding who gets CLT status, but performance reviewers will have a big part to play. With more than 38,900 teachers registered on the scheme and hundreds of people now having the status, Chartered London Teacher provides recognition for the capital's teachers and has the potential to change the culture of teaching and shape development in London.

THRESHOLD ASSESSMENT

Early professional development is meant to help teachers make progress towards the threshold standards and the upper pay scale. The threshold is the next assessable point after induction. Crossing the threshold is not an automatic process. To be eligible people must have qualified teacher status, be working in a state school and be at the top of the main pay scale.

Keeping the threshold standards in mind during one's career and maintaining a professional portfolio will make this process easier. Teachers are responsible for applying for threshold assessment. This involves summarizing evidence – in the form of concrete examples from day-to-day work – to show that they have worked at broadly the standards (TDA, 2007) indicated over the last two to three years. Filling in forms is something that most people hate and CPD co-ordinators may wish to organize some support for them. Kevan Bleach, assistant head at Sneyd School in Wolverhampton, runs sessions where he outlines the process, shows them exemplars and talks through different approaches that others have taken in completing the forms.

Headteachers make the assessment because they have a legal and professional responsibility for evaluating the standards of teaching and learning in the school and ensuring that proper standards of professional performance are established and maintained. However, people who manage staff have to assist the head to carry out threshold assessments.

ADVANCED SKILLS TEACHERS

If people want to stay in the classroom, becoming an advanced skills teacher is a financially viable alternative to taking the promotion route into management. Advanced Skills Teachers (ASTs) have their own pay spine. Each AST is paid within a five point range which is based primarily on the nature of the work to be undertaken, the scale of the challenges to be tackled, the professional competencies required and any other recruitment considerations. ASTs receive an increase when the pay scales are uprated and may also be awarded one or two pay points each September for high quality performance.

The government wants 3–5 per cent of the teaching workforce to be ASTs. The main duty of ASTs is to be an excellent teacher in their own school for four days a week. For one day a week they have to share their good practice with other teachers and help other people's professional development – not only in their own schools but also in others (see Chapter 2). They offer an area of specialism which could be a subject (for example, music, PE, science), age phase (for example, Early Years) or both (for example, literacy in Key Stage 1). Some ASTs have been appointed to support initial teacher training.

If there is a very strong teacher on the staff they can apply to become an AST when they are still on the main pay scale. There is no minimum period of time that teachers have to have worked before they can apply to be an AST, and they do not have to have passed the threshold. However, the application form is gruelling and the applicant has to provide supporting evidence under each of the standards on the lengthy application.

In most cases, strong teachers will have plenty of evidence for most of the standards. Ones such as

> Possess the analytical, interpersonal and organizational skills necessary to work effectively with staff and leadership teams beyond their own school.

may be harder to find evidence for without the opportunity to provide clear feedback, good support and sound advice to others; and help others evaluate the impact of their teaching on raising pupils' achievements. This is where CPD co-ordinators can deploy prospective ASTs to mutual advantage. They will need training and practice in these skills.

Headteachers have to agree to the application and verify each standard, perhaps with other people's advice. If the application meets the requirements, an assessor spends a day in school watching the person teach, interviewing them, pupils and others who know their work, and looking at evidence of how the standards are met.

In the next chapter we look at an alternative to becoming an advanced skills teacher: becoming a middle manager or middle leader. We do not know very much about the career plans of ASTs but it does appear that many do end up in leadership positions and that being an AST is an excellent preparation for leadership and management roles because it involves working with fellow professionals either within school (in-reach) or outside (outreach).

Emergent Leaders and Middle Managers

◆ Role definitions

◆ Training and development needs

◆ Training programmes

This chapter looks at the training and development needs of emergent leaders, subject leaders and middle managers, and at the various ways in which they can be met. After outlining the key role that middle managers can play in teaching and learning, it draws on data to examine training and development needs. Reference is also made to the range of training programmes currently available, including the course for middle leaders from the National College for School Leadership, entitled 'Leading from the Middle'.

Middle managers, of which there are said to be around 220,000 in English schools (NCSL, 2003a), have a variety of names or labels in schools and colleges: subject leaders, heads of department, year heads, pastoral heads, curriculum co-ordinators, Key Stage managers, special educational needs co-ordinators, heads of ICT or literacy, or numeracy, to name a few. Middle managers – or middle leaders as they are increasingly called – have long been recognized as crucial to a school's success but it is only comparatively recently that their importance has attracted the attention of policy makers and educational researchers, particularly those interested in school effectiveness and school improvement. This is perhaps surprising given that middle managers/leaders are uniquely placed to have a major impact on a school and the quality of its teaching and learning.

Middle managers have long been seen as 'kingpins', 'the boiler house' or 'the hub of the school'. The NCSL has stated that effective middle leaders are at 'the heart of the matter' representing 'a critical base of knowledge and expertise for schools' noting that heads 'talk about them as "the engine room of change" and a repository of expert, up-to-date knowledge capable of transforming and energising learning and teaching' (NCSL, 2003b: 1).

One of the first activities of the NCSL when it was established in November 2000 was to design and publish a leadership development framework that consisted of five stages of leadership development. The first stage, that of *emergent leadership*, was when 'a teacher is beginning to take on management and leadership responsibilities and perhaps forms an aspiration to become a headteacher' (NCSL, 2001: 7). It is the management training and leadership development needs of emerging and established middle leaders/managers that are the main focus of this chapter. But it is first necessary to consider briefly the nature of the role in both primary and secondary schools.

ROLE DEFINITIONS

The definition of middle management is problematic. All teachers are managers in that they are responsible for the management of pupils and resources, and the management of the learning process. Increasingly teachers manage support staff too, but only some have responsibility for the work of other teachers – the key factor in any definition of management. Management is often defined as the achievement of organizational aims and goals through the collaborative efforts of groups of people. Management, at senior or middle management level, is about getting things done by working with and through other people and it is likely to consist of a combination of activities such as planning, organizing, resourcing, controlling, monitoring and evaluating. It will also involve leading.

Middle managers are now seen as having a key leadership role – as *middle leaders*. It is not the case that previously leadership was unimportant – it has always been necessary to lead a subject or a department or a year group – rather it is more a matter of emphasis. The importance of leadership is reflected in the standards for subject leaders that were published in 1998, as well as the teacher standards framework (TDA, 2007). The dominant discourse is about leadership not management, and distributed or shared leadership where anyone in an organization can function as a leader outside their formal position as such.

Middle managers have always had a pivotal role in passing ideas and information 'up the line' to organizational leaders. Senior managers rely heavily on middle managers to keep them informed of what is going on at the 'chalk face' and to alert them to problems and opportunities. The ability to take on a wider organizational perspective, and not be restricted to a departmental or sectional viewpoint, is highly valued and encouraged by senior staff. Middle leaders as key brokers within organizations are, therefore, potential agents of change through their ability to control and influence the flow of information.

NATIONAL STANDARDS FOR SUBJECT LEADERS

Various models or conceptualizations of middle managers' roles have been developed over the years, both for primary (e.g. West, 1995) and secondary schools (e.g. Earley and Fletcher-Campbell, 1992) but these have been superseded by the 'subject leader' standards developed by the (then) Teacher Training Agency and published in 1998 (TTA, 1998). They have not been updated and do not have the statutory status of the 2007 teacher standards but are still useful.

The TTA defines the core purpose for subject leadership as: 'to provide professional leadership and management for a subject to secure high quality teaching, effective use of resources, and improved standards of learning achievement for all pupils' (TTA, 1998: 4). It goes on to state that:

> A subject leader provides leadership and direction for the subject and ensures that it is managed and organised to meet the aims and objectives of the school and the subject. While the headteacher and governors carry overall responsibility for school improvement, a subject leader has responsibility for securing high standards of teaching and learning in their subject as well as playing a major role in the development of school policy and practice. Throughout their work, a subject leader ensures that practices improve the quality of education provided, meet the needs and aspirations of all pupils, and raise standards of achievement in the school. (TTA, 1998: 4)

Most importantly, it is assumed that subject leaders work within a school-wide context, are able to identify subject needs but recognize these have to be weighed against the overall needs of the school.

The national standards discuss the key outcomes of subject leadership and the *professional knowledge and understanding* that subject leaders should possess (e.g. the characteristics of expert teaching in the subject; relevant research and inspection evidence; the use of comparative data to establish benchmarks and set targets; health and safety requirements; the relationship of the subject to the curriculum as a whole; school governance). There are four broad categories of *skills and attributes* which subject leaders should possess:

- leadership skills, attributes and professional competence: the ability to lead and manage people to work towards common goals;

- decision-making skills: the ability to solve problems and make decisions;

- communication skills: the ability to make points clearly and understand the views of others;

- self-management: the ability to plan time effectively and to organize oneself well.

Attributes listed as required for the successful enactment of subject leadership include: personal presence, adaptability, energy and perseverance, self-confidence, enthusiasm, intellectual ability, reliability and integrity and commitment.

The key areas of subject leadership and management are set out in detail under the four headings of:

- *Strategic direction and development of the subject* (within the context of the school's aims and policies, subject leaders develop and implement subject policies, plans, targets and practices);

- *Teaching and learning* (subject leaders secure and sustain effective teaching of the subject, evaluate the quality of teaching and standards of pupils' achievements and set targets for improvement);

- *Leading and managing staff* (subject leaders provide to all those with involvement in the teaching or support of the subject, the support, challenge, information and development necessary to sustain motivation and secure improvement in teaching);

- *Efficient and effective deployment of staff and resources* (subject leaders identify appropriate resources for the subject and ensure that they are used efficiently, effectively and safely) (TTA, 1998: 9).

Although the national standards are useful, they cannot cater for all those who fulfil a subject leadership role because they are generic and are pitched at Rolls-Royce level. Yet, there are crucial differences as to what can be expected from someone who is in charge of 15 specialist teachers and a primary school teacher (with no TLR responsibility) in their second year in the profession and responsible for a subject in which they have limited knowledge throughout the school.

IMPROVING TEACHING AND LEARNING

A key aspect of the role is how can middle leaders influence and evaluate effective teaching and learning outcomes. Turner (1996) outlined several ways in which department heads influence teaching and learning outcomes. These included discussion of department vision and how to achieve it; encouragement of teamwork; informal discussions; use of meetings to plan curriculum, share good practice, discuss marking policy and teaching methods used; engage in staff development; feedback on performance; direct classroom observation and classroom appraisal.

Monitoring performance, feedback and classroom observation is generally recognized as problematic. Turner (2003: 14–15) suggests that the reasons for this 'reluctance' might be the desire not to damage team morale or upset relationships amongst colleagues or because of the fear that observational evidence might be used at a later stage in any formal procedure relating to decisions about pay or performance. It may also be due to lack of time to engage in such activities as it is known that middle managers are given little non-contact time to devote to the management and leadership responsibilities of their respective areas.

But attitudes towards monitoring and evaluation of colleagues are changing. This has been brought about by a number of factors, most significantly external school inspection (Ferguson et al., 2000), but performance management and the drive to raise standards (school improvement) have also had a role to play. Wise (2001) highlights the tensions or internal role conflict that this can cause to subject leaders who find themselves caught between a strong expectation from senior staff that monitoring of teaching and learning will take place and team members who may feel uncomfortable about their teaching being monitored by their line manager. Much will depend on the culture of the department and the school and the extent to which observation is mutual and seen as being primarily for *developmental* purposes and not for accountability (Bubb, 2005a).

The National College for School Leadership has published a practical guide to what middle leaders can do to improve learning in secondary schools (NCSL, 2003b). It states that the guide, entitled *The Heart of the Matter*, 'confirms a shift of role from managers of resources to leaders of people' and sets out to:

- illuminate the relationship between effective middle leadership and school improvement;
- recognize the practical ways in which schools can harness the potential of middle leaders and develop their capacity to work as a team;
- explore how senior leaders can provide support and enable middle leaders to be as good as they can be (ibid.: 1).

The message of the guide is that schools need clarity, consensus and senior staff support 'in identifying what makes a difference in building schools' capacity to improve learning for all' (ibid.: 1). It asks how can middle leaders be enabled to have maximum impact on the quality of learning in schools? The practical guide sets out eight areas in which middle and senior leaders can make a difference to learning. These are:

- a focus on learning and teaching;
- generate positive relationships;
- provide a clear vision and high expectations;
- improve the environment;
- provide time and opportunities for collaboration;
- distribute leadership: build teams;
- engage the community;
- evaluate and innovate.

For each area a list is provided of what middle leaders can do and how senior leaders can support and enable them to work effectively.

TRAINING AND DEVELOPMENT NEEDS

It is generally acknowledged that over the years the training and development needs of middle managers and middle leaders have not been thoroughly addressed. The whole area of preparation, training and professional development of middle managers and emergent leaders was the subject of the 2002 DfES baseline study of school leadership (Earley et al., 2002) and its follow-up in 2005 (Stevens et al., 2005). Middle leaders were asked (using a four-point adequacy of preparation scale) to indicate how well prepared professionally they were prior to taking up their current position. The results of the two questionnaire surveys are shown in Table 13.1.

In 2002 over one-fifth (22 per cent) reported being 'very prepared', whilst one in ten regarded themselves as 'not prepared at all'. The 2005 follow-up found fewer middle managers felt very prepared (13 per cent) or not prepared at all (5 per cent) but in broad terms the figures indicate that slightly more middle managers felt better prepared (74 per cent) in 2005 than they did in 2002 (69 per cent) and fewer less prepared (25 per cent cf 31 per cent) (Earley et al., 2002; Stevens et al., 2005).

In 2002 middle managers were also asked whether in their view they had received a sufficient amount of leadership and management training before taking on their current role. Fifteen per cent of the sample perceived that training as 'quite sufficient', whilst 20 per cent regarded it as 'not at all sufficient'. A significant percentage of the sample (59 per cent) was less than happy with the amount of leadership and management training they had received before taking on their current role. The 2005 study asked middle managers how well prepared 'in reality' they were for their new leadership post and about one-quarter (26 per cent) stated they were not well prepared, whilst 12 per cent stated they were very well prepared (Stevens et al., 2005: 69). The national programme 'Leading from the Middle' (discussed later) is an attempt to meet what is a clear training need.

In the 2002 baseline study, middle managers were asked to note in which areas of the subject leader standards they would welcome further or new training and development opportunities. The results, shown in Table 13.2, indicate that with the exception of 'decision-making' and 'communication' skills, approximately one-half of the sample of middle managers would welcome further training and development opportunities in all of the specified areas. Leading and managing staff was the key area mentioned most frequently (59 per cent), with leadership skills (55 per cent) and self-management (55 per cent) the second highest scorers.

Significant on-the-job or in-school experiences were noted with many middle managers making reference to working with others (good and poor role models), including a good head; promotion or taking up a management role; and working in a good school; everyday work experience and school development planning or involvement in whole-school initiatives. When presented with a list of possible sources of ideas and inspiration, middle managers most frequently referred to other school leaders (76 per cent), headteachers (52 per cent), books and other publications (49 per cent), senior management teams (44 per cent) and local authorities (40 per cent). Clearly, their work experiences were crucial in shaping their thinking and their practice.

What professional development activities do middle leaders undertake? Table 13.3 shows that over the past three years nearly two-thirds (63 per cent) were trained by local authorities, about half (48 per cent) had training from consultants, 28 per cent mentoring from headteachers and about one in five (19 per cent) had training from HEIs, where they were most likely undertaking higher degrees. The 2005 survey found that just 15 per cent of middle managers/leaders had made use of development opportunities provided by the NCSL.

TABLE 13.1 PERCEPTIONS OF PREPARATION FOR MIDDLE MANAGEMENT

	Very prepared (1) (%)	(2) (%)	(3) (%)	Not prepared at all (4) (%)
Middle managers				
2002 (n = 229)	22	47	21	10
2005 (n = 398)	13	61	20	5
Source: Earley et al., 2002 and Stevens et al., 2005				

TABLE 13.2 FURTHER TRAINING OPPORTUNITIES WITH REFERENCE TO THE NATIONAL STANDARDS FOR SUBJECT LEADERS (N = 233)

Key area	% of sample
Strategic direction and development of the subject (within the context of the school's aims and policies, subject leaders develop and implement subject policies, plans, targets and practices)	48
Teaching and learning (subject leaders secure and sustain effective teaching of the subject, evaluate the quality of teaching and standards of pupils' achievements and set targets for improvement)	51
Leading and managing staff (subject leaders provide to all those with involvement in the teaching or support of the subject, the support, challenge, information and development necessary to sustain motivation and secure improvement in teaching)	59
Efficient and effective deployment of staff and resources (subject leaders identify appropriate resources for the subject and ensure that they are used efficiently, effectively and safely)	45

Key skills and attributes	% of sample
Leadership skills – the ability to lead and manage people to work towards common goals	55
Decision-making skills – the ability to solve problems and make decisions	39
Communication skills – the ability to make points clearly and understand the views of others	33
Self-management – the ability to plan time effectively and to organize oneself well	55

Source: Earley et al., 2002

TABLE 13.3 DEVELOPMENT OPPORTUNITIES PARTICIPATED IN, IN YOUR ROLE AS A SCHOOL LEADER DURING THE PAST THREE YEARS

n = 389	% of sample
Training from local authorities	63
Mentoring from a headteacher	28
Training from education consultants	48
Development offered by NCSL	15
Training from HEIs	19
Mentoring from business or other mentors	4
Mentoring by one of your governors	2
None of these	13

Source: Adapted from Stevens et al., 2005: 78

TRAINING PROGRAMMES

What then might an effective training programme for subject leaders and middle managers look like? Research into the current state of school leadership for the DfES (Earley et al., 2002) found that some training providers considered that middle managers did not need an overly prescriptive training and development framework, but rather one that invited the providers to respond with programmes that helped build a scaffold for future development. Several felt it would be important to accredit such training and development, perhaps in partnership with a higher education institution, as part of a postgraduate qualification. Training providers proposed the development of a spiral curriculum framework in which similar concepts were introduced, but at different levels, and developed to different degrees of complexity and depth. It was suggested that people should be identified early on in their careers and nurtured for the role in a 'fast track' kind of way.

An overriding theme emerging was the urgent need to see put in place a map of leadership development ensuring coherence, continuity, some common themes, and some choice at different stages. There was strong support for regional provision and a modular approach, beginning from early in the teacher's career. Middle managers and subject leaders, it was felt, would benefit from this approach with those who aspired to head-ship being better prepared for the position.

Effective training programmes for subject leaders have the following features:

- an emphasis on collaboration;
- involvement and support of senior management;
- flexible and intermittent training points;
- external agency;
- context related planning and development;
- necessity of enquiry and reflection;
- use of research to inform practice;
- evaluation and data analysis (Busher and Harris with Wise, 2000).

A growing number of university staff have worked as consultants with individual schools and helped them to devise their own in-house management development programmes for emergent leaders, middle managers and others who perhaps have aspirations to become a deputy or assistant headteacher (for example, Day, 2003).

The NCSL's 'Leading from the Middle' (LftM) training programme, which came fully on-stream in September 2003, is likely to have had a considerable impact with many authorities and schools choosing to re-evaluate their own provision for subject leaders in its light. It will be recalled (see Table 13.3) that by 2005, 15 per cent of middle leaders were making use of development opportunities provided by the College and many of these were likely to be LftM.

'LEADING FROM THE MIDDLE'

'Leading from the Middle' is an NCSL leadership development or learning programme designed for subject leaders from all school phases. The LftM programme was designed to take account of how adults best learn and what constitutes effective professional development. The programme represents a central commitment to distributed leadership – 'devolving responsibilities for leadership away from the head and involving leaders at many levels in the organisation' (NCSL, 2003a: 2) – and is intended to give middle leaders a broader understanding of the school context which will help them to combine teaching and management responsibilities with a more strategic role. The programme encourages 'middle leaders to work with and through other people, equipping them to manage change and creating a culture of leadership designed to bring about improvements in pupil learning' (NCSL, 2003a: 2).

The purpose of the 'learning' programme is to develop participants' leadership expertise and capability by:

- increasing their confidence and competence in collaborative leadership and management;
- equipping them with the knowledge and understanding, skills and attributes for learning-centred leadership within a school setting;
- enabling them to find, make and take their role in leading the transformational agenda.

A unique aspect of the programme is the requirement for teams rather than individuals to take part. School teams consisting of two or three subject leaders and a senior leader in a coaching role enrol on the programme. 'Leading from the Middle' takes place over three terms and is delivered at a number of regional centres. The programme employs what NCSL calls a 'blended' learning technique that combines face-to-face and online learning. The elements of the programme include a virtual school providing a simulation of leadership-centred learning activities; learning-centred leadership materials provided online, which incorporate the knowledge, understanding, skills and attributes outlined in the National Standards for Subject Leaders; online communities; face-to-face tutoring and leadership coaching. It also includes a school leadership project that is at the heart of the learning model (NCSL, 2003a).

It is an exciting development and a central plank of the College's efforts to develop the leaders of English schools. It is hoped that some of the participants will wish eventually to take up more senior leadership positions in our schools. Both national and local evaluations of the programme have pointed to the benefits of LftM, particularly the in-school coaching component and the development of a coaching and mentoring school culture (Earley and Weindling et al., 2005; Simpkins, 2006).

More recently the NCSL has introduced a course entitled 'Leadership Pathways' which is aimed at experienced or established middle leaders. It attempts to provide a bespoke programme of leadership development, post LftM and prior to enrolling on the development stage of the National Professional Qualification for Headship (NPQH). It is aimed at those aspiring to headship but who require further development before applying for NPQH. It covers the four learning areas of: extending the community; leading learning and teaching; stepping up to leadership; and resourcing change.

CONCLUSION

Middle leaders are crucial to the success of schools and colleges: they are the kingpins and provide a crucial conduit between senior management and the troops at the chalk face. They are also the future deputies and the heads of tomorrow. Their experiences at middle leader level and the training and development they receive will be crucial in preparing them for a more senior role in schools. It is the leadership development of heads and other senior staff that we now turn to in the next chapter.

14

Leadership Development for Heads and Deputies

> ♦ What we know about leaders' needs
>
> ♦ Professional development for leaders at different stages
>
> ♦ What universities and professional associations offer
>
> ♦ What LAs offer

Heads and deputies have important needs, yet Her Majesty's Inspectorate have found that provision is patchy. For instance, 'the support programme offered by LEAs for new headteachers is characterized by inconsistency, with no LEA having good practice in all aspects and one-quarter of LEAs providing unsatisfactory support' (Ofsted, 2002d).

One of the first activities of the National College for School Leadership when it was established in late 2000 was to design and publish a leadership development framework that consisted of five stages of leadership development (NCSL, 2001). The first stage, that of emergent leadership, was considered in Chapter 13. It is the management training and leadership development needs of the other stages of leadership that are the main focus of this chapter.

The importance of careful and accurate needs identification has been referred to on several occasions in this book. This also applies to school leaders and more attention has been given to this recently, including the growing use of tools and techniques to ascertain feedback on performance, sometimes called 360-degree appraisal or feedback. Many of the NCSL's national programmes for example now include elements of needs identification. In the first section we look at leaders' needs and wants, drawing on the DfES baseline studies (Earley et al., 2002; Stevens et al., 2005) and the work of HMI (Ofsted, 2002d). We also look at current provision and forms of support for school leaders from the NCSL, universities, professional associations and local authorities. The NCSL's good practice guide (Earley and Evans, 2002) is drawn upon to provide examples of the latter.

Further details of all NCSL programmes, seminars and specialist courses (such as the leadership of academies and extended schools) are found on the College's website at www.ncsl.org.uk. Information can also be found about the various online communities, networked learning communities and opportunities to undertake overseas visits and conduct research.

WHAT WE KNOW ABOUT LEADERS' NEEDS

NEEDS RELATED TO THE *NATIONAL STANDARDS FOR HEADTEACHERS*

As part of the 2002 DfES baseline study on the state of school leadership, heads, deputy heads and NPQH candidates (deputies aspiring to headship) were asked about their development needs matched to the 1998 National Standards for Headteachers. The standards where further or new training and development opportunities were most commonly welcomed, were to 'promote and secure good teaching, effective learning and high standards of achievement' (58 per cent of headteachers and 49 per cent of deputies) and to 'manage time, finance, accommodation and resources and ensure value for money' (66 per cent of NPQH respondents).

The first baseline study (Earley et al., 2002) also interviewed various people who train heads and deputies. This group considered that leaders needed more help with ICT development and performance management. They felt there was a need for leadership development that stressed instructional leadership – what the NCSL calls learning-centred leadership – and personal and interpersonal development. Providers stated that mentoring, coaching and shadowing schemes should be more widely available and that there should be more international opportunities for development. They were concerned to learn more about ways to enable and empower school leaders to have the courage to be creative and flexible. They felt that deputies and heads concentrated too much on developing skills for particular tasks and were unable to see how their role relates to others in the school.

Since the first baseline study new national standards have been published for headteachers (NCSL, 2004) but these were not used to identify training needs in the 2005 follow-up study. However, school leaders were asked about their training experiences and these are discussed in the next section.

◼ MOST POWERFUL DEVELOPMENT OPPORTUNITIES

In the initial baseline study school leaders were asked what they perceived to be the single most powerful development opportunity of their career, both on the job and off the job, in helping to forge their understanding of leadership. The responses have interesting implications for CPD co-ordinators and others within schools.

On-the-job activities included (in order):

- working with an effective headteacher;
- working in an effective leadership or management team;
- everyday work experience;
- working in a good school;
- being an acting headteacher.

Off-the-job opportunities included (in order):

- postgraduate study (for example, an MA in leadership and management);
- involvement in the national programmes, such as NPQH and LPSH (see later for details);
- CPD or INSET courses in general;
- visiting other schools;
- networking (which involves a range of activities, both informal and formal);
- working with other headteachers;
- being a parent and 'general life experience';
- working on specialist tasks (such as for the local authority or professional association).

The main leadership development opportunities in which school leaders had participated over the last three years were explored in both the 2002 and 2005 studies. Findings from the latter are shown in Table 14.1.

TABLE 14.1 LEADERSHIP DEVELOPMENT OPPORTUNITIES PARTICIPATED IN DURING THE PAST THREE YEARS

Opportunities provided by:	Heads	DHs (% of sample)	NPQH
	(n = 911)	(n = 446)	(n = 287)
Local Education Authorities	74	62	75
Education consultants	48	41	46
Mentoring from (other) headteacher(s)	46	46	48
NCSL	47	30	46*
Mentoring from business or other mentors	20	3	7
Higher Education Institutions	13	21	23
Mentoring by one of your governors	9	3	4
None of these	4	11	7

Note: * Other than NPQH
Source: adapted from Stevens et al., 2005

School leaders participated in a wide range of leadership development activities and professional development opportunities. The 2005 baseline study found that three-quarters of headteachers and NPQH candidates, and nearly two-thirds of deputy heads had undertaken training offered by their local authority in the last three years. Just under half had taken up training from education consultants or been mentored by headteachers. The follow-up study found that since 2001, nearly half of headteachers and NPQH candidates, and 30 per cent of deputies had undertaken training provided by the NCSL. Fewer school leaders made use of opportunities provided by higher education institutions or mentors from business leaders or governors.

Overall, school leaders found the leadership development opportunities that they had taken up in the last three years to be useful. Above all else, mentoring from a headteacher was regarded as the most useful professional development opportunity. In contrast training provided by the local authority was less likely to be rated positively. Headteachers were wary of wasting both time and money on poor quality training but finding out what was of good value was problematic and often depended on recommendation by others.

PROFESSIONAL DEVELOPMENT FOR LEADERS AT DIFFERENT STAGES

THE FIVE STAGES OF LEADERSHIP

The model of continuing professional development underpinning this book is that learning is lifelong – 'from the cradle to the grave'. This model or continuum obviously also applies to leadership development and learning and the NCSL's five stages of school leadership (NCSL, 2001) provide a useful means of analysing different groups in schools and their training and development needs.

Provision of training and development and other support mechanisms can be discussed around the five stages in a school leader's career, namely:

1 *Emergent leadership*, when a teacher is beginning to take on management and leadership responsibilities and perhaps forms an aspiration to become a headteacher (see Chapter 13).

2 *Established leadership*, comprising assistant and deputy heads who are experienced leaders but who do not intend to pursue headship.

3   *Entry to headship*, including preparation for and induction into the senior post in a school.

4   *Advanced leadership*, the stage at which school leaders mature in their role, look to widen their experience, to refresh themselves and to update their skills.

5   *Consultant leadership*, when an able and experienced leader is ready to put something back into the profession by taking on training, mentoring, inspection or other responsibilities (NCSL, 2001: 7).

We have organized the CPD opportunities for each stage, identifying the appropriate NCSL programmes and examples of what local authorities offer, since they are the main providers.

STAGE 2: ESTABLISHED LEADERSHIP

This comprises assistant and deputy heads who are experienced leaders but who do not intend to pursue headship. The NCSL has designed the 'Established Leader Programme' for assistant and deputy headteachers who have chosen not to become a headteacher. It acknowledges the importance of their role as experienced leaders and seeks to support their professional development through consideration of five broad themes that relate directly to the NCSL's Leadership Development Framework – vision and values; learning; leadership for learning; sharing leadership; and future(s) leadership. The programme is delivered in single-phase regional groups of 16 who undertake one two-day residential course and four further face-to-face days over a 12-month period. Approaches to training include: action learning sets; peer support through the development of mentoring, coaching and critical friendship; study group work on think pieces and case studies from successful practice elsewhere; visits to other schools; and self-reflection. Online materials and an online community provide important further dimensions to the programme. The expectation is that candidates will become involved in dialogue with others to develop professional understanding and mutual learning.

Deputy head networks, personal career guidance and counselling for deputy heads are in place in some LAs. Essex, for instance, offers development modules in coaching, mentoring, managing the performance of others, working in other schools (interim management), the art of consultancy, managing yourself (personal effectiveness), developing training skills, project management, information management and recruiting staff.

In some LAs opportunities are available for staff to train together and for leadership teams to have 'away days'. Courses specifically for senior management and leadership teams are available. Warwickshire LA has a programme entitled 'Leading change – developing effective leadership teams'. This gives SMTs and leadership teams the chance to work together intensively on the theme of change management. Its focus is on school improvement and teamworking; it is cross-phase and consists of two residential workshops plus one and a half days' follow-up. Buckinghamshire has developed (with a private partner) a bespoke programme that examines the effectiveness of leadership teams. Although such programmes are expensive, their impact is high as they are designed to meet a school's specific needs. The NCSL has developed a 'top team' programme for leadership teams – Working Together for Success – which was part of the leadership strategy of the London Challenge (DfES, 2003a; Earley et al., 2005).

STAGE 3: ENTRY TO HEADSHIP

As noted earlier, acting headship has been found to be a very good source of on the job professional development. Some LAs make regular use of deputies as acting heads, and these positions are seen as practical placements for professional development, but only a few run workshops specifically for them.

The NCSL's National Professional Qualification for Headship – mandatory for all headship applicants since April 2004 – is for those in the 'entry to headship' stage who are seeking to become headteachers. The training is focused on candidates' development needs and the programme is underpinned by the *National Standards for Headteachers* (NCSL, 2004). It includes online learning, school-based assessment and visits to successful schools. Participants can use the NPQH for credits towards a higher degree.

There are different types of support offered to new heads:

- needs assessment;
- an induction training programme;
- mentoring;
- networking;
- link adviser support.

NEEDS ASSESSMENT

Her Majesty's Inspectorate (Ofsted, 2002c) found that it was often erroneously assumed that needs assessment had been done via NPQH or other programmes. Even when it had been, it was not necessarily used to inform local authority programmes. Needs assessment was often informal and conducted with the school's link adviser. Where it was done well:

- heads assessed themselves against the national standards;
- the assessment was informed by NPQH outcomes;
- the identified development needs took account of the school's context;
- a written report was produced, leading to a personal development plan.

Headteachers found needs assessment most useful when it was conducted one to two terms after taking up their posts, and they welcomed the opportunity to involve the leadership team or SMT in this and elements of the induction programme.

INDUCTION PROGRAMME

Her Majesty's Inspectorate found that good headteacher induction programmes included:

- early contact, including meeting with the head before taking up post;
- useful information packs and documentation;
- effective introductory meetings;
- use of needs assessment to inform subsequent training;
- regular meetings and training opportunities;
- additional support from the school's link adviser;
- involvement of experienced heads in the process, and not just as mentors;
- opportunities for heads to include senior staff in elements of the programme;
- monitoring and evaluation of the programme leading to improved provision.

Weaknesses to avoid included:

- insufficient recognition of the needs of particular phases and types of school;

- a programme tied to September only starts (not January or Easter);

- insufficient guidance and information on opportunities available (for example, heads were often unclear about the potential uses of HEADLAMP funds) (Ofsted, 2002c).

In 2003 the National College replaced HEADLAMP with the 'Headteacher Induction Programme' which provided new heads with a grant of £2,500 that could be used with a range of training and development providers. The HIP was an entitlement for all new headteachers appointed to their first permanent post. Since 2005, HIP has become EHP, the Early Headship Programme, which includes the New Visions programme. This is open to those in their first three years of headship and is a year-long programme rooted in an innovative model of learning based on enquiry and reflection into the practical experiences of headship. It has been very positively received (Bush et al., 2006). The early headship programme aims to support heads through the first years of headship by personalizing provision to improve leadership effectiveness.

■ MENTORING

Her Majesty's Inspectorate found that mentoring or one-to-one 'executive coaching' was rarely well developed and its effectiveness extremely variable. Most conceptions of a mentor were as 'critical friend' but some examples were found where it was linked to a planned programme for school improvement. Her Majesty's Inspectorate considered that effective mentoring had:

- a selection process with formal training for mentors;

- written guidance for new heads and their mentors;

- structured and purposeful meetings, that have a clear agenda;

- careful costing, including funding for supply cover;

- monitoring and evaluation of the process, leading to improvement (Ofsted, 2002c).

Mentoring practices include formal arrangements and informal 'buddy' relationships. In Warwickshire, for example, this is arranged locally and, unlike formal mentors, buddies are often colleagues from local schools. The whole process is managed by an executive group of heads 'to enable a new head to feel comfortable and supported in their first year of their new post through a professional relationship with a colleague' (cited in Earley and Evans, 2002: 19). The mentor is funded for three days of supply cover. Heads choose a mentor from a booklet that contains names and profiles. The purposes of mentoring include: acting as a confidential sounding board; to help plan professional development; to reduce stress; and to help meet needs. In another authority, all new heads are approached by the school's link adviser who discusses pairings mentioned by the mentor steering group, which also quality-assures the process.

Where it works well, headteacher mentoring is often highly valued by both mentees and mentors: 'What worked was having a very experienced head from a similar school that could provide professional and personal support' (headteacher); 'We don't have a problem finding heads to work as mentors; they see it as part of their continuing professional development' (LA inspector, quoted in Earley and Evans, 2002: 19). Most local authorities offer training for those heads wishing to become mentors of new heads. Specialist mentoring for acting heads and for those operating in challenging circumstances is found in a few LAs.

Coaching too has become more prevalent. Barrie Joy notes that this emphasizes 'learning rather than instruction and the importance of starting to facilitate learning from where the learner is' (Joy, 2006). It is about unlocking people's potential to maximize their own performance. The principles of successful coaching and its key elements are outlined by the NCSL in *Leading Coaching in Schools* (NCSL, 2006b).

NETWORKING

Although heads report good support through networks (for example, phase, cluster, diocese), these rarely focus on induction and tend not to be developmental. Very few new headteacher groups exist but they can be very useful for discussing common issues, identifying needs, and so on.

LINK ADVISER SUPPORT

Overall, HMI found support from local authority link advisers to be good and more consistent than induction programmes. Heads value the support and see it as focused on their own and the school's needs. Good features include:

- link advisers being involved in the head's appointment;
- careful matching of link advisers to headteachers;
- additional entitlement of link advisers' time for new headteachers;
- differentiated support which depends on school and head's needs;
- effective needs assessment by the link advisers, leading to the development of a planned induction programme (Ofsted, 2002c).

STAGES 4 AND 5: ADVANCED LEADERSHIP AND CONSULTANT LEADERSHIP

The NCSL's 'Leadership Programme for Serving Headteachers' (LPSH) ran from 2002 to 2006. It was updated and replaced by 'Head for the Future'. Both programmes help heads in the advanced leadership stage to reflect on their personal leadership effectiveness and impact. Evaluations of the four-day LPSH programme found it to be a challenging, revealing and personally motivating experience, and many heads have referred to it as the best leadership training they have ever had (NCSL, 2003c: 9). Both programmes include self-directed learning where headteachers support and challenge each other in co-coaching groups. The programme design enables headteachers to embed the change and developments into everyday school leadership practice. It offers headteachers: online learning opportunities and access to NCSL's web-based support; 360-degree feedback from colleagues, including personal self-assessment; a three-day residential with follow-up sessions over planned intervals to ensure sustainability of learning. Participants are provided with opportunities to learn collaboratively with others in a confidential setting, to focus on personal development and leadership styles and how they impact on school climate, and to experiment and test hypotheses in leadership and school development. 'Head for the Future' includes pre-programme preparation and learning; a residential; follow-up sessions and post-residential opportunities. It allows heads to focus on their own personal development and provides insights into their professional characteristics, leadership styles, school climate and how they impact on school performance. It also enables them to identify the variety of opportunities and roles open to them across the school system and in the future.

The NCSL's 'Strategic Leadership of ICT' programme was devised jointly with BECTA. It helps heads to take a strategic lead of ICT with the aim of improving school effectiveness and teaching and learning. It is not a skills-based course but is based around the principles of vision, audit and planning and is a self- and peer-review learning programme. Self-assessment and reflection are key throughout.

The 'Consultant Leader Development Programme' enables experienced school leaders to take responsibility for the future development of the profession while remaining in post (NCSL, 2003c: 10). The NCSL sees such leaders as fundamental to building leadership capacity in schools and throughout the education system. Since autumn 2003 the programme has been developed for experienced advanced skills teachers, experienced deputy heads and for primary head consultants as part of the primary national strategy leadership programme (NCSL, 2006c).

The two most common ways that these two stages of leadership are supported in local authorities are through mentoring (and buddying), and acting as 'associate heads'. Mentoring is available to provide assistance for heads (temporary or permanent) of schools in need of support. In such circumstances heads often acted as consultants. Formal links between headteachers officially lasted six months, although informally they lasted much longer.

In some authorities a register of expertise is kept and there are lists of heads and deputies who would be willing, if approached, to operate as acting or temporary heads. This is generally recognized as powerful professional development and, in the case of deputies, the best preparation for headship. Associate heads and consultant heads are being used in a variety of ways but usually to assist other heads or to take over the headship of failing and weak schools. (See Earley and Weindling, 2006 for a further discussion of consultant leaders.)

The NCSL's provision attempts to meet the future challenges of school leadership and its programmes are constantly changing in the light of new developments. Most recently it has offered programmes for educational leaders of extended schools, academies, schools facing complex contexts and diverse communities, remodelling the workforce, multi-agency working and the integration of children's services and the *Every Child Matters* agenda. It is worth looking at the College's website on a regular basis.

However, despite wide-ranging and ever-changing provision, the current NCSL leadership development framework offered to school leaders seems to be lacking in provision for experienced heads. The NCSL has piloted a programme for 'Advanced Leaders' but at the moment it appears there is little, post LPSH or Head for the Future, for experienced leaders. Such a programme could be seen as a natural follow-on from NPQH (Part 1) or Head for the Future (Part 2). Part 3 would provide opportunities for heads with their colleagues to explore the changing nature of their role. In fact there is little mention by the NCSL of developing heads in their roles as heads or in helping them maintain their expertise, motivation and enthusiasm for their role.

In one of the rare studies considering this group of school leaders – advanced leaders and experienced heads – Vince Stroud (2006: 91) examines their needs 'so that professional development can be appropriately tailored to overcome the possibility of any decline' in performance. In a small-scale study he found that experienced heads 'felt that coaching and feedback on their professional practice was the key to much of their professional development' (Ibid: 93). It appears that heads – all heads, both experienced and inexperienced – want three things: non-judgemental relationships; 'permission to find the job difficult'; and time put aside for their own professional development (Wallace, 2006).

What is needed for experienced heads – indeed it could be argued for all school leaders *and* teachers – is a differentiated solution to professional or leadership development. One size does not fit all. Heads in Stroud's study wished for:

> A more personalised type of training and professional development, where they have the opportunity to shape their own professional development and have a sensible debate with their experienced colleagues.
>
> (Ibid.: 94)

Having a coach–mentor (and being one too) was very powerful and offered a bespoke opportunity to analyse their needs and to discuss ways of responding to them. Heads were also keen to work as training providers and coaches and consultants as a part-time addition to their headteacher role, as a means of professional stimulation and keeping them up to date.

But are we doing enough to provide professional development and refreshment opportunities for experienced heads? This is an area that has grown hugely in the last few years. It is known, for example, that by 2003 over 400 heads had been trained as 'consultant leaders' to engage in a range of NCSL 'level 5' activities, such as NPQH tutoring, coaching and mentoring, 'school improvement partners' and Primary Strategy Consultant Leaders (PSCLs) of which there are now 1900 (Earley, 2006).

WHAT UNIVERSITIES AND PROFESSIONAL ASSOCIATIONS OFFER

Higher education institutions have traditionally provided leadership development and management development opportunities for teachers and school leaders, whether accredited or not. These will vary from place to place and depend on the offerings of your local university and HEIs but a smaller percentage of heads (13 per cent) than deputies (21 per cent) and NPQH candidates (23 per cent) has been involved with them over the past three years. The NCSL has been working closely with a group of ten universities – the universities partnership group – to ensure continuity and complementarity between the national programmes (such as NPQH and LftM) and higher degrees such as MAs and MBAs. As earlier noted, it is now possible to use the possession of an NPQH for credits towards a Master's degree, and for those individuals with a higher degree in leadership and management to count towards the NPQH. The partnership group is also looking at ways to accredit other NCSL offerings within a national accreditation framework.

Master's programmes are usually studied over a minimum of two years (or one year full time) and often consist of a modular framework made up of core and optional modules. The MA in Educational Leadership and Management at the Institute of Education in London, for example, which can be taken via distance learning or face to face (or a combination of the two), has three core modules each of a term's duration:

- Leading and managing educational change and improvement.
- Leadership for the learning community.
- Understanding education policy.

In addition to the core modules a number of options are available (for example, human resource management; leading in diverse cultures and communities; finance and budgeting for schools; developing management skills and insights). Finally, to complete the MA a research-based report or dissertation is required.

PROFESSIONAL ASSOCIATIONS

Like universities, the various professional associations but especially the heads' associations (the Association of School and College Leaders [ASCL] – formally the Secondary Heads Association [SHA] and National Association of Head Teachers [NAHT]), have traditionally provided courses and conferences which cover management and leadership issues as well as current concerns. Examples of their courses can be found on their websites. The baseline studies found that school leaders but especially heads – over one-third – had made use of such professional development opportunities and valued them highly.

WHAT LAs OFFER

Many local authorities have devised extensive programmes for primary, secondary and special school leaders. The local authority, it will be recalled, is still a major provider of professional development and training for most schools (see Chapter 5). However, authorities increasingly are using a variety of external organizations to meet the professional development needs of school leaders, in particular the NCSL (through such national programmes as *Leading from the Middle*) and individual consultants (Stevens et al., 2005).

The good practice guide, entitled *LEAding Provision*, gives many examples of local authority provision for school leaders (see Earley and Evans, 2002). The programme in Essex, for example, is structured around role focus, professional focus and course objectives. The programme differentiates between induction, development and progression, and outlines the key themes and skills that individual school leaders are expected to develop. These include:

- mentoring and coaching;
- consultancy skills;
- training skills;
- intervention strategies;
- recruitment and selection;
- developing personal effectiveness;
- developing organizational effectiveness;
- career development and management.

No matter at what stages of leadership individuals are placed, local authorities are able to support their school leaders in a variety of ways. These include providing support groups and networks, disseminating good practice and offering opportunities to be involved in a variety of initiatives and programmes.

NETWORKS AND SUPPORT GROUPS

Headteachers, other school leaders and teachers have always made good use of networks and found them a valuable form of support when and where they exist. In Warwickshire, for example, a range of networks are currently on offer with local patch meetings seen as an effective self-supporting network, with colleagues from different phases meeting to discuss common concerns and issues. A number of authorities supported applications from groups of schools to join the NCSL's Networked Learning Communities (NLC) initiative (see Chapter 2) and, more recently, the primary schools network. Opportunities for subject and curriculum specialists to get together are particularly difficult in small authorities and some have entered into partnerships with others in order to make such provision.

GUIDANCE AND ADVICE

Many documents and working papers are available to support school leaders on such topics as utilising data to support school improvement, school improvement planning, and target-setting at Key Stage 3. Local authorities have traditionally been good at offering advice and guidance to their schools. They produce a wide range of helpful documents and guides available on all aspects of school leadership and management. In themselves these can be useful professional development tools. More recently, authorities are advising schools on how to complete the self evaluation form (SEF) in preparation for inspection (Bubb et al., 2007; MacBeath, 2006).

■ WORK–LIFE BALANCE AND WELLBEING

A growing number of authorities are concerned about issues to do with work–life balance and general wellbeing. 'Peer counselling for heads' was a small-scale pilot research project in Wiltshire involving eight primary headteachers who met for a day's training to consider such matters as peer counselling, how it relates to self-esteem, good communication, constructive feedback and building peer support. This one-day conference was followed by the heads pairing up, visiting each other's schools, and then meeting a term later to evaluate and write up their findings. The heads spoke positively of the experience.

■ ASSISTANCE FOR ETHNIC MINORITY GROUPS AND WOMEN LEADERS

The London Centre for Leadership in Learning has a programme called *Investing in Diversity*, which is designed specifically to support staff from black and minority ethnic backgrounds to reach leadership positions. It is for aspiring heads but a programme for middle leaders has recently been developed as part of the leadership strategy of the London Challenge (DfES, 2003a; Earley et al., 2005). Only a few authorities are providing opportunities for minority groups and women – one set up a 'centre for women leaders' whilst another, in conjunction with a university, is providing mentors for minority ethnic teachers in their second and third years in the profession. Another appointed a race equality officer and was looking at what needed to be done to help such staff manage career progression.

■ DISSEMINATION OF GOOD PRACTICE

Local authorities are well placed to disseminate the good practice within their schools. Involvement in the NCSL's national initiative, Networked Learning Communities, also helped to disseminate good practice (see Chapters 2 and 7). Strategies for the latter include:

- making good use of training and specialist schools;
- using heads and deputies as coaches and mentors;
- naming and acclaiming publications;
- undertaking research and publication;
- producing training videos;
- providing opportunities for CPD;
- benchmarking with family groups and identifying good practice;
- encouraging school self-evaluation;
- promoting quality circles and networking groups;
- setting up research and development groups and Action Research projects;
- developing HEI partnerships;
- devising a good practice website;
- promoting quality standards, for example, IiP, EFQM, Basic Skills quality mark;
- appointing ASTs and leading teachers (for literacy, numeracy and early years).

Dissemination of good practice was however, said to be made more difficult by the 'inverse proportionality principle' whereby local authorities are discouraged from going into good schools (one visit per annum to effective schools was the norm) and to focus their efforts on underperforming, seriously weak and failing schools.

■ RESEARCH-BASED ENQUIRY

Some authorities are heavily committed to encouraging school-based research and enquiry and are promoting action research in schools – what Graham Handscomb in Chapter 7 refers to as the self-researching or the 'research-engaged school' (see also NCSL, 2006d). For example, Buckinghamshire linked together ten schools that successfully applied for Best Practice Research Scholarships. A common theme was investigated across the projects and an action learning set established, in partnership with an HEI, for all those involved.

CONCLUSION

This chapter has examined the range of CPD opportunities or leadership development provision that is available for school leaders using the NCSL's model or framework of the five stages of leadership. Performance management was mentioned in Chapter 4 as one way of ascertaining training and development needs and ensuring that they are met. For teachers this takes place with their team leader or line manager. For heads it involves the governing body who is assisted in the process by an external adviser or a school improvement partner (who often is a consultant leader). As with the performance management of teachers, heads may wish to draw up an objective in the professional development area. This is significant, as previously heads have had a tendency to put the CPD needs of others before themselves (Barthes, 1990). However, as we argued in Chapter 2, it is crucially important for all school leaders to demonstrate that they are learners too, and to work towards developing a culture that attaches great importance to continuing professional development and personal growth.

15

Governors' Training and Development

♦ Why training, development and support are so important for governors

♦ Diagnosing governors' needs

♦ How to meet needs

This chapter aims to demonstrate why CPD co-ordinators should be as interested in the training and development of members of their school's governing body as they are in that of their professional (and paid) colleagues. Governors, like staff, are part of the school's human resource, and as such their training, development and support are very important if they are to fulfil their responsibilities effectively.

Governors play an important role in relation to continuing professional development and training in several ways. They are, or should be, concerned about their own training and development, but equally important is the priority they give, and show they are giving, to CPD within the school as a whole. Most schools will have policies and procedures that relate, for example, to staff development and training, induction, the use of supply teachers and performance management. More specifically, 'appointed' governors have responsibility, with the help of an adviser or school improvement partner, for the performance management of the headteacher when the head, like teachers, will be asked about professional development objectives.

All these 'people' or human resource matters are the concern of the governing body, which is responsible for developing and ratifying such policies and also for ensuring that they are successfully implemented. When a school is applying for Investors in People status, for example, assessors will want to seek the views of governors and ascertain the importance that the governing body attaches to the development of its people, both teachers and other staff. But assessors will also be interested in exploring how governors' training and development needs are being met, if there is a training and development plan for the governing body, and whether or not this is an integral part of the school's development or improvement plan.

This chapter explores these issues further. First, it considers why training, development and support are so important for governors. What do governors do that is so significant to warrant such concern and interest from busy CPD co-ordinators? What role does training, development and support play, and what do we know about what works in relation to both whole-school governing body development and training to meet the needs of individual governors? How are new governors inducted into their roles and what part can school self-evaluation play in governing body development?

WHY TRAINING, DEVELOPMENT AND SUPPORT ARE SO IMPORTANT FOR GOVERNORS

KEY ROLES

Training, development and support are important for governors because without them the governing body is unlikely to operate as effectively as it might. It is important for the governing body to work well because it performs a number of key roles and responsibilities that help the school ensure it is an effective and an improving school. This is not the place to go into these in great detail and they have been discussed elsewhere (see, for example, Earley and Weindling, 2004). Briefly their key responsibilities have been encapsulated in terms of three roles:

1   To provide a sense of direction for the work of the school (strategic role).

2   To support the work of the school (critical friend role).

3   To hold the school to account for the standards and quality of education it achieves (monitoring and accountability role).

Training materials produced by the DfES, and available for local authorities to use with newly appointed governors, have centred explicitly on the three key roles of governing bodies (DfES, 2001). This way of conceptualizing the governing body's role has been enshrined in legislation (Education Act 2002) and inspection. The most recent inspection framework, which has applied to schools since September 2005, asks 'How effective are leadership and management in raising achievement and supporting all learners?' and inspectors evaluate the effectiveness with which governors discharge their responsibilities (Ofsted, 2005). Inspectors assess the extent to which the governing body:

- helps shape the vision and direction of the school;

- ensures that the school fulfils its statutory duties;

- has a good understanding of the strengths and weaknesses of the school;

- challenges and supports the senior management team (Ofsted, 2003a).

But what do we know about how governors and headteachers perceive and enact these key responsibilities and how they conceptualize the governing body's roles?

> Governors in about 90 per cent of schools have a satisfactory or better understanding of the strengths and weaknesses of their school, but they are less effective in shaping the direction of the school … Where governors do not contribute effectively to shaping the direction of the school, they often have little knowledge of the school's main development priorities, agree plans and policies unquestioningly, and rely too much on the headteacher as the source of their information about the school.
>
> (Ofsted, 2002e: 10)

These key roles are therefore unlikely to be undertaken effectively without some form of training and support. Governors serve on governing bodies for a period of four years, and although it is known that many stay on for a further term of office (Scanlon et al., 1999) it is important to ensure that governors are 'fully functioning' as soon as possible. This is why induction of new governors is so important.

BENEFITS OF A GOOD GOVERNING BODY

Research into school governance (for example, Creese and Earley, 1999; Ranson et al., 2005; Scanlon et al., 1999) shows there are a number of advantages to having a good governing body:

- a critical and informed sounding board for the headteacher;

- offering support for the school;

- helping to break down the isolation of the head;

- being a link with parents and the community;
- working with the staff to provide direction and a vision for the school;
- provide a forum within which the teachers can explain their work;
- bringing to the school a range of non-educational expertise and experience (Scanlon et al., 1999: 27).

One of the most important attributes of a governing body is that it is largely composed of individuals who bring different perspectives to the headteacher and the school and therefore the opportunity to learn from different people with different backgrounds. Sometimes the professionals were too close to the issues or had tunnel vision: 'you simply can't see the wood for the trees'. Having a group of people with a variety of skills and experience was an added resource for headteachers. This could enhance their role and make their jobs easier.

Overall headteachers are beginning more fully to appreciate the benefits of having a good chair and an effective governing body in what could, otherwise, be a lonely and at times vulnerable position. They can find sympathy and understanding, as well as challenge and stimulus, from a body of hard-working and committed laypeople who have the best interests of the school at heart.

Effective schools and effective governing bodies make a difference – they add value. There is already a considerable body of research into what makes a school effective. Although there has been less research into the effectiveness of governing bodies, it is possible to identify (for example, Ranson et al., 2005; Scanlon et al., 1999) a number of factors that are present in effective governing bodies. These include:

- a positive attitude towards governors on the part of the headteacher;
- efficient working arrangements;
- effective teamwork within the governing body;
- governors who are committed to the school.

Governing bodies which make a conscious effort to improve their performance in these areas *do* become more effective as can be seen from the case studies described in Creese (2000). In his study of governing bodies that became more effective Creese pointed to four common factors which were significant: teamwork, positive relationships, efficient working arrangements and the important input of the chair of governors.

Many research studies (for an overview see Earley and Creese, 2003) have identified the key role which the headteacher plays in determining the effectiveness, or otherwise, of the governing body. The nature of the relationship between the headteacher and the chair of governors in particular is crucial. Joan Sallis, the well-known governor trainer and agony aunt, notes that schools boast about their governing body's quality because the quality of the governing body, like the quality of the staff, gives evidence of the head's leadership and management (Sallis, 2001). Relationships between staff in general and the governors are also important. Governors should be encouraged to visit their schools regularly and so become well known to the staff who trust them and respect their input.

A useful way of conceptualizing governing bodies as regards their effectiveness is in terms of where they are located on the pressure and support spectrum (see Figure 15.1). Effective governing bodies are those that provide high pressure but with high support. Governing bodies have to offer both support and challenge to the schools, but getting the balance between these two is not always easy.

low	*SUPPORT*		*high*
1. Supporters club 'We're here to support the head!'		**4. Partners or critical friends** 'We share everything - good or bad!'	
low	*CHALLENGE*		*high*
2. Abdicators 'We leave it to the professionals!'		**3. Adversaries** 'We keep a very close eye on the staff!'	

FIGURE 15.1 THE EFFECTIVE GOVERNING BODY (CREESE AND EARLEY, 1999: 8)

To work effectively as critical friends there is a need for trust, sensitivity and openness. This cannot be legislated for, or introduced overnight. What is more, once achieved there is no guarantee that such qualities will persist – changes of personnel mean that they have to be continuously re-established. Effective governing bodies are not heads' supporters' clubs, abdicators or adversaries but, as shown in Figure 15.1, the partners or critical friends offering 'high support – high challenge' (Creese and Earley, 1999: 8).

? POINTS FOR REFLECTION

How would you describe your governing body?

DIAGNOSING GOVERNORS' NEEDS

SELF-EVALUATION

Another common theme for whole governing body training, perhaps also partly brought about by Ofsted, has been school self-evaluation and in particular evaluating the effectiveness of themselves – how are they currently operating as a governing body and what are their strengths and weaknesses? Are their working arrangements efficient and are they able to ensure their limited time and efforts are focusing on those things that matter most? Considering that governors are unpaid volunteers, the demands on them are high – and some may not think that CPD is a priority.

Most local authorities already have in place self-evaluation programmes for their governing bodies. Some LAs and other bodies, such as the governor associations and training organizations, have published appropriate criteria against which governors can judge their effectiveness or have developed self-review procedures or good governance guides which ask a series of questions governors might want to ask about their schools: for example, questions on issues such as the curriculum, finance, premises, staff development, development planning and, perhaps most importantly, school performance. Self-review or evaluation against a set of criteria can have a marked effect on enhancing the effectiveness of school governing bodies. Those that take part in such activity (and it probably tends to be those who are already pretty effective) are able to build on their strengths and recognize those areas where development is needed.

One of us (Peter Earley) was involved in a self-evaluation exercise that identified governors' awareness of the school, and monitoring and evaluating as major weaknesses. Such identification was the first step in bringing about action to alter this state of affairs. Governing bodies that take part in such activities will tend to be more questioning of heads and other staff, and of themselves, and have developed better procedures for asking such questions as why, where, how, what and, perhaps most importantly, 'How well are we doing?'. These naive questions can make heads and senior school staff think very carefully about what they are doing and planning to do and why. The key question that an effective and efficient governing body will want to ask at all times is: 'Is the way we operate as a governing body allowing us to focus on making our school more effective?'

With the above in mind it is interesting to note the moves to promote a national (albeit voluntary) model of governing body self-evaluation (Little, 2002). This is known as the 4Ps framework (see Table 15.1) and the Index of School Governance, and has been piloted in over 30 LAs in England. The framework – also known as 345 – consists of three key roles (strategic overview, accountability and critical friend), four aspects or Ps (strategic Planning, ensuring Progress, real Partnership and sound Practice), and five criteria for each of the four Ps (see below). The index, developed by Catherine Burt, is both a product and a facilitated process for governing body self-evaluation. It will be interesting to see how it develops and whether it becomes the preferred or dominant model but clearly self-evaluation for governing bodies is here to stay!

Good relationships between governors and staff are fundamental to improving the effectiveness of the governing body. Although finding the time is hard, governors need to visit the school during the day to see pupils at work and talk to, and get to know, the staff. Governors benefit from being offered guidance on how to get the most out of their visits.

Jane Phillips, formerly of NAGM (now the National Governors' Association) has drawn up this list to prompt governors into thinking about their school as a learning organization:

1 Are there regular opportunities for staff to examine and reflect together on classroom practice and pupil learning?

2 Are governors involved?

3 Is there dialogue across departments and within and between Key Stages?

4 Are governors informed of this dialogue?

5 Do staff actively turn to each other to solve problems?

6 Do governors actively turn to each other to solve problems?

7 Is there a common understanding between staff as to what counts as progress for pupils?

8 Do governors share this understanding?

9 Do pupils experience the same high expectations of their progress across departments and within and between Key Stages?

10 Do governors share these high expectations?

11 Does the school measure what it values – not those things that are easily measured?

12 Do the values of the staff and the values of the governing body coincide?

13 Do staff have opportunities to read about, examine and share 'best practices' within and beyond the school?

14 Do governors have an understanding of 'best practice' in teaching?

15 Is there feedback from pupils about the quality of their learning experiences in school?

16 Is this feedback shared with the governors?

17 Is the relationship between parents and staff a learning relationship – that is, do they learn from each other?

18 Are governors involved?

19 Is the relationship between governors and staff a learning relationship – that is, do they learn from each other?

20 What is the head's role in all of this? (Phillips, 1999)

TABLE 15.1 GOVERNING BODY SELF-EVALUATION – THE 4Ps

Planning	Progress	Partnership	Practice
1. Direction	1. Monitoring	1. Representation	1. Teamwork
2. Improvement	2. Target-setting	2. Participation	2. Relationships
3. Documentation	3. Efficiency	3. Communication	3. Meetings
4. Decision	4. Impact	4. Accountability	4. Organization
5. Statute	5. Equality	5. Advocacy	5. Development

INDIVIDUAL GOVERNORS' NEEDS

It is worth remembering that governors, who may be parents, support staff, teachers, members of the local community or businesspeople, come onto the governing body from a variety of backgrounds with a wide range of experience. Some will have an educational background – indeed, a recent study found that nearly 40 per cent of governors work in education or have an education-related occupation (Earley and Creese, 2003). Most, however, will have limited knowledge of education, although all of course will recall their own school days!

NEW GOVERNORS

The first matter to be attended to therefore is how to induct new governors into their role and ensure they become knowledgeable about the school and about education in general. We should not aim to make them educational experts; that is not their role – the strength of the governing body as Joan Sallis and others have argued lies in the fact that it is made up of non-experts, its 'precious light of ordinariness'. But newcomers need to 'get up to speed' as quickly as possible. Most LAs offer a programme of training for new governors, often based on the training materials developed by the DfES (2001), which focus on the aforementioned three key roles.

CHAIRS OF GOVERNORS

The relationship between the headteacher and the chair of governors is crucial and affects how the whole school operates. Chairs provide 'an ear to bash, a shoulder to cry on and someone to bounce ideas off' (Sallis, 2001). They require certain key qualities: they need to be accessible, keen and interested.

The chair of governors is often the prime mover in enhancing the effectiveness of the governing body and 'it is difficult for a governing body to improve or become more effective if the role of the chair is poorly enacted' (Scanlon et al., 1999: 5). It is not always easy to chair effectively meetings of a group of disparate volunteers, such as a governing body. It may include some governors with little or no experience of meetings, who find difficulty in expressing their views, whilst at the other end of the spectrum there are those with considerable experience of serving on committees. A good chair will be able to ensure that all governors are able to contribute to meetings which have clear objectives and outcomes achieved within a reasonable space of time.

Chairs need to set up efficient working arrangements, which allow governors time to concentrate upon the key issues for their school. The setting up of a pattern of meetings, and delegation to sub-groups, enables governors to give time to the important issues. Chairs need to run meetings well with all governors being given the opportunity to contribute. Including timings for the various items on agendas and indicating clearly specific responsibilities for follow-up in the minutes of meetings are two examples of good practice in this area.

The majority of LAs offer training specifically targeted at chairs, in the form of briefings about forthcoming issues and/or guidance on how to run meetings, and so on. Greater stress may need to be laid upon the factors linked to the effectiveness of the governing body, and the steps necessary to enhance effectiveness. In particular, chairs may need reminding of the importance of good teamwork, and of having working arrangements which allow governors time to concentrate upon the key issues in their schools. These are aspects of the work of the governors that should be stressed in any evaluation of the effectiveness of the governing body. The DfES funds Governornet, which has a wealth of training opportunities such as the National Clerks' Training Programme, as well as resources, links and discussion boards (www.governornet.co.uk).

HOW TO MEET NEEDS

There are many training opportunities for chairs and other governors and a growing amount of support. The DfES produces a termly newsletter entitled *Governors* and there is lots of very useful information on their website (www.governornet.co.uk) as well as the websites of the governor organizations (nga.org.uk; governors.fsnet.co.uk) and the *Times Educational Supplement* (www.tes.co.uk). There is a 24-hour hotline available for governors (on www.schoolgovernorline.info or 0800 0722 181) to answer any questions governors may have about any aspect of school life.

Much governor training provided by local authorities focuses largely on what might be termed the 'nuts and bolts' of governance – issues such as governors' legal responsibilities, budget management and so on. Here is one authority's list of courses:

Induction Training for New Governors

Curriculum

The Experienced Clerk

Exploring Church School Distinctiveness

Exclusions

Extended Schools

Finance – Budgeting and Finance for Governors

Health and Safety

Performance Management Training

Personnel Management

The Role of the Clerk

The Role of the Chair

Managing Staff Reductions

Safeguarding Children

Special Educational Needs

Supporting Vulnerable Children

Warwickshire, for instance, has a governors' website and offers a free helpline to all governors on all aspects of the governing body's role and responsibilities as well as:

- Advice and practical help with restructuring the governing body's committees and working parties.

- An information pack and induction of new governors.

- Programme of more specialist courses including personnel and finance, and school improvement topics including self-evaluation.

- Up to the minute briefings available on all the latest topics/issues including Children Act, Extended Schools, Child Protection.

- A termly newsletter for all governors.

- An annual training programme sent to all Warwickshire governors, available to purchase by subscription or on a buy as you go basis.

The wider but more fundamental issue of governors' involvement may receive less attention. A further difficulty lies in the constant turnover of governors. With new governors being appointed on a regular basis, there is an on-going need for induction programmes, a need that has been partly filled by a national programme which LAs are free to use (DfES, 2001). New governors inevitably take time, perhaps as long as two years, to get to grips with their role. If they only serve one four-year term, they can only offer two years when they are in a position to undertake the sort of tasks which effective governance requires.

In most LAs, governor trainers offer training sessions aimed at the whole governing body, on such matters as:

- preparing for an Ofsted inspection: what governors need to know;

- developing the governing body's strategic role;

- governors' school visits;

- being a good employer: staffing issues for the governing body;

- understanding your school performance data;

- the critical friend role in practice.

Such collective training sessions are invaluable as part of the essential team-building process. It is also worth noting that social events, of various sorts, contribute to helping governors get to know one another and to find a common sense of purpose. There is no reason why governing bodies should rely solely upon external agencies for developmental work in team building. Experienced headteachers and governors can gain in terms of their own development by organizing training sessions for their governing body. For example, headteachers have to explain more fully to laypeople what the professionals have too often taken for granted, to make things more explicit, translate the coded language and jargon of education, and fill in background details so that governors can make informed decisions.

TEAM BUILDING

There is no reason to suppose that governors will automatically form themselves into a team with shared beliefs and a common sense of purpose – indeed, the opposite is more likely to be the case. Some form of team-building process must take place if the governing body is to become an effective team. Many governing bodies arrange training sessions of one sort or another for the whole governing body, in addition to the training attended by individual governors. Good teamwork can be strengthened through having sound procedures and good communication systems, which are understood by all. Some LAs have sessions run by an experienced trainer who will work with governing bodies in a series of challenges and problem-solving exercises designed to give you insights into the skills and behaviour deployed as a governor in meetings.

ROLE OF 'LINK' GOVERNORS

Most governing bodies appoint or select a 'link' or training governor whose responsibility is to bring to the attention of individual governors the various training opportunities available and encourage them to attend. This person will work with the CPD co-ordinator to manage the training budget, and if the school is signed up to the authority's training and support programme, will wish to ensure the school is getting value for money for its annual subscription.

The link governor ensures that all new governors are provided with documentation about the school and the governing body, whilst being careful not to overload them. This school-based induction pack should be seen as complementing that provided by the local authority. In addition a growing number of governing bodies are setting up 'buddy' or mentoring systems whereby an experienced governor will be attached to a new one. The other essential feature of induction is arranging for the new governors to visit the school at the earliest opportunity. Indeed, all governors 'new' or 'old' should be encouraged to give high priority to visiting the school in order to see the pupils at work and to talk with the staff.

WHOLE GOVERNING BODY TRAINING

Training can also be an integral part of the way the governing body operates – for example, by having an item on the agenda of the full governing body meeting which allows those governors who have attended courses to feed back to others; or by having a five minute item which examines a particular topic (for example, school visits, sex education, equal opportunities, links with the school). Effective governing bodies are known to share information about recent developments in education and elsewhere which are likely to impact on the school. Headteachers, chairs of governors, link governors, indeed all governors may make copies and circulate relevant (short) articles and overviews. Matters are made easier as more governors and school staff acquire email addresses and access to the web.

The training and development of individual governors, especially new ones, are very important but training for the whole governing body can be tailored more specifically to its needs. Research has found a strong link between perceptions of governing body effectiveness and involvement in whole governing body training (Scanlon et al., 1999). It also identified a trend where more and more governor training was of this kind and now nearly all LAs (as part of the package that most schools purchase) offer such a service at least once a year to the school if requested. Effective governing bodies are likely to use their limited training funds carefully to ensure a balance between school-based training and off-site sessions for individual governors. Both are clearly needed and the role of the link governor and the CPD co-ordinator/headteacher is important here. Also important is that experienced heads, CPD co-ordinators and governors can gain in terms of their own development by organizing training sessions for their governing bodies. It can be even more valuable if it is occasionally held in conjunction with staff.

Another advantage of whole governing body training is that it promotes team building and teamwork. It can also help develop positive relationships between governors, the head and senior staff. As earlier noted, teamwork is a characteristic of effective governing bodies but there is of course no guarantee that this disparate (albeit well-meaning) group of governors will automatically form themselves into a team with shared beliefs and a common sense of purpose. Some form of team building process must take place if the governing body is to become an effective team. Some arrange events so as to bring governors together to get to know each other and to develop a common purpose thus enhancing their sense of identity as a team. These include meetings (some on Saturdays) and a variety of other working sessions and/or social events. Others arrange training events around a theme of concern to the governing body such as the school improvement plan or, commonly, preparation for inspection. If there is one thing Ofsted inspections have done for schools and governing bodies it is to get them to unite against a common foe – an unintended but positive consequence perhaps! Similarly, the appointment of a new headteacher – for which the NCSL has recently published a guide for governors (NCSL, 2006a) – can bring the governing body together very effectively.

CONCLUSION

Governors need to access high-quality training to carry out their roles effectively, especially with regard to such difficult areas as monitoring and evaluating the work of the school. Training will help to raise governors' awareness of their roles and their statutory responsibilities as well as increase their confidence to play a full part in the life of the school and the governing body. Acting as critical friends or asking pertinent questions to heads and teachers is not easy and governors need lots of help and support – from within the school, the LA and governor organizations – to do this effectively. Headteachers and CPD co-ordinators should therefore consider the training needs of governors in the same way they would those of paid employees of the school. As noted above, Creese (2000) in his study of governing bodies that became more effective, pointed to four common factors which were significant: teamwork, positive relationships, efficient working arrangements and the important input of the chair of governors. Training can make a significant impact on all of these. The key to effective governance is therefore the development of a partnership between the school, its staff and governors, one built on positive relationships and trust which enables a supportive, yet challenging and questioning, culture to exist. For this to occur training is crucially important. It is also very important for governors to demonstrate by their actions that they are interested in the CPD of school staff and that they work towards being 'good employers' of people. As we said at the beginning of this book, people matter!

References

Adams, M. (2005) 'Identifying training and development needs in your school', *Professional Development Today* **8**(1): Autumn/Winter.

Balshaw, M. and Farrell, P. (2002) *Teaching Assistants: Practical Strategies for Effective Classroom Support*. London: David Fulton.

Barthes, R. (1990) *Improving Schools from Within*. San Francisco, CA: Jossey-Bass.

Baxter, G. and Chambers, M. (1998) 'Setting the standard for coordinators', *Professional Development Today*, **1**(2): 79–84.

Bentley, P. (2002/2003) 'Continuing professional development: views from the front', *Professional Development Today*, **6**(1) 57–62.

Berrill, D. and Whalen, C. (2003) 'Professional identity/personal integrity: towards a reflective portfolio teaching community'. Paper presented at AERA, Chicago.

Bezzina, C. (2002) 'Rethinking teachers' professional development: agenda for the 21st century', *Journal of In-service Education*, **28**(1): 57–78.

Blatchford, P., Bassett, P., Brown, P., Martin, C., Russell, A., Webster, R. and Haywood, N. (2006) *The Deployment and Impact of Support Staff in Schools RR776*. London: DfES.

Bleach, K. (2000) *The Newly-Qualified Teacher's Handbook*. London: David Fulton.

Bolam, R. (1993) 'Recent development and emerging issues', in *The Continuing Professional Development of Teachers*. London: GTC.

Bolam, R. and McMahon, A. (2003) 'Recent developments in CPD', in C. Day and J. Sachs (eds), *International Handbook of the Continuing Professional Development of Teachers*. Maidenhead: Open University Press.

Bolam, R. and Weindling, D. (2006) *Synthesis of Research and Evaluation Projects Concerned with capacity-building Through Teachers' Professional Development*. London: GTC.

Bolam, R., McMahon, A., Stoll, L., Thomas, S. and Wallace, M. (2005) *Creating and Sustaining Effective Professional Learning Communities*. Nottingham: DfES.

Boyle, B., White, D. and Boyle, T. (2003) 'A longitudinal study of teacher change: what makes professional development effective?', Paper given to American Education Research Association, Chicago, April.

Brown, S. and Earley, P. (1990) *Enabling Teachers to Undertake INSET*. Slough: NFER.

Bubb, S. (2000) *The Effective Induction of Newly Qualified Primary Teachers: An Induction Tutor's Handbook*. London: David Fulton.

Bubb, S. (2001) *A Newly Qualified Teacher's Manual: How to Meet the Induction Standards*. London: David Fulton.

Bubb, S. (2003a) *The Insider's Guide for New Teachers: Succeeding in Training and Induction*. London: TES/Kogan Page.

Bubb, S. (2003b) *A Newly Qualified Teacher's Manual: How to Meet the Induction Standards*. Reprint. London: David Fulton.

Bubb, S. (2003c) *The Insider's Guide to Early Professional Development: Succeed in Your First Five Years*. London: TES/RoutledgeFalmer.

Bubb, S (2003d) 'Helping overseas-trained teachers get QTS', *Managing Schools Today*, **12**(4): 40–4.

Bubb, S. (2005a) *Helping Teachers Develop*. London: Sage/Paul Chapman.

Bubb, S. (2005b) CPD, *Education Review*, London: NUT.

Bubb, S. (2006) 'The virtual staffroom', *Times Educational Supplement*, 23 June.

Bubb, S. (2007) *Making Performance Management Work for You*. London: ATL.

Bubb, S. and Earley, P. (2004) *Managing Teacher Workload: Work–Life Balance and Wellbeing*. London: Sage/Paul Chapman.

Bubb, S. and Earley, P. (2005) 'How schools take responsibility for staff professional development'. Paper presented at ECER conference.

Bubb, S. and Earley, P. (2006) 'Induction rites and wrongs: the "education vandalism" of new teachers' professional development', *Journal of In-service education*, **32**(1): March. pp. 5–12.

Bubb, S. and Hoare, P. (2001) *Performance Management*. London: David Fulton.

Bubb, S. and Porritt, V. (2006) 'Recognising and nuturing urban teachers: Chartered London Teacher Status'. Paper presented at BELMAS conference, Aston.

Bubb, S. Earley, P. Ahtaridou, E., Jones, J. and Taylor, C. (2007) 'The self evaluation form: how are schools handling the SEF?', *Managment in Education*, **21**(3).

Bubb, S., Heilbronn, R., Jones, C., Totterdell, M. and Bailey, M. (2002) *Improving Induction*. London: RoutledgeFalmer.

Bush, T., Briggs, A. and Middlewood, D. (2006) 'The impact of school leadership development: evidence from the "New visions" programme for early headship', *Journal of In-service Education*, **32**(2).

Busher, H. and Harris, A. with Wise, C. (2000) *School Leadership and School Improvement*. London: Paul Chapman/Sage.

Butler, S., and Geeson, J. (2002) 'Why everyone needs mentoring', *Secondary English Magazine*. **5**(3).

Carnell, E. (2001) 'The value of meta-learning dialogue', *Professional Development Today*, **4**(2): 43–54.

CfBT Lincolnshire School Improvement Service (2006) *CPD Impact Evaluation: A Guidance Pack for Schools*. Lincoln: CfBT.

Child, A. and Merrill, S. (2002) 'Making the most of ITT', *Professional Development Today*, **5**(2): 17–20.

Connor, D. (1997) 'Becoming a professional development co-ordinator – the challenge', *Professional Development Today*, **1**(1): 47–52.

Cordingley, P. (2001) 'CPD reformed? An interview with Carol Adams', PDT **4**(2): 79–84.

Cordingley, P. (2003) 'Bringing research resources to school based users', *Professional Development Today*, **6**(3): 13–18.

Cordingley, P., Bell, M., Rundell, B. and Evans, D. (2003) *The impact of collaborative CPD on classroom teaching and learning*. London: EPPI.

Cordingley, P., Bell, M., Thomason, S. and Firth, A. (2005) *The impact of collaborative continuing professional development (CPD) on classroom teacher and learning*. London: EPPI.

Cordingley, P., Bell, M., Thomason, S. and Firth, A. (2006) *How do collaborative and sustained CPD and sustained but not collaborative CPD affect teaching and learning?* London: EPPI.

Craig, M. (2002) 'Crisis for challenging schools', *Professional Development Today*, **5**(2): 29–34.

Creese, M. and Earley, P. (1999) *Improving Schools and Governing Bodies: Making a Difference*. London: Routledge.

Creese, M. (2000) 'Enhancing the effectiveness of governing bodies', *Professional Development Today*, **3**(3): 49–58.

Davey, J. (2000) 'Evaluating staff development: a case study', *Professional Development Today*, **3**(2) 33–40.

Davies, B. (2006) *Leading the Strategically Focused School*. London: Sage/PCP.

Day, C. (2006) *Commitment, Resilience and Effectiveness: The Importance of Context for CPD*. London: GTC.

Day, C., Sammons, P., Stobbart, G. et al. (2006) *Variations in Teacher's Work, Lives and Effectiveness*. Nottingham: DfES.

Dennison, B. and Kirk, R. (1990) *Do, Review, Learn, Apply: A Simple Guide to Experential Learning*. Oxford: Blackwell.

Department for Education and Employment (DfEE) (1989) *Elton Report*. London: DfEE.

Department for Education and Employment (DfEE) (1998) *National Standards for Headteachers*. London: DfEE.

Department for Education and Employment (DfEE) (2000) *Code of Practice on LEA/Schools Relations*. London: DfEE.

Department for Education and Employment (DfEE) (2001a) *Learning and Teaching: A Strategy for Professional Development*. London: DfEE.

Department for Education and Employment (DfEE) (2001b) *Good Value CPD: A Code of Practice for Providers of Professional Development for Teachers*. London: DfEE.

Department for Education and Skills (DfES) (2001) *National Induction Programme for Governors: Toolkit for Trainers*. London: DfES.

Department for Education and Skills (DfES) (2002a) *Staff Health and Wellbeing*. London: DfES.

Department for Education and Skills (DfES) (2002b) *The EPD Pilots*. London: DfES.

Department for Education and Skills (DfES) (2002c) *Using Supply Teachers to Cover Short Term Absences*. London: DfES.

Department for Education and Skills (DfES) (2003a) *The London Challenge – Transforming London Secondary Schools: London Data*. London: DfES.

Department for Education and Skills (DfES) (2003b) *The Induction Support Programme For Newly Qualified Teachers. Guidance 0458/2003*. London: DfES.

Department for Education and Skills (2004) *National Standards for Headteachers*. London: DfES.

Department for Education and Skills (2005a) *London's Learning: Developing the Leadership of CPD in London Schools* (CD). London: DfES.

Department for Education and Skills (DfES) (2005b) *The Common Core of Skills and Knowledge for Every Child Matters*. London: DfES.

Department for Education and Skills (DfES) (2006) *School Teachers' Pay and Conditions Document*, London: HMSO.

Department for Education and Skills (DfES) (2006a) *Performance Management*. London: DfES.

Department for Education and Skills (DfES) (2006b) *Families of Schools*. London: DfES.

Department for Education and Skills (DfES) (2006c) *Chartered London Teacher Poster*. London: DfES.

Department for Education and Skills (DfES) (2007a) *School Workforce in England*. London: DfES.

Department for Education and Skills (DfES) (2007b) *Chartered London Teacher Guidance*. London DfES.

Department of Education and Science (DES) (1972) *Teacher Education and Training (James Report)*. London: HMSO.

Earley, P. (1995) *Managing our Greatest Resource: The Evaluation of the Continuous Development in Schools Project*. Oxford: CBI Education Foundation/NFER.

Earley, P. (1996) 'Introduction', in P. Earley, B. Fidler and J. Ouston (eds), *Improvement Through Inspection? Complementary Approaches to School Development*. London: David Fulton.

Earley, P. (2005) 'Continuing professional development: the learning community', in M. Coleman and P. Earley (eds.), *The Leadership and Management of Educational Organisations: Cultures, Change and Continuity*. Oxford: Oxford University Press.

Earley, P. (2006) *Headship and Beyond: The Motivation and Development of School Leaders*. London: Institution of Education.

Earley, P. and Creese, M. (2003) 'Lay or professsional? Re-examining the role of school governors', in B. Davies and J. West-Burnham (eds), *Handbook of Educational Leadership and Management*. Harlow: Pearson.

Earley, P. and Evans, J. (2002) *Leading Provision: School Leadership Development in LEAs: A Good Practice Guide*. Nottingham: NCSL.

Earley, P. and Fletcher-Campbell, F. (1992) *The Time to Manage? Department and Faculty Heads at Work*. London: Routledge.

Earley, P. and Weindling, D. (2004) *Understanding School Leadership*. London: Sage/Paul Chapman.

Earley, P. and Weindling, D. (2006) 'Consultant leaders: a new role for headteachers?', *School Leadership and Management*, **26**(1): 37–53.

Earley, P. and Weindling, D. with Bubb, S., Coleman, M., Crawford, M., Evans, J., Pocklington, K. and Woodroffe, L. (2005) *An Evaluation of the Leadership Strategy of the London Challenge*. London: IoE.

Earley, P. Evans, J., Gold, A., Collarbone, P. and Halpin, D. (2002) *Establishing the Current State of School Leadership in England*. Nottingham: DfES.

Earley, P., Fidler, B. and Ouston, J. (eds) (1996) *Improvement through Inspection? Complementary Approaches to School Development*. London: David Fulton.

Ebbutt, D. (2003)'The development of a research culture in secondary schools', *Education Action Research*, **10**(1).

Eraut, M., Pennycuick, D. and Radner, M. (1988) *Local Evaluation of INSET: A Meta-evaluation of TRIST Evaluation*. Brighton: University of Sussex.

Ferguson, N., Earley, P., Ouston, J. and Fidler, B. (2000) *Improving Schools and Inspection: The Self-inspecting School*. London: Paul Chapman/Sage.

Fielding, M., Bragg, S. Craig, J., Cunningham, I., Eraut, M., Gillinson, S., Horne, M., Robinson, C. and Thorp, J. (2005) *Factors Influencing the Transfer of Good Practice, RB615*. London: DfES.

Frost, D. and Durrant, J. (2003) *Teacher-led Development Work*. London: David Fulton.

Furlong, J., Salisbury, J. and Coombes, L. (2003) *Best Practice Research Scholarships – Evaluation*. London DfES.

General Teaching Council for England (GTCE) (2001) *A Professional Development Entitlement for Teachers*. London: GTC.

General Teaching Council (GTC) (2003) *Teachers' Professional Development Learning Framework*. Birmingham: GTC. Available at www.gtce.org.uk

Glaser, R. (2002) *Designing and Facilitating Adult Learning*. Pennsylvania: HRDQ.

Goodall, J., Day, C., Harris, A., Lindsey, G. and Muijs, D. (2005) *The Impact of Professional Development*. Research report. Nottingham: DfES.

Guskey, T. (2000) *Evaluating Professional Development*. New York: Corwin.

Guskey, T. (2002) 'Does it make a difference? Evaluating professional development', *Educational Leadership*, March, 45–51.

Guskey, T. (2005) 'A Conversation with Thomas R. Guskey', *The Evaluation Exchange* **XI**(4): 12–15, Winter.

Hallgarten, J. (2002) *Supply Teachers: Symptom of the Problem or Part of the Solution?* London: IPPR.

Handscomb, G. (2002/03) 'Learning and developing together', *Professional Development Today*, **6**(1): 17–22, Winter.

Handscomb, G. (2007a) 'Enlightening Autonomy – Collaboration and Enquiry Symposium', 20th Annual World ICSEI Congress, January, Portorož, Slovenia.

Handscomb, G. (2007b) 'Every Child Matters – The Professional Development Challenge', *Professional Development Today*, **10**(1).

Handscomb, G. and MacBeath, J. (2003) *The Research-Engaged School*. Forum for Learning and Research Enquiry, Essex LEA.

Handscomb, G. and Sharp, C. (2006) 'Broadening Horizons – The role of Local Authorities in Encouraging Research Communities'. Symposium at 19th Annual World ICSEI Congress, January, Fort Lauderdale, Florida.

Hargreaves, D. (1998) 'Creative Professionalism: The Role of Teachers in the Knowledge Society'. DEMOS Arguments series 22.

Harland, J., Ashworth, M., Atkinson, M., Halsey, K., Haynes, J., Moor, H. and Wilkin, A. (1999) *Thank You for the Days: How Schools Use their Non-contact Days*. Slough: NFER.

Harris, A. (2002) *School Improvement: What's in it for Schools?* London: Routledge/Falmer.

Harris, B. (2000) 'A strategy for identifying the professional development needs of teachers: a report from New South Wales', *Journal of In-service Education*, 26(1): 25–47.

Hay McBer (2000) *Effective Teachers*, London: DfES.

Hobson, A., Malderez, A., Tracey, L., Kerr, K. and Pell, G. (2005) *Becoming a Teacher, RB673*. Nottingham: DfES.

Honey, P. and Mumford, A. (2006a) *Learning Styles Helper's Guide*. Maidenhead: Peter Honey.

Honey, P. and Mumford, A. (2006b) *The Learning Styles Questionnaire*. Maidenhead: Peter Honey.

Hopkins, D. (2002) Presentation at the launch of the Networked Learning Communities initiative, National College for School Leadership.

Hustler, D., McNamara, O., Jarvis, J., Londra, M., Campbell, A. and Howson, J. (2003) *Teachers' Perceptions of Continuing Professional Development*. Nottingham: DfES.

Hutchings, M., Smart, S., James, K. and Williams, K. (2006) *General Teaching Council for England Survey of Teachers 2006: Contents and Executive Summary*. London: GTCE.

Investors in People UK (IiP) (2006) *The Investors in People Standard*. London: IiPUK.

Jallongo, M. (1991) *Creating Learning Communities*. Indiana; National Education Service.

Jones, T. (2003) 'Continuing professional development in Wales: an entitlement for all', *Professional Development Today*, 6(1): 35–42.

Joy, B. (2006) 'Mentoring and Coaching', *NSIN Research Matters*, No. 27.

Kabra, K. (2002) 'From initial teacher training to a learning community', *Professional Development Today*, 5(3): 31–6.

Kay, J. (2002) *The Teaching Assistant's Handbook*. London: Continuum.

Kellow, M. (2003) 'Developing learning: school and teacher development through networking learning communities', *Professional Development Today*, 6(2): 6–12.

Kelly, S. (2006) *The CPD Coordinator's Toolkit*. London: Sage.

Kendall, L., Lee, B., Pye, D. and Wray, M. (2000) *Investors in People in Schools*. Research Report 207. Nottingham: DfEE.

Kerry, T. (2001) *Working with Support Staff*. Harlow: Pearson.

Kerry, T. (2003) 'Releasing potential', *Managing Schools Today*, 12(6): 25–7.

Knowles, M. (1984) *Andragogy in Action*. San Franciso, CA: Jossey-Bass.

Lieberman, A. (1999) 'Networks', *Journal of Staff Development*, 20(3).

Little, J.W. (1990) 'The persistence of privacy: autonomy and initiative in teachers' professional relations', *Teachers College Record*, 91(4): 509–36.

Little, R. (2002) 'Accelerated learning', *Governors' Agenda*, (22), April: 10–11.

Lorenz, S. (1998) *Effective In-class Support*. London: David Fulton.

MacBeath, J. (2006) *School Inspection and Self-Evaluation: Working with the New Relationship*. London: Routledge.

Madden, C. and Mitchell, V. (1993) *Professions, Standards and Competence: A Survey of Continuing Education for the Professions*. Department for Continuing Education, University of Bristol.

McIntyre, D. (2001) MEd presentation. Essex LA/University of Cambridge.

McMahon, M. and Forde, C. (2005) 'Chartered teacher: enhancing practice, enriching professionalism', *Professional Development Today*, 9(1): 14–21.

Miliband, D. (2003) 'School improvement and performance management'. Speech to the Performance Management Conference, Bournemouth. Available at info@dfes.gsi.gov.uk

Minnis, F. (2003) 'Early professional development'. MA dissertation, Institute of Education, University of London.

Moor, H., Halsey, K., Jones, M., Martin, K., Stott, A., Brown, C. and Harland, J. (2005) *Professional Development for Teachers Early in their Careers*. Research brief and report no. 613. Nottingham: DfES.

Moss, S. and Silk, J. (2003) 'What can coaching bring to continuing professional development in education?', *Professional Development Today*, **7**(1): 19–22.

National College for School Leadership (2001) *The Leadership Development Framework*. Nottingham: NCSL.

National College for School Leadership (2003a) 'Leading from the Middle, a supplement to LDR', May. Nottingham: NCSL.

National College for School Leadership (2003b) *The Heart of the Matter: A Practical Guide to What Middle Leaders can do to Improve Learning in Secondary Schools*. Nottingham: NCSL.

National College for School Leadership (2003c) *School Leadership*. Nottingham: NCSL.

National College for School Leadership (2004) *National Standards for Headteachers*. Nottingham: NCSL.

National College for School Leadership (2005) *National Framework for Coaching and Mentoring*. Nottingham: NCSL.

National College for School Leadership (2006a) *Recruiting Headteachers and School Leaders: Seven Steps to Success*. Nottingham: NCSL.

National College for School Leadership (2006b) *Leading Coaching in Schools*. Nottingham: NCSL.

National College for School Leadership (2006c) *Leading Beyond the School: Evaluating the impact of the Primary Strategy Consultant Leaders*. Nottingham: NCSL.

National College for School Leadership (2006d) *Leading a Research-engaged School*. Nottingham: NCSL.

National Education Research Forum (2001) The Impact of Educational Research on Policy and Practice. Sub-group report of NERF. Slough: NFER.

National Staff Development Council (2001) *Standards for Staff Development*. Ohio: NSDC.

Naylor, D. (1999) 'The professional development needs of midday assistants', *Professional Development Today*, **3**(3): 51–60.

Office for Standards in Education (2002a) *Continuing Professional Development for Teachers in Schools*. London: Ofsted.

Office for Standards in Education (2002b) *Performance Management of Teachers*. London: Ofsted.

Office for Standards in Education (2002c) *Teaching Assistants in Primary Schools: An Evaluation of the Quality and Impact of their Work* (HMI Report 434). Available online.

Office for Standards in Education (2002d) *Leadership and Management Training for Headteachers: Report by HMI (HMI 547)*. London: Ofsted.

Office for Standards in Education (2002e) *The Work of School Governors (HMI 707) (report from HMCI)*, London: Ofsted. Available online.

Office for Standards in Education (2003a) *Inspecting Schools*. London: Ofsted.

Office for Standards in Education (2003b) *Early Professional Development*. London: Ofsted.

Office for Standards in Education (2003c) *HMCI Annual Report*. London: Ofsted.

Office for Standards in Education (2003d) *Schools' Use of Temporary Teachers*. London: Ofsted.

Office for Standards in Education (2005) *Every Child matters: Framework for the Inspection of Schools in England from September 2005*. London: Ofsted.

Office for Standards in Education (2006) *The Logical Chain: Continuing Professional Development in Effective Schools*, London: Ofsted.

Office for Standards in Education (2007a) *The School Self-evaluation Form*. London: Ofsted.

Office for Standards in Education (2007b) *An Employment Based Route into Teaching*, London: Ofsted.

Oldroyd, D. and Hall, V. (1991) *Managing Staff Development: A Handbook for Secondary Schools*. London: Paul Chapman.

Pachler, N. and Field, K. (2004) 'Continuing professional development', in S. Capel, M. Leask and T. Turner, (eds), *Starting to Teach in the Secondary School*. London: Routledge/Falmer.

Phillips, J. (1999) *Is your School a Learning Organisation?* St Albans: Phillips Associates.

Ranson, S., Smith, P., Farrell, C., Peim, N. (2005) 'Does governance matter for school improvement?', *School Effectiveness and School Improvement*, **16** (3): 305–25.

Reeves, J. (2005) 'Securing Systemic Impact, paper presented at EMASA conference, Johannesburg, 11–13 March.

Reynolds (2003) 'So near but yet so far', *Times Educational Supplement*, 20 June: 23.

Riches, C. and Morgan, C. (eds) (1989) *Human Resource Management in Education*. Buckingham: Open University Press.

Riley, K. (2003) 'Redefining Professionalism: Teachers with Attitude!', GTCE website at http://www.gtce.org.uk/news/featuresDetail.asp?ezineID=107

Robins, J. (2003) *AST Groupworking Pilots*. London: DfES.

Rosenholtz, S. (1989) *Teachers' Workplace: The Social Organisation of Schools*. New York: Teachers College Press.

Sallis, J. (2001) *Heads in Partnership: Working with your Governors for a Successful School*. London: Pitman.

Scanlon, M., Earley, P. and Evans, J. (1999) *Improving the Effectiveness of School Governing Bodies*. London: DfEE.

School Development Support Agency (SDSA) (2005) *Everybody's Learning*. CPD Toolkit. East Midlands CPD Partnership. Leicester: SDSA.

Sharp, C., Eames, A., Saunders, D. and Tomlinson, K. (2006) *Postcards from Research-Engaged Schools*. Slough: NFER.

Simkins, T., Coldwell, M., Caillan, I., Finlayson, H. and Morgan, A. (2006) 'Coaching as an in-school leadership development strategy: experiences from *Leading from the Middle*', *Journal of In-service Education*. **32**(3).

Smithers, A. and Robinson, P. (2003) *Factors Affecting Teachers' Decisions to Leave the Profession*. Research brief and Research report no. 430. Nottingham: DfES.

Southworth, G. (2005) Keynote address at Certificate and Diploma of School Business Management Graduation Ceremony. Nottingham: NCSL.

Stevens, J., Knibbs, S. and Smith, J. (2005) *Follow-up Research into the State of School Leadership in England*. Nottingham: DfES.

Stoll, L. and Fink, D. (1996) *Changing our Schools*. Buckingham: Open University Press.

Stoll, L., Bolam, R., McMahon, A., Thomas, A., Wallace, M., Greenwood, A. and Hawkey, K. (2006) *Professional Learning Communities: source materials for school leaders and other leaders of professional learning*. Innovation Unit, DfES, NCSL and GTC.

Stoll, L., Wallace, M., Bolam, R., McMahon, A., Thomas, S., Hawkey, K., Smith, M. and Greenwood, A. (2003) 'Creating and sustaining effective professional learning communities: questions arising from the literature', Universities of Bath and Bristol information sheet.

Stroud, V. (2006) 'Sustaining skills in headship: Professional development for experienced headteachers', *Educational Management, Administration and Leadership*, **34**(1): 89–103.

Swann, W. and Loxley, A. (1998) 'The impact of school-based training on classroom assistants in primary schools', *Research Papers in Education*, 13(2): 141–60.

Tabberer, R. (2005) 'We have to develop the best people business' *Times Education Supplement*, 7 January, 21.

Taylor, P. (2004) 'Effective performance management and professional development: a case study', *Professional Development Today*, **7**(1): 4–10.

Teacher Training Agency (TTA) (1998) *National Standards for Subject Leaders*. London: TTA.

Teacher Training Agency (TTA) (2005) *How to Qualify as a Teacher in England*. London: TTA.

Thompson, K. (2002) 'Early professional development', *Professional Development Today*, **6**(1): 23–8.

Times Educational Supplement (TES) (2003) 'On course'. 21 March.

Tomlinson, H. (1993) 'Developing Professionals', *Education*, 24 September.

Tomlinson, J. (1993) *The Control of Education*. London: Cassell.

Totterdell, M., Heilbronn, R., Bubb, S. and Jones, C. (2002) *Evaluation of the Effectiveness of the Statutory Arrangements for the Induction of Newly Qualified Teachers*. Research brief and report no. 338. Nottingham: DfES.

Training and Development Agency for Schools (TDA) (2006) *Career Development Framework for Support Staff*. London: TDA.

Training and Development Agency for Schools (TDA) (2007a) *Teacher Standards Framework*. London: TDA.

Training and Development Agency (TDA) (2007b) *Higher Level Teaching Assistant Standards*. London: TDA.

Turner, C. (1996) 'The roles and tasks of a subject head of department in secondary schools: a neglected area of study?', *School Organisation*, **16**(2): 203–17.

Turner, C. (2003) 'A critical review of research on subject leaders in secondary schools', *School Leadership and Management*, **23**(2): 209–27.

Villar, A. and Strong, M. (2007) *Is Mentoring Worth the Money?* Santa Cruz: University of California.

Wallace, W. (2006) 'Lean on me', *Times Educational Supplement*, 19 May, 6.

Waters, M. (1998) 'Personal development for teachers', *Professional Development Today*, **1**(2): 29–38.

Watkinson, A. (2002) *Assisting Learning and Supporting Teaching: A Practical Guide for the Teaching Assistant in the Classroom*. London: David Fulton.

Watkinson, A. (2003) 'Using teacher assistants: an answer to the teacher recruitment crisis?', *Managing Schools Today*, **12**(6): 29–33.

Wenger, E. (1998) *Communities of Practice: Learning, Meaning and Identity*. Cambridge: Cambridge University Press.

West, N. (1995) *Middle Management in the Primary School*. London: David Fulton.

West-Burnham, J. and O'Sullivan, F. (1998) *Leadership and Professional Development in Schools*. London: Pitman.

Williams, A. (2002) 'Informal learning in the workplace – a case study of new teachers'. Paper given at BERA conference, University of Exeter.

Williams, M. (1993). 'Changing policies and practices', in *The Continuing Professional Development of Teachers*. London: GTC.

Wise, C. (2001) 'The monitoring role of the academic middle manager', *Educational Management and Administration*, **29**(3): 333–41.

Woods D. (2000) *The Promotion and Dissemination of Good Practice*. London: The Education Network, (October).

Author Index

Subject Index